TRANSITIONS

The Family
and the Life Course
in Historical Perspective

This is a volume in

STUDIES IN SOCIAL DISCONTINUITY

A complete list of titles in this series appears at the end of this volume.

TRANSITIONS
The Family and the Life Course in Historical Perspective

Edited by

Tamara K. Hareven

Department of History
Clark University
Worcester, Massachusetts
and
Center for Population Studies
Harvard University
Cambridge, Massachusetts

ACADEMIC PRESS   New York   San Francisco   London
A Subsidiary of Harcourt Brace Jovanovich, Publishers

ACADEMIC PRESS, INC.
111 Fifth Avenue, New York, New York 10003

United Kingdom Edition published by
ACADEMIC PRESS, INC. (LONDON) LTD.
24/28 Oval Road, London NW1 7DX

Library of Congress Cataloging in Publication Data
Main entry under title:

Transitions: The family and the life course in
    historical perspective.

    (Studies in social discontinuity series)
    Outgrowth of a series of conferences sponsored
by the Mathematics Social Science Board of the
National Science Foundation.
    Includes bibliographies.
    1.   Family——Massachusetts——Essex Co.——History——
19th century——Congresses.   2.   Essex Co., Mass.
——Economic conditions——Congresses.   I.   Hareven,
Tamara K.   II.   United States.   National Science
Foundation.   Mathematics Social Science Board.
HQ555.M37F35   301.42'097445   78–13208
ISBN 0–12–325150–8

Contents

11927

5

From Fireside to Factory: School Entry and School Leaving in Nineteenth-Century Massachusetts   **135**

CARL F. KAESTLE
MARIS A. VINOVSKIS

6

Women's Work and the Life Course in Essex County, Massachusetts, 1880   **187**

KAREN OPPENHEIM MASON
MARIS A. VINOVSKIS
TAMARA K. HAREVEN

7

Family Transitions into Old Age   **217**

HOWARD CHUDACOFF
TAMARA K. HAREVEN

List of Contributors

Numbers in parentheses indicate the pages on which the authors' contributions begin.

BENGT ANKARLOO (113), Department of History, Lund University, Lund, Sweden

HOWARD P. CHUDACOFF (99, 217), Department of History, Brown University, Providence, Rhode Island 02912

GLEN H. ELDER, JR. (17), Center for the Study of Youth Development, Boys Town, Nebraska 68010

STANLEY ENGERMAN (271), Department of Economics, University of Rochester, Rochester, New York 14627

TAMARA K. HAREVEN (1, 187, 217, 245), Department of History, Clark University, Worcester, Massachusetts 01610

CARL F. KAESTLE (135), Department of History, University of Wisconsin—Madison, Madison, Wisconsin 53706

ROBERT A. LEVINE (287), Graduate School of Education, Harvard University, Cambridge, Massachusetts 02138

KAREN OPPENHEIM MASON (187), Population Studies Center, 1225 South University Avenue, Ann Arbor, Michigan 48109

JOHN MODELL (99, 245), Department of History, University of Minnesota, Minneapolis, Minnesota 55455

PETER UHLENBERG (65), Department of Sociology, University of North Carolina, Chapel Hill, North Carolina 27514

MARIS A. VINOVSKIS (135, 187), Department of History, University of Michigan, Ann Arbor, Michigan 48104

Foreword

The family is a compelling object of historical study. Families figure importantly in most of the major transitions that people face in their lives. Families figure in those transitions as cause, effect, context, and source of support. The fact is obvious for marriage, divorce, and the death of a parent, child, or spouse. But a child's entry into school, a first job, a retirement from work, a change of residence are also, by and large, family events; their impact on the individual depends significantly on how other family members deal with them. The history of the family offers us the hope of learning which of the experiences we face as twentieth-century family members are general and durable, which ones vary extensively, quickly, and easily, and which ones are changing according to powerful long-term trends. The history of the family even offers the hope of learning *why* family affairs work as they do: whether, for example, the place of a family in the surrounding economy largely determines the texture and sequences of the experiences its members encounter. The answers to those sorts of questions help us understand our own experiences, help us appreciate those of our forebears, and help us recognize the opportunities—and the limits on the opportunities—to create different family lives. Because much is at stake, historical analyses of family life often make us skeptical and anxious at the same time as they rivet our attention.

The past with which the essays on this volume deal is recent enough to encourage us to reflect on their relevance for contemporary family experience. Most of the essays concentrate on Massachusetts families of about a century ago. Today's readers can find the equivalents of their grandparents and great-grandparents in these Yankees, Irish, Canadians, and others who left their traces in the records of Lynn, Salem, Lawrence, and surrounding towns. There they are, marrying (relatively late, by recent standards), divorcing (rarely, by twentieth-century rates) watching their children leave home (late in the parents' lifetimes, by comparison with our own time), and confronting the nineteenth-century equivalents of other joys, crises, and transitions. The comparison between contemporary family life and the Essex County evidence underlines important changes we and our parents have gone through: the increasingly uniform timing of major life events, the lengthening of the years still available to a couple when their children leave home definitively, and so on. Although our authors stress the close analysis of their nineteenth-century evidence, we readers can hardly help darting back and forth past and present.

Tamara Hareven and her collaborators have undertaken a difficult but promising synthesis. They are trying to merge the analysis of family structure with the treatment of the changing course of individual lives. That requires them to deal seriously with at least three different social units: the nuclear family, the household, and the individual. (In this book, the nature of the evidence does not permit them to say much about the fourth obvious candidate, the kin group.) Each has its own history, on the small scale and the large scale as well. Despite the tendency of Europeans and Americans to form households consisting of a single nuclear family, and that alone, the life history of a given household never coincides exactly with that of a given nuclear family or a given individual. Family members come and go. So—abundantly so in nineteenth-century Massachusetts—do nonmembers of the nuclear family: boarders, servants, grandparents, and other kinsmen. The authors therefore have to examine the overlap and interdependence of three social units, each of which has its own logic and trajectory.

The move from the notion of "family cycle" to the idea of "life course" sums up the authors' intentions. The useful concept of a family cycle concentrates on the stages in the experience of an hypothetical average nuclear family. The markers between the stages are the average ages of the couple at certain crucial events: marriage, birth of last child, death of first spouse to die, and so on. This simple device clarifies the impact of such changes as declining age at marriage, rising life expectancy, and increasing concentration of childbearing in the early years of marriage on the overall experience of nuclear families. An examination of the family cycle, for example, makes it easier to understand that some of the twentieth-century rise in the divorce rate results from the voluntary termination of marriages that would have ended just as soon by the death of one of the spouses under the life expectancies prevailing in the nineteenth century. But the family cycle scheme gives a poor picture of the *range* of nuclear family experiences, and of how the frequency of alternative paths through the family cycle changes. That tempts us to treat less frequent cases—one-parent households, teenage marriages, and so on—as not only rare but deviant. Furthermore, the family cycle scheme provides an inaccurate summary of individual lives: Most people spend major parts of their lives in at least two distinct nuclear families, many people spend years away from their various nuclear families, and, in any case, at the individual level there are so many different paths from event to event that the average sequence is by no means the sequence of the majority.

The idea of a life course shifts the focus emphatically to the individual. The differences from the family-cycle scheme are important. Although the life-course analyst also uses the ages at which crucial events occur as markers, the concept of standard stages disappears, and the notion of a *distribution* of ages at which the events occur enters importantly into the analysis. In the particular applications of life-course analysis reported in this book another device also becomes prominent. It is the careful distinction and comparison of the experiences of successive *cohorts*—typically, but not exclusively, birth cohorts. Implicitly, our analysts are posing these sorts of questions: For the set of people born in 1850, what was the distribution of ages (and combinations of ages) at which they entered school, left school, went to work, married, bore their first children, and so on through the life course? What about the birth cohort of 1860? How did these individual experiences compound into changing compositions of nuclear families and households? And did those changing characteristics of households and families themselves reshape individual experience? That is the interplay of life course and family structure.

The central body of evidence shared by Hareven and her collaborators sets stringent limits on the answers they could find. They had common access to a sample of household schedules from the 1880 census. Although the evidence made it just as easy to look at individuals as at households, the evidence did not provide direct observations of change over time. Nor did it regroup easily and surely into observations on nuclear families as such. As a result, many of the analyses in this book compare the characteristics of different age-groups (as the best available approximations of birth cohorts) at the same point in time. Others go to addition sources for evidence on individual experiences and on change over time. Still others use aggregate data for Massachusetts or for the United States as a whole to identify the changes whose traces are frozen into the 1880 census. The limitations of the evidence, then, produce some benefits: They clarify what sorts of additional evidence we need in order to carry on a successful integration of life course and family structure. They also give the authors an opportunity to show how much information skilled and thoughtful investigators can wring from limited evidence.

Fortunately, I do not have to summarize, evaluate, or synthesize the authors' findings. This book is unusual: despite a tight empirical focus and despite a thematic unity which is rare in collective volumes, about half the essays in the book are syntheses of one kind or another. Most of the essays, furthermore, reflect explicitly on the connections among particular findings from the 1880 sample, general conditions of life in nineteenth-century Essex County, and the broad experience of modern America. You have your choice: read the synthetic essays, then see if the detailed analyses bear out their generalizations; study the detailed analyses, then compare the syntheses with the conclusion you have drawn from your own examination of the findings. Either way you are likely to gain insight into the relations between changing family structure and changing individual experience.

It is my job, on the other hand, to say something about the origins of this book. The papers in it grew from a series of meetings organized by Tamara Hareven under the sponsorship of the Mathematical Social Science Board (MSSB). During its 14 years of activity, MSSB sponsored many conferences, workshops, and seminars dealing with the more quantitative versions of social, political, and economic history. After 1970, MSSB gave increasing attention to demographic history, and then to the history of the family. The members of MSSB felt that in these fields the short-run challenge was not to develop or apply powerful mathematics to the existing materials and arguments. Rather, we sought to encourage a sharper formulation of arguments and models, greater rigor in the collection and presentation of evidence, more exacting standards of measurement, more careful matching of statistical procedures to the arguments and evidence, and an increase in the amount and variety of sound quantitative work being done in demographic history and the history of the family. Our sponsorship of workshops on the historical study of family structure and the life course was one of several efforts in those directions. As this book testifies, they were good efforts, but they left plenty of work to do.

On New Year's Day 1978, the Mathematical Social Science Board ceased to exist. As one family generates another, the old MSSB has given rise to a new organization: the Social Science Research Council's Committee on Mathematics in the Social Sciences. The new committee (which consists, for the moment, of the members of the late MSSB) is trying to revive and reorient the work of MSSB. That takes energy, imagination, and—not least—money. Whether the renewed effort will succeed remains to be seen. In the meantime, such volumes as *Transitions: The Family and the Life Course in Historical Perspective* stand as evidence that the effort is worthwhile.

Charles Tilly

Preface

This volume has two major components: theoretical chapters examining life-course analysis in relation to history, and a set of empirical chapters applying this approach to a common data set for late nineteenth-century American communities in Essex County, Massachusetts. The five historians and one sociologist involved in preparing this book collaborated in different configurations on the data set. In addition, a sociologist, a demographer, and an economic historian were invited to offer theoretical models and commentary on the historical patterns from the vantage points of their disciplines. Also, an anthropologist has offered cross-cultural comparisons.

In Chapter 1, Glen Elder, a pioneer in formulating sociological theory in life-course analysis, discusses life-course development in relation to historical change; in Chapter 2 Peter Uhlenberg, utilizing aggregate data for the United States for the period 1870–1930, examines historical changes in age configurations along the life course, and constructs the demographic scaffolding for analyzing family behavior and life-course transitions; and in Chapter 9, Stanley Engerman, applying models of economic behavior to the historical patterns emerging from this data set, tries to explain the choices that individuals and families make in the timing of different life-course transitions. Finally, anthropologist Robert LeVine, in Chapter 10, compares the historical chapters for Essex County, Massachusetts, with the life-course patterns of the Gusii in Kenya, providing significant insights into cross-cultural differences, in the scheduling of life-course transitions, and in their meaning. The historical chapters are all based on the same data set, which consists of a sample of the individual manuscript schedules of the United States 1880 census for eight selected towns in Essex County, Massachusetts. Lawrence was chosen as a textile center; Lynn as the major center of the shoe industry; Salem as a traditional commercial town; Lynnfield as a rural community in transition to a suburb of Lynn; and Boxford, Topsfield, Wenham, and Hamilton as rural communities. We selected these communities on the basis of their levels of industrialization and economic development. We used the same data set as a base for the different chapters in order to address our questions in a uniform context, and to avoid the usual problems inherent in the lack of comparable data.

Each of the historical chapters addressed one specific transition that individuals and/or families experience over their life course. Bengt Ankarloo, in Chapter 4, examines marriage; Carl Kaestle and Maris Vinovskis, in Chapter 5, analyze children's entry into and exit from school; Karen Oppenheim Mason, Vinovskis, and I, in Chapter 6, investigate patterns of women's entry into the labor force; Howard Chudacoff and I, in Chapter 7, examine the affect on household structure of transitions into old age.

While all these empirical chapters examine the relationship of individual to familial transitions, they vary in their emphasis. Chapters 4 and 7 examine familial transitions (transitions in and out of the family of orientation and establishment of an independent household through marriage, and household extension in the later years of life through the sharing of housing space between parents and adult children). Chapters 5 and 6 examine apparently individual transitions. The contribution of life-course analysis in this case is to view each of these individual moves as part of a larger collective-family process.

In an effort to integrate the different transitions discussed in this book, I and John Modell examine them, in Chapter 8, on two related levels: the interrelationship of different transitions with each other, and the relative role of demographic, cultural, and economic factors affecting the timing of different life-course transitions. The first level links timing to family history; the second connects the chapters to larger questions of social history.

Tamara K. Hareven

Acknowledgments

This book is the outgrowth of a continuing series of conferences and intensive advanced workshops that I directed in 1975 under a grant from the Mathematics Social Science Board (MSSB) of the National Science Foundation. The initial idea for this conference originated at an MSSB advanced seminar that I organized in 1974 to analyze demographic processes and household structure in nineteenth-century American communities. During our seminar discussions we recognized the importance of a developmental perspective in understanding family behavior. We, therefore, decided to organize an advanced workshop for the historical study of the family cycle. Our effort to apply family-cycle categories, which are based primarily on age of the household head, to the analysis of family and household structure produced a series of static snapshots of household organization and of the status of different individuals within the household. In the process, we became aware of the limitations in the use of a priori stages, and shifted our interest to the process by which individuals moved in and out of different family configurations and the roles they assumed. What became important was not merely the different stages that families found themselves in, but the timing of the transitions.

The broadening of our perspective from the family cycle to the more encompassing approach of life-course analysis, particularly our shift from *stages* to *timing*, evolved through three 2-day planning workshops which were held in the winter and spring of 1975. Our exposure to Elder's approach to life-course analysis considerably influenced the rephrasing of our original questions, and led to reorganizing our research strategies to focus on the timing of life-course transitions. Having reached this common ground, the historians ventured to examine distinct life-course transitions in the common data set. Initial drafts of the historical chapters revealed the degree to which the timing of leaving home, marriage, school attendance, women's work, and the continuation of household headship in old age were related to the family's economic strategies. We then invited Stanley Engerman to interpret the Essex chapters in the light of the kinds of choices that families and individuals within them were likely to make. Much of the time in the planning conferences was devoted to forming common strategies for analyzing and dovetailing individual chapters for the Essex County data set. The intensive seminar at Williams College in the summer of 1975 was devoted to critically discussing the first drafts of the chapters. Revised chapters were discussed again at the follow-up, 3-day conference in December, where Reuben Hill presented a commentary from the perspective of family development theory and Engerman offered commentary from an economic perspective. The essays were revised in final form, following that meeting.

We would like to express our gratitude to the Social History Committee of the MSSB for its support, particularly to Charles Tilly, chairman of the committee, for his interest in this project, and for the practical as well as conceptual advice which he offered, and to Preston Cutler at the Center for Advanced Studies in the Behavioral Sciences for administering the grant. We are indebted to the Rockefeller Foundation for supporting the History of the Family Program at Clark University, which generated the Essex County data set used in this project, while I was director of the program and Vinovskis was postdoctoral fellow, and to the computer centers at the Universities of Rhode Island and Michigan where the data was analyzed. We are especially grateful to Steven Shedd for recoding and analyzing the data, to Laurel Rosenthal for secretarial assistance, and to the Clark University secretarial pool and Joyce Ingham for final typing. We are all especially indebted to Howard Litwak for his thoughtful editorial assistance. My special thanks go to the staff of Academic Press. The Center for Population Studies has been extremely supportive during the final revising and editing.

Tamara K. Hareven

Introduction: The Historical Study of the Life Course

TAMARA K. HAREVEN

The essays in this volume shift the historical investigation of the family from the classification of household structure at individual points in time to a developmental perspective. Rather than viewing the family as a static unit, they examine it as a changing entity over the life course of its members; as Elder states in Chapter 1 of this volume, this approach views the family "as a setting of mutually contingent individual careers, whose dynamics shape the family as a unit." This book's major concern is the synchronization of individual timing with the collective timing of the family unit, as each changes within different societal and historical settings. Essentially, they explore the interaction between "individual time," "family time," and "historical time" (Hareven, 1977).

Individuals develop at different paces and assume a variety of roles over their lifetime. Their entry into and exit from such roles and the accompanying changes within the family unit are subject to biological time tables, as well as to changing social and economic conditions. Hence, family and individual decisions affecting the timing of transitions such as leaving home, entering the labor force, marrying, setting up independent households, childbearing, launching children from the home, and widowhood, are in turn affected by changing historical conditions. An understanding of this interaction between family develop-

1

TRANSITIONS
The Family and the Life Course in
Historical Perspective

ment and historical change provides insight into the dynamics of social change, as well as a deeper understanding of the major transitions that have taken place in the history of the family.

In their earlier search for a developmental framework for the analysis of changes in household and family structure over the family members' lifetimes, historians utilized the family cycle as an analytical construct. The family cycle measures changes in the family as it moves from stage to stage as a collective unit. The definition of such stages employs typologies derived from contemporary populations. The life course, on the other hand, encompasses both individual and collective family development, and the problems that arise from their synchronization. Rather than identifying *stages,* the life course approach examines *transitions:* It follows individuals' movements through different family configurations and analyzes the determinants of the timing of such movements.

In the discussion that follows I will focus first on historians' earlier use of the family cycle construct, and next, on the life course as a framework for the historical analysis of the family; finally, I will discuss methodological approaches.

The Family Cycle

Historians initially found in the family cycle a flexible construct, particularly for the analysis of changes in household and family structure. The family cycle has been valuable to historians in leading them to shift the analysis of family behavior in the past from one point in time to a developmental sequence. As developed by Hill, the family cycle measures role changes in the family unit as it moves from stage to stage over the life of its members, from family formation by marriage, to its dissolution after the death of its head (Hill, 1964).

When applying the family cycle to their examination of household and family structure in past populations, historians discovered that patterns that appeared constant at one point in time varied significantly over the lives of the household's head and its different members. Individuals living in nuclear households at one point in their lives were likely to live in extended or augmented households at other points. The family cycle construct thus introduced a developmental perspective into the historical study of the family (Berkner, 1972). This discovery revised the generalization that households have tended to be consistently nuclear over the past two centuries (Hareven, 1974).

The family cycle was also effective in leading historians to view the family as a *collective* unit, engaged in activities and decisions which change in relation to the roles and social characteristics of its members, and in response to external conditions. A collective perspective is particularly valuable in studying the population investigated in this volume, since nineteenth-century American society was familistic in its orientation. Within such a setting, collective family priorities generally dominated over individual values (Anderson, 1971). The understanding of the family's interaction with different economic and demographic regimes, especially the extent to which inheritance customs, the availability of housing, or migration patterns may have caused different family and household configurations, can be best achieved by examining changes in family behavior along its cycle, rather than at one point in time. For example, Berkner (1972) has shown that differences in inheritance patterns and land distribution affected variations in the structure of peasant households over the family cycle in late eighteenth-century Austria. In American urban communities, Modell and Hareven (1973) found that the structure of late nineteen-century households varied along the family cycle in accordance with patterns of migration, the availability of housing, and changing economic needs. Households that were nuclear at one point in their heads' lives were augmented with boarders and lodgers at a later point. In Chapter 7, Chudacoff and Hareven found that despite the overall nuclear configuration of households, considerable household extension occurred in old age.

The family cycle also proved especially valuable for the identification of those stages in its life when the family unit was economically vulnerable. This examination of the family economy along its cycle, stemming from Frederick LePlay through B. S. Rowntree (1901) into American sociological and economic literature on the family has also influenced historical analysis. Modell (forthcoming) for example, followed the family cycle in analyzing patterns of labor force participation and family expenditure of United States workers in the late nineteenth century. He identified changing economic strategies of the family, and the rhythms of insecurity over the family's cycle.

Despite its continuing utility, the family cycle also has limitations. Elder sees one of its major failings in its measurement of stages: "As operationalized, the family cycle uses age information from the parents. Indeed, this is a major deficiency—we may know where the children are in terms of age-patterned roles, but not where the parents are. Timing enters the family cycle model in relation to the children. Its full meaning requires, however, knowledge of event timing among the parents as well. From this perspective, the family cycle fails to do justice to its primary target, the temporal features of stages of parenthood." [1]

An effort to apply it to the nineteenth-century population groups studied in this volume also revealed a limitation: As Uhlenberg (1974) points out, the differences between a priori stages as defined by family-development sociology, based on contemporary populations, and the diversity of patterns in the late nineteenth century pose a problem. Glick's model, which has been followed by demographers, measures *mean* patterns of change in stages of the family cycle since the late nineteenth-century, but does not examine variance from the norm, or differentials by ethnicity or occupation within specific time periods (Glick, 1947, 1955, 1977; Glick and Parke, 1965). In Chapter 2 of this volume, Uhlenberg shows the extent to which voluntary and involuntary demographic factors caused age configurations in the family, which were considerably different from the "normal" twentieth-century pattern. Uhlenberg concludes that a sequence of marriage, family formation, child-rearing, launching, and survival until age fifty with the first marriage still intact unless broken by divorce, although always modal, was by no means prevalent for the majority of the population before the beginning of the twentieth century.

Prior to the late nineteenth-century declines in mortality and fertility, discontinuities between different stages of the family cycle seem to have been less clearly marked. Higher birth rates meant that children were spread along a broad age range within the family; frequently the youngest child was starting school at the same time that the oldest was preparing for marriage. Today, parents generally complete childrearing with one-third of their lives still ahead (Glick and Norton, 1977). Nineteenth-century parenthood, on the other hand, encompassed most of the adult life span. The combination of a later age at marriage and larger numbers of children rarely provided an opportunity for an empty nest stage to occur. Prior to the increase in life expectancy at the beginning of the twentieth century, marriage was frequently broken by the death of a spouse even before the end of the childrearing period. Fathers surviving the childrearing years rarely lived beyond the marriage of their second child. The boundaries between one's family of orientation and one's family of procreation were not as clear as they are today, and transitions from one stage of the family cycle to the next were more rigidly timed. For example, leaving home did not necessarily precede marriage, and the launching of children from the home did not necessarily leave the nest empty (Modell et

---

[1]Personal communication from Glen H. Elder, Jr. to Tamara K. Hareven, 1978.

al., 1976). Frequently, a married child would return to the home, or the parents would take in boarders or lodgers.

Given these limitations in applying a priori stages to historical populations, we directed our questions to the synchronization of individual life careers with those of the family as a collective unit. Rather than restrict the examination to stages of the family cycle, we turned to the life course.[2]

The Historical Study of the Life Course

In Chapter 1 of this volume, Elder formulates the conceptual framework of life-course analysis and its application to historical research. According to Elder (see Chapter 1) the life course is "a concept of interdependent careers that vary in synchronization." The life course approach encompasses individual development as well as the collective development of the family unit. It focuses on the meshing of individual careers with the family as it changes over time, and especially on the coordination of several possibly distinct roles in peoples' lives, such as work and family. An understanding of these patterns also provides important insights into the process of decision making within the family, especially where such decisions affected individual as well as collective behavior (insofar as the process can be ascertained from the available historical data).

I will now turn to three essential features of life-course analysis that are most relevant to historical research: the synchronization of individual with family transitions; the interaction between life-course transitions and historical change; and, ultimately, the cumulative impact of earlier life-course transitions on subsequent ones.

The first feature concerns the timing and synchronization of transitions. The interrelationship of individual transitions and changing family configurations perhaps can be seen as the movement of schools of fish. As individuals move through their life course in family units, they group and regroup themselves. The functions that they take on in

[2]There is currently a disagreement among scholars about the continuing utility of the family cycle. Vinovskis (1977) argues that life-course analysis should completely replace the family cycle. Elder, who has given conceptual and methodological coherence to the life-course construct, does not see the life course and the family cycle as mutually exclusive. He argues that the family cycle represents stages of parenthood, which are encompassed in the life course. When coupled with temporal considerations (e.g., age patterns of family members), the family cycle construct represents one dimension of the multi-dimensional life course.

these different clusters also vary significantly over their life course. Most individuals are involved simultaneously in several configurations, fulfilling different functions in each. A married adult, for example, is part of both a family of origin and a family of procreation (and occupies a different position and fulfills a different role in each); in addition, such an individual also figures in his or her spouse's family of orientation, and in the spouse's kin network. When a son leaves home, his departure changes the configuration of his family unit. Depending on the status he held, his family might find itself less one bread winner, or less one dependent. When he marries and forms a new family unit, his roles and obligations differ from the ones which he held in his parents' unit. This seemingly individual move impinges upon the collective conditions of at least three family units—his family of origin, his newly founded family, and his wife's family of origin. In situations where remarriage follows death of a spouse or divorce, the new spouse's family enters the orbit of relationships, while the former spouse's family does not necessarily disappear completely from the picture. In case of divorce, a woman would stop relating to her former husband's mother as her mother-in-law, but may continue to relate to her as her child's grandmother. In the period under study here, where familial assistance was almost the exclusive source of security, especially during critical life situations, the multiplicity of obligations that individuals incurred over their life course may have been more complex than under the present welfare state.

The picture is complicated further because life-course changes are not limited to family transitions. Movement in and out of schools, in and out of the labor force, and changes in housing and migration also involve different patterns of timing. It is important to identify both the synchronization of individual with familial moves, and of familial with nonfamilial transitions; the degree to which taking a job is related to leaving home, for example, or whether retirement from the labor force is accompanied by changes in housing and family organization.

Conjunction of several transitions is also a significant aspect of life-course analysis. As Engerman notes in Chapter 9 of this volume, within a given family unit, the entry of a 6-year-old child into school, the mother's entry into the labor force, and the taking in of a boarder might all occur at the same time. While analytically, this book treats each of these decisions separately, the reality probably involved simultaneous decisions.

The second important feature of life-course analysis is the impact of historical processes on the timing of individual or family transitions. Life-course transitions are timed through the interaction of demographic, economic, and social factors as well as cultural and familial norms. Fertility can abstractly account for the number of children and the proportion of the life course spent on childbearing, but the commencement of childbirth (within biological limits) and the spacing of children are socially and culturally determined. Age at leaving home and age at marriage are also subject to interactions among demographic, social, cultural, and economic factors. One of the difficult assignments would be to understand the relative role of these factors. For example, at what point did demographic patterns take priority over economic considerations or cultural values? To what extent were cultural norms about timing of life-course transitions violated or stretched under economic constraints? How conscious were individuals of the existence of general patterns of timing, and of the specific historical circumstances facilitating or handicapping the timing of their transitions?

The life-course approach is historical by its very nature, since it encompasses change over an individual's entire life as it is influenced by historical conditions. A short-term historical process, stretching merely over an individual's lifetime, is best understood as part of a larger process of change over time. Individual choices may be either facilitated or thwarted by such external conditions. Patterns of timing can be reenforced or violated by specific historical circumstances such as wars and economic depressions, and, on a more local scale, migration. As Hill puts it, "each cohort encounters at marriage a unique set of historical constraints and incentives which influence the timing of its crucial life decisions [1970: 322]."

It is the historian's task to identify the interaction among demographic, social, and economic conditions within specific historical periods as it affects patterns of timing along the life course. Social change has an important impact on patterns of timing in several areas: demographic changes in mortality, fertility, and nuptiality; cultural changes in norms of timing; economic changes in the opportunity structure affecting employment and retirement; overall changes in the economy; institutional changes affecting different age groups in society (schooling, child labor laws, retirement). Ryder (1965) has suggested that change occurs when there is a marked discontinuity between the experiences of a cohort and those of its predecessor. A historical extension of Ryder's approach would argue that social change could occur through important discontinuities within the same cohort. The cohort that reached adulthood during the Great Depression experienced major discontinuities in family and work life that were not only part of an overall process of social change, but also may have catalyzed social change in turn. Or, consider the cohort that reached 65 around 1910 and was faced with mandatory retirement. This cohort would have found imposed retirement at a set age far more traumatic than subsequent cohorts that came of age early in the twentieth century, when entry into the labor force and exit from it were more strictly age-defined and legislated. Intra-cohort variation is thus extremely significant for the understanding of social change. The impact of change is not uniform; variations in exposure to events, in social class, and in community background would effect important differences among members of the same cohort.

This leads us to the third feature of life-course analysis: the cumulative impact of earlier transitions on subsequent ones. A life-course approach views a cohort not merely as an aggregation of individuals, but as an age group moving through history. The social experience of each cohort is influenced not only by contemporary conditions, but also by the cumulative experience of earlier life-course transitions. These transitions are affected, in turn, by a set of historical circumstances specific to their own time. This complex pattern of cumulative life-course effects can be grasped on two levels. First, the direct consequences of earlier life-course experiences on subsequent development must be taken into account. Elder's *Children of the Great Depression* (1974) documents the impact of Depression experiences in childhood and early adulthood on subsequent adult experiences.

Second, one must consider the experiences of a cohort at one point in time, as they relate to previous life-course experiences. For example, within the same cohort of unemployed adults caught in the Great Depression, coping with unemployment would have differed not only in terms of available resources, personality, and family background, but also in terms of earlier transitions experienced, such as how long they had been working; whether their career had been continuous and stable, or whether they had already experienced earlier job dislocations and disruptions; and what historical circumstances had affected such earlier discontinuities.

The life-course framework thus has a multiple utility for historians. First, it offers a comprehensive, integrative approach that steers one to interpret individual and family transitions as part of a continuous interactive process, even if they are observed only at one point in time. Second, it helps one view an individual transition as part of a cluster of other concurrent transitions, and as part of a sequence of transitions affecting each other. Finally, it treats a cohort not only as belonging to the specific period of study, but also as located in earlier times, its experience shaped by different historical forces.

Methodology

The crucial issue for historians is how to utilize this approach. The questions generated within the life-course framework are best answered from data following individuals and families over time. Life-course analysis at its best depends on the reconstruction of individual and family careers over entire lives and across generations. The data utilized by Elder for *Children of the Great Depression* was constructed as a longitudinal set to investigate the impact of early life-course events on subsequent adult development. In the absence of such complete data sets, historians have several choices: (a) to find occasional longitudinal data sets; (b) to generate such sets through linkages; or (c) to use cross-sectional data. The best-known historical linkage technique, family reconstitution, enabled historical demographers to reconstruct family units from baptismal, marriage, and death registers. Such reconstitution does not generate a complete longitudinal data set, but it allows the reconstruction of sequences of demographic events within the same family over time. When linked with land records as in Greven's study (1970) of colonial Andover, Massachusetts, family reconstitution can illustrate the conflict in the timing of three interrelated life-course transitions for sons, leaving home, marrying, and setting up an independent household, with one transition in their father's life, retirement from active farming. This method further enabled Greven to trace variations over four generations, illustrating the impact of historical changes in the community and of the distribution of land on those patterns of timing.

Similar large scale reconstitutions of longitudinal patterns have not been undertaken for nineteenth-century American populations. Historians studying nineteenth-century family patterns primarily utilize decennial census schedules that when combined with state censuses (where available) can provide information for every 5 years. Attempts to trace the same population group from one census to the next have generally rendered limited results because of the high population turnover and uncertainty in the identification of specific names. Several modest attempts at linkage of census schedules with marriage records have revealed how useful such linkages can be, even if limited in number, in illuminating life-course patterns of presumably stationary populations. For instance, by tracing marriage records to the census for Providence, Rhode Island, in 1880, Chudacoff (forthcoming) has documented the tendency of children who had left home to return and reside near their parents after marriage. In Chapter 4 of this volume, Ankarloo linked marriage records with census household schedules, thereby examining the timing of marriage in the context of previous and subsequent family transitions.

For the twentieth century, Hareven constructed a longitudinal data set out of cumulative individual employee files (dating from 1910–1936) of the Amoskeag Manufacturing Company in Manchester, New Hampshire. Reconstructing individual work careers from these files, subsequently linking them with marriage and birth records, and, wherever possible, tracing them back to the household schedules of the 1900 Federal Census, enabled her to examine changes in individual work careers in relation to the timing of family transitions, and to document the role of kin configurations in the workers' adaptation to industrial work. Such longitudinal data further enabled her to document the relationship between individual work careers and changing methods of employment and production in the corporation (Hareven, 1975a, 1975b).

Since such longitudinal data are generally not available to historians, life-course analysis must frequently be carried out with cross-sectional data. Cross-sectional data are more appropriate for analysis of the distribution of attributes, than for examination of transitions between states. They capture individuals, families, and household groups at one point in time, often resulting in a static picture of family behavior. Even when the same population sample is compared in two different censuses, the pattern that emerges still only presents individuals or families in two different stages, without revealing how they made their transition from one stage to the next.

Despite this limitation, as this volume demonstrates, it is possible to infer certain longitudinal patterns from cross-sectional data. Since age is such a powerful variable affecting life-course transitions, one could attempt to differentiate life-course-related transitions from family statuses at one point in time. In an analysis of boarding and lodging, Modell and Hareven (1973) reconstructed a life-course exchange-pattern between young men and women in the transitional state between leaving home and marrying, and older heads of household whose children had left home. In Chapter 6 of this volume, Mason, Vinovskis, and Hareven, in analyzing women's labor force participation in relationship to age and marital status, ethnicity, literacy, and family's economic status, found that, overall, whether women were gainfully employed was primarily a function of marital status. Unless confronted with economic exigencies, most women stopped working for remuneration after their marriage (assuming their husband was present and working). Chudacoff and Hareven (Chapter 7 of this volume), using head of household's age as a variable in measuring the family arrangements of older people, found that household extension frequently occurred in the lives of older heads. The use of their household space was related to changing needs along the life course.

The task of reconstructing sequences of transitions is more difficult, especially the ways in which one transition affects others, and timing affects subsequent timing. In Chapter 8 of this volume, Hareven and Modell attempt to combine the timing patterns of the individual transitions discussed in the respective historical essays, by constructing a "synthetic life-course sequence" for Essex County, relating the different transitions to one another. The degree of concurrence and congruity of certain transitions must still be examined, however (see Modell et al., 1976).

If used creatively, cross-sectional data can also make important contributions to life-course analysis, especially where the family, rather than the individual, serves as the unit of analysis. A cross-section of any family at a particular point in time represents a configuration of individuals related to each other, who are each in a different phase of their own life course. The study of the interacting of such individual life patterns within a family framework can reveal the different age-related roles and tensions involved in the orchestration of individual life careers within the family collective. For example, the analysis by Kaestle and Vinovskis in this volume (Chapter 5) examines a child's school attendance in relationship to a number of age and role configurations within the family unit, such as mother's work, number of other children present in the household working, presence of other children of pre-school or school age, presence of other kin working, or presence of boarders and lodgers. In this respect, cross-sectional data analyzed from a life-course perspective, can give one a better grasp of the simultaneous transitions among different family members that might be taking place in a family unit at one point in time. In fact, such analysis of age configurations within the family at different cross-sections has been pursued by those following the family cycle. At this point, the life course and the family cycle intersect, since the family cycle actually represents a slice of the life course.

Cohort analysis, a methodology frequently employed by demographers, can be followed for both cross-sectional as well as longitudinal analysis, but it must not be confused with life-course analysis. Life-course analysis provides an overall approach which uses a variety of methodologies, one of which is cohort analysis. Historians could follow cohort analysis to identify cross-sectional patterns at one point in time and to cast them into a longitudinal sequence by comparing the experiences of different cohorts over time. Its use enables one to isolate specific age groups and to measure their interaction with historical conditions, rather than simply to examine an undifferentiated population. A *cohort* provides an age-specific group for the analysis of certain experiences, while a *generation* can encompass a variety of individuals with a significant age spread. Ideally, cohort analysis could also be longitudinal, measuring the changes in the life course of a specific cohort over time, and comparing them with those of other cohorts. But, one can carry out cross-sectional cohort analysis as well. Historians could analyze the status and experience of a cohort in one census year, and compare it with that same age group two decades later. Uhlenberg's (1974) comparison of the family transitions of cohorts of white American women from 1870 to 1930 illustrates the power of this methodology in measuring social change. To understand subsequent life-course patterns of a specific age group in a specific location, 10-year-olds in 1880, for example, one can compare them with 20-year-olds in 1890, as a proxy for their subsequent careers. Unfortunately, of course, due to high mobility, one would be comparing two different groups, rather than following the same cohort. If cohort analysis is restricted to one point in time, one would assume that the experiences of 10-year-olds in 1880 would be in 10 years like those of 20-year-olds in 1880, and so on. Analysis of a cross section of the population in 1880, for example, would reveal the coincidence of a number of different cohorts at one point in time. It is, therefore, possible to differentiate between the experience of different age cohorts, as they are affected by the historical conditions specific to that point in time, or as they affect each other.

Agenda for Future Research

The innovative character of this volume imposes several limitations, especially on the empirical chapters. The first major limitation stems from the use of a cross-sectional data set, and its lack of comparability with other time periods. Except for Chapter 5 on school attendance, the historical chapters examine the experiences of different cohorts at one point in time, in 1880. Future research could compare the 1880 patterns with those in 1900, and with earlier census decades.

Second, the examination of one of the crucial life-course transitions is missing from this volume, namely the transition to parenthood. The pace of this transition has been calculated by Uhlenberg (1974) for the entire population on the aggregate level, but has not been analyzed on the 1880 data set because of the difficulty reconstructing such transitions from household level census data. The 1900 census lends itself more effectively to such analysis because it lists the number of years married, total number of children born, and total number of children living. However, the 1900 census did not become available to scholars in time to be used in this volume.

A third data limitation is the absence of explicit economic characteristics such as property or income data for the population studied here. Some of the chapters use occupation as a proxy for economic status and class (a technique usually followed by historians analyzing nineteenth-century population groups). To overcome this limitation, the chapters on school attendance and women's work utilized a "consumption" and "dependency" index, as a measure of economic need within the family.

A fourth limitation of the historical data is their confinement to the household level. Most of the analyses of "family" in these chapters are actually restricted to the household unit. The use of the census manuscript causes this limitation, precluding the possibility of analyzing patterns of kin interaction as they change over the life course.

Despite these limitations and gaps, this volume represents the first collaborative interdisciplinary effort to apply longitudinal questions to cross-sectional historical data, and to compare such patterns among different communities. It is also the first attempt to do so on a common data set, relating different transitions for the same population group, and integrating them into a sequence. It thus points the way to a more dynamic analysis of household data. Its contribution lies not merely in its findings, but also in its perspective and in the questions it raises.

The contributors share several common assumptions that lend added coherence to this volume: First, they assume that many apparently "individual" life course transitions do not represent merely individual careers, but are strongly linked to collective strategies of the family unit. Second, they assume that such collective strategies are influenced by economic, demographic, and cultural (ethnic) traditions. Rather than considering families as passive respondents to external conditions, the authors assume that families took an active role in responding to economic and demographic conditions. Families exercised some degree of choice in charting the life courses of their members. No doubt, the ways in which they formulated these choices and the priorities that they set for their different members were influenced by cultural (ethnic) considerations. However, in trying to reconstruct the choices that families made, it is difficult to isolate the basis for decision-making. This question remains subject to future research.

The understanding of different patterns of the timing of family

transitions within the context of the interaction of demographic, economic, and cultural factors becomes exceedingly complex, because in
the major part of evidence used, we have to rely on behavioral rather
than on phenomenological data. Thus, it is impossible for us to reconstruct the actual perceptions, decision-making processes, and conflicts
of the different population groups studied here. At best, we can infer
preferences and choices, but we are unable to recapture the meaning of
different life-course transitions and related choices to people. This is
precisely where anthropology has made a valuable contribution to the
understanding of phenomenology. Chapter 10 by LeVine not only provides an important comparison of behavioral patterns, but also provides a model for the analysis of perceptions within the culture.

Because of the limitations of the historical data used here, this book
raises many more questions than it can answer. It is important, nevertheless, to address these questions to the study of the family and social
change. One set of questions concerns the history of the family, while
another set relates more broadly to nineteenth-century American society. Specifically, how do changes in the timing of life-course transitions expand our understanding of historical changes in the family?
What do changes in timing tell us about family organization and internal
family strategies? With the recent emphasis on the uniformity of household structure over the past three centuries, variations in timing serve as
a major indicator of historical change.

Further questions arise as to the broader implications of these life-
course and family patterns for our understanding of historical change
in American society. Were there significant differences in timing
among different ethnic and socioeconomic groups? Was there a normatively established pattern of timing in life-course transitions? If such a
model pattern existed, in what ways did different ethnic and
socioeconomic groups deviate from the established norms? Did the
process of Americanization involve a gradual adaptation of immigrant
"time" to native American "time"? Similarly, did the adoption of
middle-class norms change patterns of timing in working-class
families? Have changes in the economy, especially increasing affluence, changing wage structures, and consumption patterns caused an
increasing conformity in family time? Are we witnessing, in 1880 in
Essex County, Massachusetts a population in transition to the more
homogeneous and "modern" life-course pattern that according to
Uhlenberg characterizes the American population in the twentieth century?

While the sociological, demographic, and economic chapters in
this volume provide theoretical supports for these questions, the empir-

ical historical chapters mostly offer answers within a restricted time period. Wherever possible, however, they interpret these cross-sectional patterns with longitudinal questions in mind.

References

Anderson, Michael S.
    1971   Family Structure in Nineteenth Century Lancashire. Cambridge, England: Cambridge University Press.
Berkner, Lutz K.
    1972   "The stem family and the developmental cycle of the peasant household: an eighteenth-century Austrian example." American Historical Review 77:398–418.
Chudacoff, Howard
    Forth-   "Newlyweds and family extension: the first stage of the family cycle in
    coming   Providence, Rhode Island, 1864–1865 and 1879–1880." In Tamara K. Hareven and Maris Vinovskis (eds.), Family and Population in Nineteenth-Century America. Princeton, New Jersey: Princeton University Press.
Elder, Glen H., Jr.
    1974   Children of the Great Depression. Chicago: University of Chicago Press.
Glick, Paul C.
    1947   "The family cycle." American Journal of Sociology 12:164–174.
    1955   "The life cycle of the family." Marriage and Family Living 18:3–9.
    1977   "Updating the life cycle of the family." Journal of Marriage and the Family 39:5–13.
Glick, Paul C., and Arthur J. Norton
    1977   "Marrying, divorcing, and living together in the U.S. today." Population Bulletin 32 (October):1–39.
Glick, Paul C., and Robert Parke, Jr.
    1965   "New approaches in studying the life cycle of the family." Demography 2:187–212.
Greven, Philip
    1970   Four Generations: Population, Land and Family in Colonial Andover, Massachusetts. Ithaca, New York: Cornell University Press.
Hareven, Tamara K.
    1974   "The family as process: the historical study of the family cycle." Journal of Social History 7:322–329.
    1975a   "The laborers of Manchester, New Hampshire, 1900–1940: the role of family and ethnicity in adjustment to industrial life." Labor History 16:249–265.
    1975b   "Family time and industrial time: family and work in a planned corporation town, 1900–1924." Journal of Urban History 1:365–389.
    1977   "Family time and historical time." Daedalus 106 (Spring):57–70.
    Forth-   "The dynamics of kin in an industrial community." American Journal of
    coming   Sociology.
Hill, Reuben
    1964   "Methodological issues in family development research." Family Process 3 (March):186–206.

1970   Family Development in Three Generations. Cambridge, Massachusetts: Schenkman.

Modell, John

Forth-   "Patterns of consumption, acculturation, and family income strategy in late
coming   nineteenth-century America." In Tamara K. Hareven and Maris Vinovskis (eds.), Family and Population in Nineteenth-Century America. Princeton, New Jersey: Princeton University Press.

Modell, John, and Tamara K. Hareven

1973   "Urbanization and the malleable household: boarding and lodging in American families." Journal of Marriage and the Family 35:467–479.

Modell, John, Frank Furstenberg, and Theodore Hershberg

1976   "Social change and transitions to adulthood in historical perspective." Journal of Family History 1:7–32.

Riley, M. W., M. E. Johnson, and A. Foner (eds.)

1972   Aging and Society: A Sociology of Age Stratification. New York: Russell Sage Foundation.

Rowntree, B. S.

1901   Poverty: A Study of Town Life. London: Macmillan.

Ryder, Norman B.

1965   "The cohort as a conception in the study of social change." American Sociological Review 30:843–861.

Uhlenberg, Peter

1974   "Cohort variations in family life cycle experiences of U.S. females." Journal of Marriage and the Family 36:284–292.

Vinovskis, Maris A.

1977   "From household size to the life course: some observations on recent trends in family history." American Behavioral Scientist 21:263–287.

1
Family History and the Life Course

GLEN H. ELDER, JR.

Change within families over the life course has been documented by studies since the turn of the century, in particular the sequential change in family relationships, adaptive options, and material welfare that occurs through the addition, aging, and loss of members. Rowntree's (1901) study of York, England is generally acknowledged as the earliest antecedent of research in the family-cycle tradition, most of which has been carried out since 1955. Later evaluation of the family cycle model[1] has served to underscore two requirements that are basic to a process-oriented perspective on the family in historical context.

First, and most important, is the development of constructs and models that represent processes of family adaptation and change over time; the timing, arrangement, and duration of events in the life course; the ever-changing pattern of interdependence and synchronization among the life histories of family members; and the cycle of genera-

Financial support in the development of this chapter was provided by the National Institute of Mental Health (Grant MH-25834).

[1]The family cycle was examined critically in some papers that were presented at the thirteenth International Family Research Seminar, Paris, France (September, 1973). For a selection of these papers see Cuisinier (1977). In a forthcoming essay, I describe the emergence of a temporal perspective on the family life course as one of the turning points in the trend among sociologists toward genuine historical research on the family.

17

tional exchange and succession. The second requirement concerns the need for greater sensitivity to transactions between historical change and the family unit, to the historical location of husband and wife (as defined by their birth cohort, for example) and their career stage at points of change.

These perspectives are expressed in the general analytic framework of the life course. The first part of this chapter reviews basic distinctions, concepts, and analytic strategies that define the life course as a framework for the study of individuals and families over time, within a single generation, and across the historical contexts of successive generations. I begin with the life course of the individual: the life path or career line and models of role transitions; the interdependence of multiple life paths or careers, with their problems of coordination and resource management; and normative influences in the timing and arrangement of events. The life course of the family is viewed in terms of the interdependent life histories of its members. This approach brings sensitivity to the continual interchange between the family and other institutional sectors, to the interdependence of individual life history and family history, and to the impact of historical change in life patterns.

In the last half of the chapter, I turn to a critical examination of the most popular concept of the family through time, that of the family cycle, and relate it to the more general life-course formulation. As a concept, the family cycle offers a distinctive analytical contribution to the study of family change when it makes explicit reference to cyclical *intergenerational* processes: (a) generational succession through childbearing and socialization of the young to maturity; and (b) the intergenerational flow of resources, including inheritance. However, typologies of the family cycle generally represent static models that provide "snapshots" of family structure in particular stages; they tell us very little about the course of a family's history. Families with an identical history, as defined by a sequence of stages, vary markedly in their respective life course. Much of this variation is due to life-course differences in the timing and arrangement of events, variables typically excluded from stage classifications of the family cycle. Operational models of the family cycle primarily depict stages of parenthood—before the birth of children, the childbearing and childrearing years, and the postparental phase which begins when the last child has left home. Though seemingly obvious, this interpretation has not been applied to theory on the relationship between family stages and behavior. The focus on stages of parenthood suggests another limitation: Stage models of the family cycle neither represent nor sensitize research to the multiple, interlocking career lines of a couple and the family unit as a whole. A final restriction also applies to the emphasis on parenthood: Most stage models of the family cycle are based on the conventional script of a marriage that bears children and survives to old age.

In life-course and family-cycle studies, observed variation in family patterns by stage (whether defined by role structure, the timing of marriage or ages of marriage partners, or both) is subject to interpretations that are based on historical context and change (Berkner, 1972; Hareven, 1974). With the emergence of a cohort-historical approach in life-course analysis, sociologists have become more attentive to historical location and change in family life (Elder, forthcoming). Hareven (1977) has applied the life-course approach to the understanding of different patterns of timing of family transitions, and Vinovskis (1977) has reviewed some implications of a cohort-historical approach to family and intergenerational patterns. As these studies make clear, to understand the impact of historical change on family life we must know something about the process by which this effect occurred, a process which varies according to both family stage and individual situation at the point of change.

The conceptual framework of life-course analysis is deeply rooted in the study of individual histories and careers, particularly within the Chicago tradition of sociological analysis (with such major figures as W. I. Thomas, Ernest Burgess, and Everett Hughes). Significant features of the early Chicago school of sociology include its orientation to the study of individuals, groups, and social organizations in concrete social situations; its sensitivity to historical context and interest in processes of social change; and its pragmatic approach to method and theory.[2] From the standpoint of life-course analysis, the most important early work is William I. Thomas's (with F. Znaniecki, 1918–1920) *The Polish Peasant in Europe and America,* a project that opened up new vistas in relation to the temporal study of individuals and groups in situations of drastic change.

Five developments since 1960 bear upon the life course as a framework for the study of lives and families: the evolution of family

[2]In a historical review of the early years of Chicago sociology (1920–1932), Faris writes that the faculty "renounced the principle of authority and encouraged open, modest searching in the spirit of an inductive science. Their students were taught to venture into the complex world of actuality, to bring in new information in quantities, and to devise and improve methods of extracting durable generalizations from it [1967:128]." Within the Chicago tradition, other significant contributions to the temporal study of lives and families have been made by Cottrell (1942), Hill (1970), Farber (1961), Clausen (1972), Goffman (1961), Wilensky (1960), Becker (1960), and Glaser and Strauss (1971), among others.

development as a theoretical framework, cohort analysis of life patterns, life-span developmental psychology, life-history methods in data collection and retrieval, and time allocation research. Since the 1960s, temporal aspects of family life (the sequential phases in role transitions, the multiple, interlocking career lines of the family unit, etc.) have become a central feature of the developmental approach in family studies. This process view of the family is represented by Rodgers's (1973) overview of the developmental literature and by Hill's (1970) three-generation study. As outlined in this chapter, the life-course perspective is consistent with the developmental approach to the family and builds upon the newly emerging sociological specialty of age stratification (Riley et al., 1972). An important contribution of the latter is the development of methods and concepts for research on cohort life patterns. Rapid social change differentiates the historical context of successive birth cohorts, of individuals born within the same time interval. Successive cohorts encounter change at a different life stage and are consequently influenced in different ways. As N. B. Ryder (1965:846) observes, "the cohort is distinctly marked by the career stage it occupies when prosperity or depression, peace or war, impinge on it." The importance of this contribution will become apparent in our examination of historical change in life patterns.

Within the field of developmental psychology, life-span theoretical interests have generated research on antecedent–consequent relations that extend beyond specific age categories such as childhood and old age (Goulet and Baltes, 1970; Nesselroade and Reese, 1973; and Baltes and Schaie, 1973). Programmatic statements identify this approach by its concern with the description and explanation of age-related behavior change from birth to death. In practice, however, most life-span studies have neglected tasks that are basic to life-course analysis; they are insensitive to the diverse career lines of individuals and their psychological effects, and have generally failed to explicate the process of developmental change. To date, little progress has been achieved in identifying linkages between historical conditions and age-related behavioral change. We still find major studies of personality development from childhood to the adult years (Kagan and Moss, 1962; Block, 1971) that have been carried out as if human behavior could be understood without reference to historical context and the varied sequence of life events.

Life-history analysts have developed methods that facilitate the collection, retrieval, and quantification of detailed life-history information. Sophisticated data collection forms have been constructed so as to link events and transitions in the life course (changes in jobs, marital status, number of children) to both chronological and historical time.[3] Significant contributions to this method and its application have come from the Johns Hopkins project (Blum et al., 1969; Karweit, 1973), the Monterrey study of occupational histories (Balan et al., 1969), and from the Norwegian life-history study (Ramsøy, 1973). In view of the material cost and time required for prospective longitudinal research, this approach offers a valuable alternative in generating life records. Some of the difficulties in analyzing life-history data are discussed at length by Carr-Hill and Macdonald (1973) in a survey of the literature and work in progress.

Studies of the temporal structure of life events are paralleled on the microlevel by the analysis of time allocation in activities. This field of research is concerned with the daily round of activities, with behavior patterns that emerge from records of individual and collective activity as it evolves over the course of a day (Szalai, 1972:1; Robinson, 1977). Types of activity are viewed in terms of their timing, duration, and frequency; their synchronization, management, sequential order, situational context, and participants. Time budgets have been used in cross-national research on the activity patterns of male workers in different occupations, and of housewives and employed, married women.

The Life Course as a Perspective

The life course refers to pathways through the age-differentiated life span, to social patterns in the timing, duration, spacing, and order of events; the timing of an event may be as consequential for life experience as whether the event occurs and the degree or type of change. Age differentiation is manifested in expectations and options that impinge on decision processes and the course of events that give shape to

[3]In addition to the use of life-history information to characterize the course of a person's life, the subjective biography has long been regarded by some clinical psychologists as "the ultimate criterion of truth about an individual [Dailey, 1971:xii]." As one of the pioneering analysts, John Dollard viewed the life history as "a deliberate attempt to define the growth of a person in a cultural milieu and to make theoretical sense of it. It might include both biographical and autobiographical documents.... [A life history is not merely] an account of a life with events separately identified like beads on a string.... The material must, in addition, be worked up and mastered from some systematic viewpoint [1949:3]." Within this framework, retrospective biographical descriptions have been employed in the study of aging (Lieberman and Falk, 1971) and in research on psychopathology (Roff and Ricks, 1970; Roff et al., 1972). For an overview of methods in the use of life histories for the study of lives, the most thorough current source is Dailey's *Assessment of Lives* (1971).

life stages, transitions, and turning points. Such differentiation is based in part on the social meanings of age and the biological facts of birth, sexual maturity, and death. These meanings have varied through social history and across cultures at points in time, as documented by evidence on socially recognized age categories, grades, and classes. Childhood, adolescence, youth, and old age are major foci of research on stages of the life course in American society (Elder, 1975a, 1975b; Hareven, 1976). Very little is known about the role of age criteria in structuring life patterns in the middle years, a period characterized by substantial variation among age mates in social roles and accomplishments. Over the life course, age differentiation also occurs through the interplay of demographic and economic processes, as in the relation between economic swings and the timing of family events. Sociocultural, demographic, and material factors are essential elements in a theory of life-course variation.

The Career Line

Traditionally, the life course of an individual has been viewed in terms of a single life path, such as the course of a person's worklife or marriage. This approach neglects a central feature of life experience in complex societies—that of multiple, interdependent pathways from birth to death—and is completely inadequate for handling the complex process of marriage and family dynamics. However, it is far superior to simple life-span comparisons of events or status. For example, comparisons of first and last job obscure the varied paths followed by workers over their productive years (see Thernstrom, 1973). Even if the first job is highly predictive of the last job, the full implications of the last position—both social and psychological—are contingent on the worker's history of jobs and employers. An orderly work history of functionally related jobs in a status hierarchy obviously differs in implications from that of a disorderly worklife (see Wilensky, 1960). Analysis of the life course is oriented to the process of situational change, and consequently to the much neglected task of explaining such change. This objective is consistent with that of analytical history, to identify "the causes and meaning of events in order to understand change [Tuma, 1971:50]."

The course of life experience is most accurately represented by temporal constructs that depict the situations traversed. Unfortunately, our theoretical language has little to offer in temporal formulations beyond the concept of career. In its most general sense as an attribute of the individual, career refers to a sequence of activities or roles through social networks and settings. From this vantage point, a career line is equivalent to an individual's life history in each role domain, such as marriage, parenthood, consumption, and worklife. This usage of the concept is not restricted to lines of action that are orderly and entail a well-defined sequence of functionally related roles. Whatever the form of a person's worklife of jobs and employers, it represents his occupational career.[4]

The personal and social implications of a particular career line arise in large part from its relation to institutionalized specifications for such activity in the social order. Though lacking adequate documentation, these specifications constitute a framework of social rules, standards of evaluation, and expectations that link behavior to rewards and negative sanctions, that is, a normative schedule on the timing and arrangement of marriage and births. From this structural perspective, an occupational career entails a "succession of related jobs, arranged in a hierarchy of prestige, through which persons move in an ordered, predictable sequence [Wilensky, 1960:554]." The work pattern thus provides a measure of stability, social support, and predictability in the life course. The expectation of "continuous, predictable rewards" engenders an acceptance of the investment costs of extensive training and solid performance, of a long distance outlook in which immediate gratifications are sacrificed for more substantial payoffs in the future. The structure of such career paths, which are mainly found among occupations in the higher social strata, makes especially costly events that force career shifts or that impede expected progress in work experience. A case in point is the adverse effect of a lengthy "time out" to bear and rear children on the professional advancement of highly trained women.

Career lines are structured by the realities of historical times and circumstance; by the opportunities, normative pressures, and adaptive requirements of altered situations; and by those expectations, commitments, and resources which are brought to these situations. "Some people come to the age of work when there is no work, others when

---

[4]The literature includes a number of variations on the career theme. For example, Hanson and Simmons have proposed the concept of role path in depicting migration to urban communities. A role path

specifies the history of events and associated attribute changes depicted as movements within and between role contexts. A role path traces the flow of experiences producing changes in personal attributes and related life condition variables. A regular, generalized sequence of events leading to a change within a role context is a social process which is part of the total larger process of urbanization [1968:155].

there are wars. . . . Such joining of a man's life with events, large and small, are his unique career, and give him many of his personal problems [Hughes, 1971:124]." A good many of these problems are associated with the timing disturbances of historical change. Examples include those women who delayed childbearing during the 1930s, as well as the men who lost ground in career advancement in the Depression decade and soon found themselves in competition with members of a younger cohort. The interplay between historical forces and career lines invites study of the process by which these forces are expressed in the structure and dynamics of lives over time.

From a subjective standpoint, a career perspective might take the form of a projection of future events and their anticipated significance, or a vantage point based on interpretations of experience as one moves through life. Regarding the latter, Hughes (1971:137) refers to the subjective career as "the moving perspective in which the person sees his life as a whole and interprets the meaning of his various attributes, actions, and the things which happen to him." Expectations in a career projection are influenced by childhood experience and have some bearing on subsequent interpretations of accomplishments. One study (Elder, 1974:261–262) found that the retrospective emotional career of middle-aged adults varied according to their family situation in the Great Depression, as remembered and actually experienced. Depression experiences seemed to have established "a frame of reference for defining life periods as relatively good or bad times," quite apart from actual adult achievements. Adults who remembered the Depression as a traumatic experience or who grew up in a hard-pressed family were most likely to view their life course as more satisfying in adulthood than in the early years.

The timing of events marks transition points in the life course, a topic that has generated a substantial literature of uneven quality, particularly in relation to the adaptive problems of entry and exit from a single role: entry into the first job (Granovetter, 1974); marriage (Rausch et al., 1963); parenthood (Rossi, 1968); departure of the last child from home (Lowenthal and Chiriboga, 1972); and retirement (Carp, 1972). In relation to life paths, Rossi (1968) has proposed that a social role be viewed in terms of four phases—anticipatory, plateau, disengagement, and termination. Following the assumption that the life span resembles a multistage cycle, with each stage defined by unique tasks and obligations, she argues that the role sequence represents a cycle. While it is clear that the stages depict the course of a career, in what sense do they constitute phases of a cycle? The phases of parenthood, marriage, and work do not represent a cycle in the sense of recurring states or conditions, unlike the process of generational succession. The metaphorical reflection of an aged Quebec farmer captures the essence of this cyclical process: "Life is like a turning wheel. The old turn over the work to the young and die, and these in turn get old and turn over the work to their children [Miner, 1939:85]."

Role transitions or sequences entail both entry and exit, some measure of rejection and acceptance, separation and integration. Their psychosocial effects are contingent on the nature of the change and the adaptive potential of the individual, as defined by resources, social preparation, and support. Cottrell (1942) and Burr (1973: Chapter 11) have formulated a preliminary model of role transitions that specifies conditions that facilitate effective adaptation; these include rehearsal of the role, clarity of expectations, and minimal normative change. An important distinction between incremental and decremental transitions (marriage versus widowhood) has been made by Lowenthal and Chiriboga (1973) in their study of adaptive processes throughout the adult years. Developments in this area of investigation offer a promising base for the construction of general models that apply to the full range of role transitions in the life course. Such models are essential in the conceptualization of concurrent or overlapping transitions, such as entry into marriage and parenthood, departure of the youngest child, and divorce.

The multiphased decision process is an example of formulations along this line which are well suited to the explanatory analysis of status change within a context of interdependent careers. In the case of childbearing, it is assumed that each birth occurs in a different context and is thus influenced by a different set of conditions. Apart from change in family composition, the context of each birth may be differentiated by parental competence and outlook, by socioeconomic conditions, worklife prospects, and consumption priorities. In rejecting the assumption that a couple makes a firm decision after marriage on how many children to have, Namboodiri (1972:198) has recently outlined a process perspective; each step of the decision process deals with the "addition of a (another) child to the family." This decision model would also apply to the spacing of children. Likewise in the study of unwed motherhood, this status has been depicted as an unplanned outcome of a sequence of decisions or actions in a distinctive moral career (Rains, 1971; Furstenberg, 1976): premarital sexual experience (versus nonexperience); sex without contraceptives (versus such protection); pregnancy (versus not pregnant); the decision to give birth to a child out of wedlock (versus abortion or motherhood in marriage). Lines of action followed in each phase of the career require different explanations; factors that explicate premarital sexual experience obviously differ from those that bear on the choice among options following birth of a child out of wedlock. Another significant application of the multiphased decision model is seen in Goode's (1956) classic study of marital dissolution as social process—disenchantment, consideration of divorce, adjustments within the framework of marriage, separation, and postdivorce adjustments.

Interdependent Careers

In complex societies social differentiation takes the form of multiple-age structures and timetables, across institutional domains, and thus requires a multidimensional concept of the life course; a concept of interdependent careers that vary in synchronization and thus in problems of resource management. An individual's life course is multidimensional since movement through successive life stages entails the concurrent assumption of multiple roles, from those of son or daughter, age-mate, and student during years of dependency to adult lines of activity in major institutional domains of society. One's life history is thus a product of multiple histories, each defined by a particular timetable and event sequence—histories of education and work-life, marriage and parenthood, residence and civic involvement. The utility of a differentiated concept of the life course is suggested by the biography and anticipated pathways of adolescents in complex, industrial societies.

Late adolescence or the stage of youth is characterized by a high degree of social differentiation along institutional sectors: Differentiation of life paths increases sharply as the child becomes an adolescent and then enters the stages of youth and young adulthood. The late adolescent is in the process of entering multiple lines of adult activity, of work and civic responsibilities, marriage and parenthood. At any point in time, a cross section of the youth population would show wide variation in stages across dimensions of the life course. Marriage may occur before economic independence or the completion of education, and parenthood before marriage. For the individual, the stage of youth frequently provides striking examples of asynchrony and its implications for social identity, public approval, and opportunities.

Differentiated paths in the life course imply some differentiation in social worlds and significant others whose demands compete for the individual's scarce or limited resources—his time, energy, affections. The demands of parenthood are frequently in conflict with those of marriage, work, and civic duties. In a theoretical essay on role strain,

Goode (1960) argues that an individual's system of relationships is both "unique and overdemanding." Since it is not possible to satisfy all demands, he must "move through a continuous sequence of role decisions and bargains, by which he attempts to adjust these demands [Goode, 1960:495]." Within the constraints of social structure (e.g., the interests and sanctioning power of third parties such as kin and friends), the individual may attempt to reduce strain by scheduling or selecting relationships that are most supportive or least conflicting, and by working out the most rewarding bargain with each significant other. An additional assignment, or obligations to one more party, may be accepted in order to weaken the onerous claims of present involvements. The filter or buffer function of an intermediary, compartmentalizing conflicting demands, delegating responsibility, and withdrawing from interaction, represent other strategies in the management of finite resources and role strain. Both choice and circumstance in shaping the course of life are expressed in strategies of this sort, particularly at points of role transition.

The full significance of event-timing in the life course is seen within the context of interdependent careers. With multiple career lines, the scheduling of events and obligations becomes a basic problem in the management of resources and pressures. Scheduling involves the timing, spacing, and arrangement of events, both within and across life paths; the life stage in which to marry, for example, and its temporal distance and order relative to other events, such as the bearing of children, employment, and material acquisitions. As shaped by choice and circumstance, the decision process of life-course management takes the form of event patterns across career lines—the relation among marital, parental, socioeconomic, and consumption events.

The Timing and Order of Events:
Cause and Consequence

Demographic, material, and normative forces shape both the temporal structure of the life course and its consequences. Demographic constraints are expressed in the age–sex structure of a social context, in size variations across successive cohorts, and in the changing social composition of cohorts across points in time. Within a specific birth cohort, the usual mating gradient on age (men select younger mates) has direct consequences for the marital options of women who delay marriage until their late twenties or early thirties; the greater the delay, the more restricted the pool of age-eligible men. Material influences are illustrated by the well-known correlation between cyclical variations in the economy and rates of marriage, childbearing, and divorce. Normative determinants take the form of social expectations that specify appropriate times and arrangements for life events and transitions; there is an appropriate time for the completion of education, for leaving home and achieving economic independence, for marriage and bearing children, for the postparental years and retirement (Neugarten and Datan, 1973). As individuals move through the age structure, they are made aware of whether they are early, on time, or late in role entry and accomplishments by an informal system of rewards and sanctions.

Normative influence, proscriptive and prescriptive, represents a favored explanation of patterned choice in the life course among sociologists and demographers. Failure to take this influence into account has been cited as a major weakness of the new economic models of fertility and life-course events. If such norms were "fixed in time and space, one could readily take them as given (meaning essentially to forget them), but they vary from culture to culture, from subculture to subculture, from class to class, and they vary through time.... So thoroughly are they embedded in our lives that they verge on the invisible, and this is one of the major sources of their strength [N. B. Ryder, 1974:77]." Unfortunately, empirical evidence regarding normative influence also verges on the invisible; assertions or platitudes far exceed demonstrable evidence. Far more is known about demographic constraints—age–sex ratios, etc.

Instead of measuring norms, sanctions, and control networks, and including such measures in the analysis, studies have tended to offer general statements based on imprecise or sketchy documentation. For example, reference is made to normative life patterns or to the presumed fact that the birth of a first child is expected early in the childbearing years by society (Ritchey and Stokes, 1974). Claims of this sort completely disregard the assumption of normative variation by social context—between the South and non-South, small towns and metropolitan areas. Available evidence clearly points to community size as a key variable in the normative regulation of life events, from the cultural homogeneity and informal control networks of rural communities to the cultural diversity of large urban centers. However, at present, the literature does not include even one large-scale study of age expectations and sanctions relative to events in the life course. This deficiency is a matter of some irony when we note the longstanding prominence of cultural norms in social theory.

The preferred sequence of events and activities implied by a normative timetable suggests a number of problems that warrant investigation; in particular, deviant sequences or disarrangements, such as motherhood before marriage, which may arise from external pressure, social disruptions and disorganization, and faulty socialization (Furstenberg, 1976). The effects of a deviant sequence are contingent on its timing, on the temporal phase of the life course in which it occurs. In this respect, unwed motherhood represents a very different event for the adolescent than for a woman in her late twenties or early thirties. Through its social stigma and burden, teenage illegitimate birth deprives the mother of social support and severely restricts access to training and developmental experiences that determine life prospects.

Without substantial evidence on age norms and sanctions across historical time and place, it is difficult to judge the significance of other deviant or atypical sequences, such as marriage before economic independence or completion of education. In particular, the meaning of such arrangements may have little to do with norms per se; events may depart from shared understandings of the usual life course and entail hardships of one kind or another, but not as a result of normative sanctions. Judging from the evidence at hand, event sequences appear to have become more variable since the nineteenth century in America. The transition to adulthood is characterized by less temporal differentiation between events (leaving home, marriage, completion of education, entry into work) among contemporary young men, when compared with the experience of their counterparts in late nineteenth-century Philadelphia (Modell et al., 1976), and is thus distinguished by a greater probability of variant sequences—of completion of education after marriage and even parenthood, and of parenthood before marriage. Matters of timing, sequencing, and coordination have emerged as key aspects of the decision process among youth in advanced industrial societies.

Temporal Patterns in Marriage and the Family

Up to this point we have focused on the life course of the individual—on the course of a single life path and the dynamic interdependence of multiple career lines or pathways. In applying the life-course perspective to marriage and the family unit, we begin with the interdependent life histories of their members; problems of coordination and resource management at the group level emerge from this temporal interdependence. Analysis of the young couple centers on the social patterns formed by the joining of life histories through mate selection and their consequences for marital interaction, child rearing, and kin relations. Each status relation between husband and wife acquires distinctive meaning within a particular social and cultural configuration. Thus the significance of marriage into a lower-status family is partly contingent on the relative education and occupational achievements of each spouse. Within the context of social patterns at marriage, the course of marital life is shaped by subsequent developments in the interdependent careers of husband and wife. A life-course framework views the family unit in terms of mutually contingent careers, their differentiating characteristics and problems of management. It facilitates study of divergent or nonconventional family patterns, as well as the conventional, by working with the life histories of individuals, and brings greater sensitivity to the continual interchange between family and other institutional sectors—marriage and the economy, child rearing and formal schooling.

The joining of life histories in marriage presents two major lines of inquiry[5] on the determinants and consequences of conjugal patterns. Mate selection and resulting patterns of social homogamy (on class, education, age) have been viewed generally in terms of cultural norms and ecological factors (such as propinquity) that structure the field of eligibles. More recently, interest has centered on the extent to which marital choice is influenced by its timing within a specific historical context. The marriage market changes from early to late marriage; as unmarried members of a cohort age, marriageability declines and pressures to marry increase. The usual mating gradient (men marry younger women) suggests that the selection of younger husbands is most prevalent among women who marry relatively late and that the age superiority of husbands is likely to be most pronounced among couples in which the wives married relatively early. These differences were obtained in a nationwide cohort of white women who were born during the late 1920s (Elder and Rockwell, 1976). Well-educated women who delayed marriage minimized the risk of a less-educated mate by tending to select their husbands from a younger age category. Apart from the advantage of family status and higher education, late-married women were far more likely than other members of the cohort to secure through marriage a position in the upper-middle class.

[5]Ernest Burgess (cited in Bogue, 1974:209) has consistently emphasized the marital significance of the premarriage life histories of husband and wife. Among the domains that warrant study, he cites "the relative status of husband and wife which may involve initially and perhaps permanently the difference in standing of the families of the couple" and the "relative cultural transmission" through the husband and wife which stems from the fact that at marriage each is "already a person with a history." The formation of particular social patterns in mate selection thus represents a strategic point at which to study marriage as mutually contingent careers.

Life-course analysis underscores the relevance of status relations in marriage, as against the individual characteristics of each spouse. Status differences between partners on social origins, age, and education favor marital incompatibility to the extent that they produce divergent interests or conflict with valued expectations (Pearlin, 1972, 1975).

Marriage also establishes a set of mutually contingent careers (Farber, 1961), with their problem of coordination. Strategies of career management involve the timing of marriage and births, the spacing of children, the acquisition of goods and services according to need and income, the husband's employment and job changes, the wife's entry and reentry into the labor force, and decisions regarding residential change. In a study of three generations of families from the Minneapolis–St. Paul area, Hill (1970) observed wide variations within each generation in career management and the achievement of long-term goals. Some families perceived themselves as being "ahead of schedule," others "on schedule," and still others "behind schedule." Family progress in achieving goals on schedule was dependent on effective career management, the synchronization of transitions and activities in a manner which enables the multiple career lines of the family to be mutually supportive of movement toward life-style objectives. Within a well-defined timetable, family adaptations to the recognition of "being ahead of or behind schedule" may take the form of shifts in outlook and plans; progress ahead of schedule supports a future-oriented perspective in which evaluations are phrased in terms of potential achievement; distance from career origins is more likely to serve as a basis of evaluation for families that find themselves behind schedule.

Scheduling dilemmas in life-course management are a common theme among families in which both husband and wife are involved in occupational careers—the dual-career family (Rapoport and Rapoport, 1969). The peak demands of worklife generally occur during the early phase of career establishment and advancement, a phase which frequently corresponds with the peak demands of childbearing and child rearing. Any decision to sequence the demands of parenthood and occupational career entails both costs and rewards. If children are postponed until the pressures of career advancement have diminished, problems may arise from the difficulty of adapting established routines to the needs of dependents and from the wide age difference between parent and child. Other costs are encountered in the sacrifice of one partner's career prospects for the advancement of the other, and in the placement of preschool children in day-care centers.

The life-course approach is well-suited to research on conventional and variant family forms because of its perspective on the life histories of both individuals and family units. Through the early death of one partner, divorce, and remarriage, some persons are affiliated with different family units and forms over their life course. With the expansion of historical and comparative work on the life course, we have become more aware of the necessity for conceptual models and modes of analysis that take such variety into account, as well as the course of a marriage which endures to old age and produces at least one child. For example, Uhlenberg (1974) has identified five life-course types in a comparison of white and nonwhite cohorts of American females— 1890–1894 through 1930–1934; *early death*—female dies between the ages of 15 and 50; *spinster*—female survives, does not marry before the age of 50; *childless*—female survives and marries, but has no live births; *unstable marriage, with children*—female survives, marries, bears at least one child, but first marriage is broken before the age of 50; and *preferred*—female arrives at age 50 living with first husband and as parent of at least one child. A comparison of the successive birth cohorts shows a trend toward the preferred form among white and nonwhite women. These types present an illuminating portrait of the diversity of cohort life patterns. Further work along this line should incorporate other data to flesh out the course of each life pattern; in particular, information on variations in the timing and arrangement of events.

Life-course analysis directs research toward temporal assessments of interactions between family and environment, such as the economy and social institutions. The general tendency has been to view this relation at a point in time instead of as a sequence of interchanges and reciprocal adaptations over time. For the most part, the impact of occupational or economic position on family patterns has been studied without considering the socioeconomic history of the family. From a historical standpoint, the lower-middle class includes families that are upwardly and downwardly mobile; some have experienced the social and economic insecurity of a disorderly worklife, and others a steady advancement in living standard. The same imprecision is found in generational comparisons which include only parents and offspring. Some parental families are members of the first generation in the middle class, while others have a middle-class background of three or more generations.

Relevant to this potential diversity is Wilensky's assertion that

> a man's current job, his immediate work situation, place of residence, even his
> class position, while they count for something, tend to be ephemeral.... Yet
> no studies have focused ... on the interdependence of behavior and attitude in
> the separate spheres of modern society over the life span of the person—
> interlocking cycles of work, family life and consumption, and community par-
> ticipation [1960:549].

With few exceptions, this conclusion also applies to the contemporary
literature (Young and Wilmott, 1973; Kanter, 1977). Wilensky's own
study of worklife and social integration (1961; see also Pahl and Pahl,
1971) suggests some of the advantages of taking a life history perspective on contingent careers. Men with orderly careers (jobs which are
functionally related in a hierarchy of prestige) tended to participate in
more social activities than workers with disorderly worklives, even
apart from variations in age, income, and occupational status; they
were more likely to be involved in local church and school functions, to
be members of friendship circles in which each person knows the
other, and to have a wide range of social contacts both within and
outside of family and kin.

Examples of the interplay between work and family include the
relation between work timetables and the temporal structure of family
life, the problem of "role overload" in the dual work patterns of husband and wife (Rapoport and Rapoport, 1969), the timetable and demands of women's gainful employment as factors in childcare and
marital relations (Hoffman and Nye, 1974), and the effect of generalized
economic dislocations on worklife and family. The impact of an irregular work schedule on family activity is suggested by Young and Wilmott's (1973: Chapter 7) study of shiftworkers in London, England.
Most of these men claimed that their jobs markedly interfered with
family life, with their social roles in the home, and with family routines
(nearly twice the proportion of other workers). A high level of strain
also occurred between career lines in families where the wife was employed full-time in a professional career. Among well-educated
couples in England (Bailyn, 1970), some evidence suggests that marital
satisfaction and the wife's career prospects are most heavily contingent
on the husband's mode of relating to work and family; both outcomes
are enhanced when the husband assigns priority to the family and is
able at the same time to achieve rewards in his worklife.

Up to this point, we have outlined some basic features of life-course analysis, as it applies to the individual (multiple, interlocking life paths or career lines) and to the couple and family unit. This approach joins two traditions of sociological inquiry—life-history analysis originating in the Chicago school and the study of social differentiation. Age differentiation centers attention on age distinctions in social roles, options, and sanctions, and more generally on the timing of our lives, with its normative and demographic constraints. The schedule of events provides a skeletal representation of life and family process. In complex societies, social differentiation necessitates a multidimensional concept of the life course, of multiple life paths. With an increase in life-course differentiation comes an increase in problems of coordination and resource management.

Age differentiation also takes the form of differences in historical experience because age locates the individual in a specific historical context. This brings us to the problem of social change in the life course, and, more specifically, to a methodology for linking historical events to life patterns.

Social Change in the Life Course

Everett Hughes's observation on historical events in life experience (that "some people come to work when there is no work") reflects a more general sensitivity among life-history analysts to historical forces. This consciousness is found in notable early works, such as Thomas's (with Znaniecki, 1918–1920) and Mannheim's essay on "The Problem of Generations" (1928/1952). But the most cogent statement of this perspective was made some years later by C. W. Mills in The Sociological Imagination:

> The biographies of men and women, the kinds of individuals they have become, cannot be understood without reference to the historical structures in which the milieux of their everyday life are organized. Historical transformations carry meanings not only for individual ways of life, but for the very character—the limits and possibilities of the human being [1959:175].

Such awareness of the historical imprint was uncommon among sociologists up to the 1960s, and consequently had no visible effect on research. Most studies of life experience and family patterns were conducted without any appreciation of historical context and variation. By the late 1960s, a rudimentary approach to the study of life-course change had emerged in the form of a cohort–historical framework (N. B.

Ryder, 1965; Riley et al., 1972; Elder, 1975a). This perspective employs age and vital data as social indicators and biological facts in the study of life patterns, age cohorts, and their corresponding age strata. Chronological age provides a rough index of life stage and aging, while birth year or entry into the social system (as through marriage or graduation from secondary school) locates the individual in historical context as a member of a particular cohort. Three sets of issues, in particular, warrant consideration in the study of historical events and the life course: (a) cohort and subgroup comparisons, with emphasis on the explanatory advantage of intracohort analysis; (b) the problematic meaning of age differences that reflect both historical context and career stage; and (c) cohorts and generation–lineage as social units in the study of change in the life course.

Cohort Life Patterns and Subgroup Variations

With cohort members, the individual is exposed to a slice of historical experience in the process of moving through a sequence of roles and events. The meaning and significance of birth year and cohort membership are derived from knowledge of historical events and trends at the time, and from cohort characteristics, such as composition and size, that are themselves a product of historical circumstances. Successive birth cohorts encounter the same historical event at different points in their life course, which suggests that the event's impact is contingent on the career stage of the cohort, which is indexed by age and social roles, at the point of historical change. In this regard, Hill observes that each cohort in periods of rapid change "encounters at marriage a unique set of historical constraints and incentives which influence the timing of its crucial life decisions, making for marked generational dissimilarities in life cycle career patterns [1970:322]." Two birth cohorts of American women illustrate this point: 1915–1918 and 1925–1928. The oldest cohort attained the usual age of marriage during the worst years of the Great Depression, conditions that often required the postponement of matrimony and childbearing; whereas the younger cohort came of marriage age during World War II, a period of rapid economic growth, full employment, and a decline in the age at which women entered marriage.

The complexity of assessing social change in family patterns stems in part from the diverse life stages, social roles, and historical experience of family members at points of change. The presence of older adolescents or youth, in particular, adds a significant dimension to the process by which historical events impinge on family life beyond that of the social roles of parents. Along with their mothers, they have played a role in the multiple-earner adaptation of hard-pressed families during periods of economic depression—the 1870s, 1890s, 1930s. This suggests that in specifying the outcome and process of social change in family patterns, we must begin with knowledge of the historical event and its relevance to the interdependent careers and life stages of family members.

Historical change also differentiates the life experience of social groups or categories *within* each cohort. Experiences in the Great Depression are known to have varied by age and sex, rural and urban residence, ethnicity, and social class. Middle-class families entered the Depression with social and economic aspirations that placed them in a more vulnerable "psychic" position with respect to income and job loss than families in the lower strata. But not all urban families in the middle class suffered heavy economic losses; with the decline in cost of living, some actually achieved a higher living standard. Economic sectors within class strata provide a degree of analytic precision which is essential for relating the experience of deprivation to family structure and the life course. This approach was employed in a longitudinal study of persons who were born during the early 1920s in Oakland, California (Elder, 1974). Within the middle and working class of 1929, the study compared the life experience and personality of persons who grew up in relatively nondeprived and deprived families. The income loss of nondeprived families averaged slightly less than 20% of 1929 income, which is roughly equivalent to the reduction in cost of living. Most deprived families in both social classes received losses that exceeded half of their 1929 income. At the time of maximum hardship in the early 1930s, the Oakland children were old enough to contribute to the household economy.

Family adaptations and conditions were viewed as linkages between economic deprivation and life experience among members of the 1920–1921 cohort. In this context, such linkages provide answers to the question of how and why economic loss influenced life patterns; they represent an interpretation of the relationship, an account of the mechanisms or process through which this historical change shaped the course of life events and development. Three general types of linkage were tested: (a) change in the division of labor—sudden loss of income called for new forms of economic maintenance that altered the domestic and economic roles of family members, shifting responsibilities to mother and the older children: (b) change in family relationships—father's loss of earnings and resulting adaptations in family maintenance increased the relative power of mother, reduced the level and effectiveness of parental control, and diminished the attractiveness of father as a model; and (c) social strains in the family—social ambiguity, conflicts, and emotional strain, as a consequence of resource losses, parental impairment, and inconsistency in the status of the family and its members. These family conditions were associated with economic deprivation in both social classes, and emerged as significant linkages between family hardship and life experience in the Oakland cohort. Four of these sequences are briefly summarized below to illustrate this intracohort approach to the study of historical change and life patterns:

1. *Mother's Prominence.* Economic deprivation increased the mother's sphere of activity and influence in the family, regardless of class position in 1929, although her emotional strain was most pronounced in the middle class. She was most likely to be perceived as the dominant parent in marital affairs and in parent–child relations by children from deprived homes. When father's misfortunes markedly reduced his role as breadwinner, mother frequently entered the labor force, and this economic function enhanced her perceived influence on family matters. In the eyes of her sons and daughters, the deprived mother was generally regarded as the most important source of counsel and emotional support. Her dominant position placed daughters more completely under her control, while tending to weaken parental control over sons.

2. *Domesticity.* Family deprivation shifted households toward a more labor-intensive economy with its domestic consequences for the upbringing of girls. The daughters of deprived parents in both social classes were more often involved in household responsibilities than were girls from nondeprived homes, and this activity partially accounts for their familistic orientation as adolescents and middle-aged adults. A quarter century after the Depression, women with deprived origins in the 1930s, whether middle or working class, were most inclined to prefer the family over work, leisure, and community activity; to regard children as the most important aspect of marriage; and to find satisfaction in homemaking tasks. These values are related to involvement in household operations during the 1930s and to the prominence of the mother. Neither differences in education nor variations on achieved status through marriage altered the familistic influence of childhood experience in an economically deprived household.

3. *Educational Disadvantage.* Family hardship impaired educational progress among boys and girls through loss of parental
support and increased household burdens, particularly in the
working class. Among girls, educational limitations stemmed in
large part from conditions that accelerated heterosexual involvement and the attractiveness of an early marriage: es-
trangement from father, a sense of emotional deprivation, and
domestic interests.
4. *Work Experience and Occupational Attainment.* Family deprivation increased the involvement of boys in gainful employment, and consequently their social independence and sensitivity to matters of vocation. This sensitivity took the form of an
early vocational focus and work commitment that led to a worklife which effectively countered the educational handicap of
family hardship, even among the sons of working-class parents.
In the long run, economic deprivation did not adversely affect
the occupational attainment of the Oakland men or the status
that women achieved through marriage.

The full array of findings from this study inevitably raise questions
concerning their generality. What about the uniqueness of the 1920–
1921 cohort on experiences in the Great Depression, a uniqueness in
developmental age at the time of economic crisis and in opportunities
at the end of the 1930s? In many respects, this cohort occupied a favorable position relative to depressed conditions in the 1930s; the members were too old to be highly vulnerable to family misfortune and too
young to enter the adult marketplace of marriage and work at the bottom of the economic cycle. In terms of future prospects, mobilization
for war occurred at a critical point and undoubtedly neutralized or at
least weakened the adverse effects of starting out life with a background of family privation (Elder and Rockwell, 1978). By comparison,
the Depression frequently had profound consequences for the worklives
of older men, including some fathers of the Oakland adults. Thernstrom's (1973) mobility study of Boston men documents the constraints
of the 1930s on the worklives of men who were born in the first decade of
the twentieth century, a group that had just entered lines of work and
family roles prior to the economic collapse.

These studies underscore the strategic value of a comparative study
of intracohort experiences for linking historical events to life patterns.
Members of successive cohorts encounter the same historical event at a
different stage in the life course, which implies cohort variations in
adaptive potential, options, and social roles. Equally important are
situational variations among members of each cohort that must be

specified to link historical change to the course of life experience. Both types of cohort variation caution against generalizations from the historical experience and life patterns of a single cohort.

The Problematic Meaning of Age Differences

Age differentiation in family patterns is often unclear as to its meaning since age indexes historical location as well as career stage. Are observed differences an outcome of historical change, of life stage, or of both? An answer to this question should have priority among the objectives of multigeneration studies, and yet it remains elusive in the cross-sectional designs that have been employed.

One such design was used to assess areas of intergenerational value change and continuity (Bengtson and Lovejoy, 1973); the sample was drawn from the Los Angeles area, represents a predominantly working-class population in the grandparent generation with substantial upward mobility across the ascending generations, and is distinguished by an age difference of nearly half a century between the youngest and oldest generations. Differential historical location and experience, socioeconomic position, and life stage are all potential explanatory factors for the value patterns observed across these generations. Such ambiguity is candidly acknowledged by Hill in relation to his cross-sectional study of three generations: "[The] extent historical circumstances have affected these three generations will be difficult to disentangle from other influences which come with maturation and aging [1970:30]."

Unfortunately there are many other studies in which the analyst shows little awareness of the interpretational problem. Pearlin's study (1972) of families in Turin, Italy is one example. Within the middle and working class, Pearlin found a sharp decline in marital companionship between couples in which the husband was less than 45 years of age and those in the older age category. Without any reference to evidence on the decline in marital companionship over the life course (see Dizard, 1968) or to career stage explanations, Pearlin advanced an interpretation that is based on the presumed effects of historical change:

> age differences capture a myriad of conditions attendant upon increased urbanization and industrialization; early exposure to these conditions, in turn, shapes attitudes toward marriage. The younger husbands, socialized and married at a time of heightened material and social development, are more disposed toward companionship. In this way age is related to companionship in marriage, but the relationship is quite indirect [1972:159].

The relationship is also subject to a number of other interpretations, including cohort differences in career stage and education.[6]

Generation-Lineage and Cohort as Social Units

Historical change in the life course has been viewed from both a generation-lineage and cohort perspective. The former approach tends to focus on modes of association and social transmission; examples include Kingsley Davis's (1940) provocative essay on parent–youth conflict, Eisenstadt's (1956) research on sociocultural conditions in generational cleavages and the rise of youth movements, and Hill's (1970) study of social transmission within three-generation lineages.

One of the most important issues in the generation tradition concerns the process of social transmission in areas of life-course change and continuity. A substantial literature has developed on the intergenerational or lineage transmission of education and occupation, as reviewed by Haller and Portes (1973), but we have no substantial evidence on the transmission of timetables. Generational differences in social position may be the most important source of intergenerational variations in the temporal structure of life events, but it is also conceivable that parental interpretations of experienced events are influential in forming the expectations and plans of the young. Are the meanings women place on events in their life course instrumental in orienting their daughters to a particular life pattern? The evidence for an answer to this question is not available, although it is clear that the timing of events is a matter of concern among middle-aged, American women (birthdates, 1925–1929) and that they share a general notion of the ideal or preferred life course (Elder and Rockwell, 1976). In view of their life history of relative deprivation (socioeconomic pressures in family of

---

[6]Comparison of birth cohorts within a cross-sectional or longitudinal sample should be also informed by knowledge of the criteria employed in the recruitment of families or individuals to the sample. Even more important is the need to examine the implications of these criteria for the outcomes under study. Terman's (1938) longitudinal sample of highly intelligent children and their parents represents a case in point. Terman assigned the mothers to three birth cohorts (1880–1889, 1890–1899, 1900–1909) and found a pronounced increase in premarital intercourse between the latter two cohorts. This outcome has been used as the basis for a strong generalization concerning change in sexual behavior. Thus Filene concludes that "the generation of women born between 1900 and 1909 did indeed mark an abrupt fork in the history of sexual behavior [1974:150]." The problem with Terman's finding is that the women were selected on the basis of having a child in secondary school, and consequently are likely to vary systematically by marital age across the three cohorts—those who married late would be more probable in the oldest cohort than in the 1900–1909 cohort. If this reasoning applies, the observed change in sexual behavior may be partly a reflection of cohort differences in marital age; premarital intercourse and pregnancy are most prevalent among those who marry early.

origin and procreation), it is not surprising that people who marry early do not look with favor upon the course they have followed. They uniformly endorsed a later marriage for their daughters, a delay in parenthood, and a smaller number of children. An earlier timetable was the most common choice of women who wed at a relatively late age—in the late twenties and early thirties; they preferred a younger age at marriage and parenthood, and a larger number of children. The optimal time schedule corresponds to that of women who married at the usual age.

Though generational studies are attuned to the transmission process between parents and offspring, they tend to neglect the realities of historical context. Generational status, in fact, is a very poor index of historical location. Individuals who occupy a common generational position in the descent hierarchy are most unlikely to share anything resembling a common historical location. Births to members of a particular cohort are distributed across successive cohorts. In periods of rapid change, biographical variations within a generation (among siblings) may exceed any intergenerational difference. The most persuasive case for distinguishing between age cohorts and generations comes from multi-generation studies (see Vinovskis's 1977 critique of Greven's *Four Generations*). For example, the grandparents in Bengtson's study (Bengtson and Lovejoy, 1973) vary in birth year by as much as 20 years, a time span that is too broad for a precise analysis of historical change in life patterns. Hill (1970) refers to the grandparents, parents, and children in his study as "generational cohorts," even though members of each generation were born within a broad sweep of American history (the age range in the parent generation is 30 years).

The middle generation in Hill's study offers striking documentation of the inadequacy of generations as units in the analysis of social change and life patterns. The parental couples actually represent two historically meaningful cohorts, defined by marriage in the 1920s and 1930s. Consistent with our knowledge of the Depression era, the pre-Depression couples ended up with a larger number of children and a more diverse set of career timetables (childbearing, childrearing, consumption, worklife, etc.) when compared with the younger couples. Even though the two cohorts were described as sufficiently different in life patterns "to constitute samples of different universes," they were treated throughout the analysis as one social unit (a decision which may have been based on considerations of sample size). The heterogeneity of this generation is likely to have obscured significant insights regarding intergenerational continuity and change.

Three points from this discussion deserve emphasis and apply more generally to the literature on social change in the life course:

1. *The analytic importance of the conceptual distinctions between generation and cohort*—analysts who refer to a generation as a cohort frequently have carried out their research as if the former unit possessed the attributes of the latter, that is, shared historical location.[7]

2. *The strategic advantages of employing both perspectives (generation and cohort) to studies of historical change in life patterns*—by specifying two birth cohorts within the grandparent generation of Bengtson's study, and thus across ascending generations, we identify "true" generational cohorts that are well suited for research on historical change in the life course.

3. *The need to invest greater effort in studies of the process by which particular forms of social change have an effect on life patterns.* In comparisons of successive cohorts, we assume that the same historical event has differential consequences for persons and family units who vary in career stage. This implies that stage variations are related to variations in the meaning of a situation, in adaptive resources and options, and thus in linkages between the event and the life course.

Career stage represents a basic construct in life-course analysis and in conventional models of the family cycle, but it is used in very different ways. Stage analysis in family cycle studies has generally neglected the historical context and social course of family units. Since models of the family cycle are currently the most popular approach in studies of families over the life span, it is important to identify what they do and do not represent in family patterns and to place them in relation to basic analytic features of the life-course framework.

The Family Cycle and Life Course

Three models of family change, as a developmental cycle, are suggested by theory and research. One depicts the cycle as an ordered

[7]The practice of equating generation and cohort with regard to historical location owes much to Mannheim's classic essay "The Problem of Generations" (1928/1952). Invariably we find this tendency in writings that use Mannheim's essay as a point of departure (see, for example, Spitzer, 1973). Since cohort refers explicitly to historical location, it should be preferred over the generational concept when this meaning is intended. Though generation has precise meaning within the domain of kinship and family, it has been associated with a wide variety of meanings, such as cultural or political era.

set of stages which are indexed primarily by variations in family composition and size. Refined by a Chicago research group in the early 1950s and by the subsequent work of Hill (1964) and his associates, this model has been widely adopted in family studies, often without recognition of its limitations.[8] One such limitation entails the neglect of family variations associated with the differential timing, spacing, and duration of events—a model of the developmental cycle which has informed Glick's cohort studies of family patterns (Glick and Parke, 1965: Carter and Glick, 1970; Glick, 1977). Glick's first paper on the subject offered "a presentation of the ages at which American married couples usually reach the several stages of the family cycle [1947:165]," as well as analyses of changes in family composition and economic characteristics. Unlike the family composition approach, variations in the timing of life events have not been identified with the family cycle concept, and one is hard pressed to find a single major study that has successfully employed the analytic strengths of both formulations. A perspective that joins these two formulations represents a third concept of the family cycle, a concept which more accurately represents the course of family life and structure.

Although the family cycle has been used most frequently in reference to patterned change in family composition and size, such change has been measured by typologies that only provide a series of stage or cross-sectional depictions of family structure. In what follows, I shall first explore some conceptual and empirical implications of stage typologies of compositional change, and then review issues and research on the dynamic interdependence of change in the composition and economy of family units. This review suggests the analytic advantage of a multidimensional concept of family stage which is informed by the differential timing and sequencing of events. As a global concept, the family cycle makes a valuable contribution to an understanding of the life course of family units when it is applied in studies to the

---

[8]The history of the family composition model can be traced from Rowntree's (1901:136–137) five alternating periods of comparative want and sufficiency in the life course of the common laborer of York, England, to Loomis's (1936) atheoretical study of the family cycle in the 1930s, Glick's (1947) initial analysis of the family cycle through the use of census materials on family composition and size, and the Chicago research team consisting of Duvall, Hill, Neugarten, and others. Subsequent refinements and theoretical contributions have been made by Hill (1964, 1970) and his students, especially Rodgers (1973, unpublished). In 1957, a paper by Lansing and Kish gave a substantial boost to the family stage approach by claiming that it accounted for more of the variance in family behavior than age of household head. Unfortunately, their typology of family stages is based partly on age data—young married with children, older married with children, etc. As such, a comparison of family stage and age is equivalent in outcome to that of an index with one of its components.

intergenerational aspects of change in the composition and economy of families.

Compositional Change and Family Patterns

Age patterns in social roles and transitions are expressed in the long-recognized sequence of changes in family composition and size that have been described as the developmental cycle of the family. Major points of change over the life span include marriage, birth of the first and last child, age-graded status transitions in the lives of dependent offspring (such as entrance into grade school), departure of the eldest and youngest child from the parental home, withdrawal of one or both parents from the labor force, and marital dissolution through the death of one spouse. The expansion phase, which ends with birth of the last child, is thus followed by a period of stability up to the departure of the last child and the subsequent phase of contraction. Anthropological essays by Fortes (1970), Goody (1958), and others have defined expansion and contraction as two of the three major phases in the developmental cycle of domestic groups; the other phase being that of replacement by families of the parents' offspring.

This change in family size or number of positions, with its consequences for social interaction, consumption, and material resources, is generally acknowledged as one criterion for identifying stages of family structure and development (Hill, 1964). A second criterion is based on change in the age composition of the family, or more specifically on shifts across major age categories by the eldest or youngest child, or by both. Major status changes on the part of the eldest and youngest child add a forbidding degree of complexity to typologies of family stages, as Rodgers (1962, 1973) has shown in his model of 24 stages, and yet some information must be drawn from the careers of these children in order to identify such fundamental stages as childbearing and the empty nest. The birthdates and status change of eldest and youngest child define the childbearing and childrearing phases, the stage in which the young establish their own domicile, and the postparental phase. The father's retirement or withdrawal from the labor force represents a third criterion that differentiates the postparental stage from that of old age.

Hill has proposed a nine-stage model of the family cycle which is based on information regarding change in family size, major change in the status of the eldest and youngest child, and the father's occupation:

I Establishment (newly married, childless); II New Parents (infant–3 years); III Preschool Family (child 3–6 and possibly younger siblings); IV School Age Family (oldest child 6–12 years, possibly younger siblings); V Family with Adolescent (oldest 13–19 years, possibly younger siblings); VI Family with Young Adult (oldest 20 until first child leaves home); VII Family as Launching Center (from departure of first to last child); VIII Postparental Family, The Middle Years (after children have left home until father retires); IX Aging Family (after retirement of father) [1964:192].

Each change in stage indicates a change in family structure. Such change may occur through the development of role sequences. For example, the aging of children entails change in the parents' role expectations, and thus establishes role sequences. Change in the role expectations of family positions (mother, father, child) modifies the role complex of the family; each stage represents a distinct role complex and their sequential pattern describes the family career.

A number of observations are suggested by this typology and relate to our discussion of the life-course approach. First, it is clear that the stage model does not use all information provided by the criterion indicators (see Hill's discussion, 1964); it is not a typology whose categories are defined by the joint occurrence of identically specified variables. For example, the stages become less and less precise in representing change in size as children are added to the family unit; as a result, the stages leave something to be desired for analytical work on the large family systems of late nineteenth-century America. With the exception of retirement, the stages do not use information on the economic careers and worklife of husband and wife. Also, the status of the youngest child is used only in the specification of one stage, that of the launching phase. While a full information model, based on all criteria, would be needlessly complex for most problems, the typology is costly in loss of precision and information. The meaning of stage differences in family patterns is likely to remain elusive when the categories include wide internal variations and are defined by a different mix of indicators.

Even more important, the model and most other stage formulations do not incorporate information on the differential timing of events. Just as age of family head provides only a rough index of family structure, the latter is by no means an accurate predictor of the head's age or career stage, especially in the middle years of the life span. The family head may have married a much younger woman (a pattern that may be associated with immigration) in which case he would have a younger family than most men his age. During the middle years of the life span, the cumulative impact of differences in the timing of events yields a broad age range by family stage or pattern—differences in marital age, in years between marriage and first birth, in childbearing span, etc. (Glick and Parke, 1965; Glick, 1977). Consequently, we would expect a cross-sectional sample of parents with an adolescent offspring to vary on life history and career stage (indexed by age), and thus on position in their socioeconomic career. Differences in the age of the family head when the youngest child leaves home may exceed 20 years. It would be strange indeed if the correlates of a particular stage did not reflect such variations in the life course of families. These variations are a primary feature of Hill's (1970) three-generation study, as we have noted in our review of the life-course approach. More recently, he has argued that "family development and the issues of categorizing such development into phases are primarily concerned with the pervasive issue of *time* [1973:3]." However, family time is neglected by stage typologies of the family cycle; they are not designed to chart the life course of individuals or the various career lines of a family unit. Family stages acquire meaning within the context of family history, and temporal constructs are needed to represent a family's life course.

Some models of the family cycle are more differentiated than others, from 3 stages to as many as 24. Such variation calls attention to the underlying rationale for stage delineation, and thus to the specific research problem. What is the theoretical relevance of compositional change to the problem at hand? What change, if any, is relevant to an understanding of marital satisfaction, power relations, and the division of labor over the life course? Judging from studies of marriage, typologies of the 8- or 9-stage variety are common, but their relevance has not been developed. Among some 13 cross-sectional and longitudinal studies that have investigated marital interaction by family stage (Rollins and Cannon, 1974), we find little, if any, discussion of the theoretical basis for this line of inquiry. Rollins and Feldman (1970:21) merely note that the family cycle has been used "to compare structures and functions of marital interaction in different stages of development." Do these stages of development refer to the conjugal pair, to parent–child relations, or to the total complex of family relationships?

The most common stage models of the family cycle are all best described as delineating *stages of parenthood*—before children, the active phase of parenting, the departure of children, and the empty nest. Moreover, these stages follow a preferred script of a marriage that bears children and survives to old age; deviant patterns are excluded—childless marriages, children before marriage, the widowed and divorced with or without children, serial marriages, an extended phase of living together that is eventually formalized by marriage.[9]

---

[9]Turner (1969:80–81) notes that the conventional script of marriage applies to approximately two-thirds of the adult population in Great Britain. The remainder of the population is divided among those who never marry (8.9%), marry but become divorced or separated (12–18%), and marry but do not bear children (9–10%).

There is no limit to the models that could be developed for life patterns that deviate from the preferred or conventional type, and Uhlenberg (1974) has made a suggestive beginning with his four alternative types: (a) early death, (b) spinster, (c) childless marriage, and (d) unstable marriage.

If current models of the family cycle depict phases of parenthood, then we should ask what it is about these stages that bears on family relations. For example, what stage characteristics account for the common observation among studies since 1960 that marital satisfaction declines after children arrive and then makes at least a partial recovery after the children leave home (see Dizard, 1968). Limited studies have documented the problematic aspects of entry into parenthood for marital relations, such as the effects of multiple and conflicting obligations, the clash between expectations and social demands, and greater role segregation (Jaccoby, 1969). Ryder's (1973) longitudinal study of young marriages found that wives after the first birth were more likely to claim that their husbands paid too little attention to them, when compared with wives without children. This outcome may indicate a change in husband's attentiveness after the first birth, an increasing need for such attention on the part of the wives, or both. In any case, there is a substantial body of literature that could be used to develop linkages between the sequence of parenthood stages and the course of marriage. If the family cycle has, as Rollins and Cannon (1974:80) conclude, "failed to become an important theoretical variable," one reason may be found in the unspecified meaning of its operations. We must ask what family cycle typologies measure and our answer should be more precise than merely a reference to structural change.[10] The principal changes are centered on transitions in the parenting roles of mother and father.

With their focus on parenthood, typologies of the family cycle do not provide an analytic framework for research on the synchronization of family or individual activities—of parental responsibilities and civic obligations, etc.; for assessments of the relation between family and

---

[10]Though construction of an analytic model is antecedent to matters of research design and analysis, research on marital interaction has centered on the latter—on problems of measurement and modes of analysis. Thus Spanier et al. (1975) devote several pages to a discussion of "curvilinear regression" techniques for assessing the relation between family stages and marital satisfaction, but have little to say in a systematic fashion on the theoretical relevance of the family cycle for marital relations or on the relation between family cycle as concept and operation. It should be noted that most studies on this topic are based on cross-sectional samples; marital change by family stage may thus be due to historical change. This is a problem of sizable proportion in view of the widespread use of cross-sectional samples in family-stage research and the tendency for researchers to ignore warnings on the interpretational problem.

individual activities, as expressed in family control and support exchange (Hareven, 1975); or for studies of interdependencies between interior and exterior aspects of the family unit—between marital companionship and sexuality, on the one hand, and socioeconomic conditions, on the other. If we add a temporal perspective to these problem areas, the common theme is that of interlocking or contingent careers. For example, the arrangement of marriage, births, and work suggests five main career types for married women with children: (a) the *stable homemaking* pattern with no work history; (b) the *conventional* pattern of marriage, homemaking with no return to work after marriage or children; (c) *double-track*, brief interruptions to have children; (d) *unstable*, alternations between full-time homemaking and employment; and (e) *delayed employment*, first employment following marriage and homemaking (Elder, 1974:234).[11] Stage analysis might supplement these temporal patterns by identifying the status and family structure of women at points in time. However, the meaning of one's status at a point in time depends on the course through which it was attained. Thus, while women in double-track, unstable, and delayed career lines may be gainfully employed during the postparental years, such employment cannot be fully understood apart from the life and family histories in which it is embedded. Some evidence on this point is provided by the life histories of women in the 1925–1929 cohort (Elder and Rockwell, 1976) that show a consistent relationship between marital timing and worklife. The economic pressure of early marriage and parenthood is most common among women who followed a double-track career, whereas the material advantage of late marriage and a relatively small family is characteristic of women who did not work at all or who remained employed only up to marriage and first birth. It is noteworthy that this life-course variation does not appear in static analyses which ignore the temporal relation of women's work to other events. Sweet's (1973:103) study based on the 1960 U.S. Census found no relationship between marital timing and women's work status at a point in time.

Studies organized around a stage typology of the family cycle frequently display an interior bias in which the stages become the source

---

[11]A number of other career typologies have been proposed in the literature (see Lopata, 1971; Sweet, 1973). Bernard (1971:181) has identified eight career patterns in the life course of professional women on the basis of four major contingencies and their order—marriage, childbearing, professional preparation, and the assumption or resumption of professional practice. The eight patterns represent variations of three general types—early interrupted, late interrupted, and uninterrupted. Length of the break should be added to this model.

of variation in family patterns. An example is found in studies of stage variations in marital interaction that do not analyze the socioeconomic careers of husband and wife, their relation to family stage or marital satisfaction (Rollins and Feldman, 1970; Rollins and Cannon, 1974). Rollins and Cannon refer to role strain in the middle stages as one possible explanation for the U-shaped, curvilinear relationship between marital sentiment and the family cycle, but they do not test this hypothesis with data on interdependent career lines. Moroever, the role strain hypothesis is derived from a multidimensional model of the family life course, not from the family-cycle model on which the study is based. A contrasting deficiency, the neglect of life stage and timing phenomena, is characteristic of studies on class and socialization. None of the studies in Bronfenbrenner's (1958) review of class and childrearing since the Depression era examined this relationship by stage in the family cycle or considered the implications of wide variations in age at marriage and births. This practice, which has changed little up to the present (cf. Erlanger, 1974), has a number of important consequences. In a cross-sectional sample of children, parents occupy a wide range of stages, from childbearing to the launching phase; family variations across these stages imply substantial differences in the socialization of children who are comparable in age. Equally significant are differences in socioeconomic position between the early and middle stages, and their relation to economic pressures, adaptations.[12]

Neither family nor socioeconomic careers can be fully understood apart from an examination of their interdependence. But as Rainwater has noted in a foreword to Young and Wilmott's *The Symmetrical Family,* studies on each topic have tended to "proceed along their separate narrow ways barely acknowledging the existence of each other [1973:xiv]." This judgment is not entirely justified, however, since there is a well-established tradition of research on the sequential interdependence of family composition and economic resources.

---

[12]The intercorrelational pattern of status dimensions (such as the head's education, occupational status, and income) varies by career stage, owing to differences in worklife progression and economic rewards across occupational categories. Skilled workers, for example, reach their economic peak at an earlier stage than do professionals; thus occupational status differences on income are much less pronounced among young workers than among men in middle age. This life pattern has not been given appropriate recognition in studies of socioeconomic status, specifically with respect to the analysis of status interrelations by age or career stage (see Kahl and Davis, 1955, and their observation that "income stands in sulking isolation" relative to head's education and occupation). More recently, Jackman and Jackman (1973) examined the relation between dimensions of objective and subjective social status in a cross-sectional sample, but did not carry out the analysis within age strata.

Change in Family Composition and Economy

The economic implications of change in the age composition and size of the family are expressed in the ratio of supply and demand, in the level of earnings and numbers of earners, and in the number of dependents, young and old. The lifetime course of the family economy is thus intimately linked to change in the age of the household head, to change in the number and age of children, and to loss of productive family members through death, disability, divorce, and the formation of new family units.

Initial impressions of the interlocking histories of family composition and economy emerged from a series of socioeconomic studies during the late nineteenth and early twentieth centuries.[13] Using budget data and demographic information, they charted variations in living standard by number of earners and young children, and thus in implication by family stage: (a) the relative prosperity of the young married years before children; (b) the often extreme economic pressure associated with the expansion phase of childbearing, a period of imbalance between supply and demand in which the family head occupies an early stage in his economic career and the earning potential of the wife is curtailed by child-care norms and duties; (c) an improvement in economic well-being as children and perhaps the wife enter the labor force; and (d) a decline in family income resulting from the departure of older children and the loss of their earnings. In the uncontrolled economy of late nineteenth-century England, Rowntree's (1901:136–137) study of York laborers produced a graphic portrait of this covariation between living standard and family composition.

Since the 1930s and major welfare legislation, studies of American families have continued to document the profound economic effects of change in family composition and size over the life course. Using annual data on income dynamics from a panel study of some 5000 American families, Lane and Morgan conclude that "most changes in family economic status result from changes in family composition [1975:50]." Significant economic declines over the 6-year period were found to be related to loss of earnings from offspring, to divorce in which the wife and mother became the household head, and to the withdrawal of husbands and wives from the labor force.[14] Among intact families, eco-

---

[13]In addition to Rowntree's study (1901), Rubinow (1916) makes reference to a large number of early socioeconomic studies that show the link between family composition and economy. Family budget research dating back to LePlay's work is reviewed by Zimmerman (1936).

[14]Within a longitudinal sample, family income is both a potential source and outcome of marital dissolution. The lower the income, the greater the likelihood of a marital

nomic change stemmed primarily from change in the number of earners (e.g., reemployment of the wife), rather than from change in the earnings of the family head. A similar pattern is reported by Modell (forthcoming; Modell and Hareven, 1973) from research on the household budgets of working-class families in late nineteenth-century Massachusetts. Family expenses varied more by family stage than by the earnings of the father.

Lack of synchronization between family income and material needs over the life course has centered attention on family management strategies and priorities (Hill, 1970; Modell, forthcoming), on ways of adapting to the disparity between income and demand. These strategies fall into three categories: (a) control or reduce demand, consumption—family constraints on living standards, deferral of material aspirations; (b) reallocate time and energy resources—provide services with family labor, change work patterns, etc.; and (c) improve the synchronization of income and outgo—savings, loans, etc. (Gove et al., 1973). Prior to the birth of children, the anticipation of future needs and economic pressures may take the form of decisions regarding the wife's employment, the saving of discretionary income, and the reduction of expenses by living in with relatives. Highly paid shiftwork, overtime, and moonlighting have been identified as adaptations to the economic squeeze associated with the childbearing phase, particularly in large families (Wilensky, 1963; Young and Wilmott, 1973: Chapter 7). Reentry of the wife into the labor market after childbearing may be motivated by the accumulation of debts and by the anticipated costs of children's education and the requirements of financial security in old age.

From the late nineteenth century to the 1930s, urban American families in the launching and postparental phases frequently took in boarders, primarily in response to economic considerations. As Modell and Hareven point out, boarding "was a social equalization of the family which operated *directly* by the exchange of a young adult person and a portion of his young-adult income from his family of orientation to what might be called his family of re-orientation—re-orientation to

---

break, which in turn lowers family income. This causal sequence is obscured in cross-sectional data; a negative correlation between family income and female-headed households reflects to some degree the negative effects of both variables. Does a low income have a stronger effect on marital instability than the latter has in lowering family income? An answer to this question (that could be provided by the Michigan panel study of family income dynamics, Lane and Morgan, 1975) is obviously much more than an academic matter in view of the policy thrust on economics in family stability and the sharply rising divorce rate.

the city, to a job, to a new neighborhood, to independence [1973:475]."
Boarding helped to stabilize family income by replacing the earnings of
a departed offspring with the payments of a guest, and enabled wives to
earn money for their domestic labor. By supplementing income with
payments for room and board, older single women and widows were
better able to maintain an independent household.

From a review of studies on family stress by stage, Aldous and Hill
(1969; see also Schorr, 1966) identified childbearing and the subsequent phase of school-age children as a period of maximum stress,
owing to insufficient material resources relative to family need. Dis-
satisfaction with material well-being tended to reach a peak in the
school-age years, followed by emotional stress in marriage during the
span of years when the children are leaving home. Since the evidence
on these stress points comes primarily from cross-sectional studies,
little is known about the long-term effect of early material deprivation
and related adaptations on the course of marriage.

The value of such longitudinal analysis would depend on whether
it explored the consequences of event timetables for the economic and
emotional implications of each family stage. Timing differentials on
marriage and childbearing are sufficient to produce wide variations
in economic well-being within each stage. For example, the socioeconomic context of childbearing differs markedly between women
who wed at a relatively early age and those who wed at a late age,
even assuming that they married men of similar occupational status.
Husbands of women who married late would be more firmly established
in worklife and economic assets than men who married much younger
women; differences in age at marriage may exceed 8 or 10 years,
a time span which could make a substantial economic difference
during the early phase of a man's worklife. Those who marry late
would also have more work experience than the early group through
which to accumulate economic assets before the arrival of children.
An economic squeeze should thus be most acute in the childbearing
stage of women who married and gave birth to their children at a relatively
early age.

Empirical documentation of this economic burden is provided by a
survey of women from the Detroit area (Freedman and Coombs, 1966;
see also Oppenheimer, 1974); the economic liability of having a child
either shortly before or after an early marriage persisted through the
first 9 years of marriage. Couples "who have their children very quickly
after marriage find themselves under great economic pressure, particularly if they married at an early age. . . . They are less able than others to
accumulate goods and assets regarded as desirable by young couples in

our society [Freedman and Coombs, 1966:648]." Judging from the results of another study (Cutright, 1973), the initial economic disadvantage of early family events appears to decline by middle age in the lives of women, even though early marriage entails a high risk of failure.

The interlocking course of parenthood and economic behavior makes a strong case for family studies that include variables in both domains and investigate their joint or interacting effects. An explanation of change in family structure and consumption requires knowledge of both sets of variables and their relation, of family income and assets in relation to the time schedule of family events, age composition, and family size. Social composition and economic effects in family behavior are partly contingent on the timing of key family events and thus on the course of family history. Problems of synchronization and coordination in family management arise from the relation between the course of events in these domains. An economic squeeze may result from loss of job or a midlife demotion, as well as from early marriage and births.

From Concept to Operation

With data requirements that clearly favor detailed longitudinal records, a life-course framework may appear to offer little to the analyst with cross-sectional materials, as in the case of nineteenth-century federal census manuscripts on households. Even when decennial records are linked, a 10-year gap between data points severely restricts the kinds of questions that can be addressed. The occupation of a man in 1870 and in 1880 obviously leaves much of his worklife or career to the analyst's imagination. Despite such constraints, there is much to be gained by linking age to events or statuses within a cross-section of a cohort or sample. Given satisfactory age data, the analyst could compare family patterns by stage within subgroups defined by different time schedules; for example, by early, on time, and late marriage (link marriage certificates to census records). More complex timetables might be developed by linking ages at marriage, first birth, and last birth, or by combining marital age with variations in the childbearing span. Though age of household head is sometimes employed as an alternative to stages of the family cycle, both head's age and family stages acquire greater utility when they are used in combination. By relating head's age to family stage, we achieve some knowledge of the differential timing of family events. The head's age should also be linked to his socioeconomic position if we are concerned with the sequential interdependence of parenthood and economic events.

In lieu of age-at-event information, a rough estimation of the temporal structure of life events in cohorts can be achieved by comparing the distribution of persons who have made a transition, such as marriage, by age category in each cohort. An elaboration of this strategy has been employed most creatively by Modell et al. (1976) in a comparison of five transitions to adult status (exit from school, entry into the labor force, departure from the family of origin, marriage, establishment of a household) among Philadelphia whites in 1880 and a United States census sample in 1970. Six aspects of the transition to adulthood are indexed in the study, including prevalence (proportion of cohort that experiences a given transition in specific age categories), timing (typical points of transition), spread (span of time required for given proportion of cohort to pass through a transition), and age-congruity (degree of overlap between transitions). The authors note that

> The ideal ending-point of this inquiry would be a distribution of *careers*, which might be categorized by starting age, sequence of transitions, and intervals among transitions. To know this distribution of careers would permit us substantial insight into how they were constructed. But our data permit us only to compare cross-sections, in order to draw implications for patterns of events within individual life courses [1976:12; emphasis added].

This study illustrates a successful adaptation of research design, measurement, and analysis to the testing of life-course questions on historical data that appear wholly inappropriate for such interests. By approaching other problems and data sets with this framework, we may find equally effective means of studying the life course in past time. As always, one of the dangers when data are ill-suited to questions of interest is the tendency to put aside data constraints in the interpretation of findings. This tendency is most vividly documented in Peter Laslett's *Household and Family in Past Time* (1972). Laslett makes repeated reference to the restricted scope of his study of English households—that it is a study of family and kinship only within the narrow boundaries of the residential household—and to the lack of adequate age data that prevent analysis of the developmental cycle. In conclusion, he notes that "almost nothing emerges from the present discussion about relationships between households, or between individual members of different households. We simply do not know from data of this kind how strong the kinship tie was between two brothers in eighteenth century England ... [1972:157]." (The reference is to brothers living in separate households.) And yet Laslett proceeds at various points to draw unwarranted inferences about kinship from

household composition, such as, "if relatives had in fact been so intimately bound up in the family cycle in pre-industrial England, then
they would surely be found more often to have actually lived within
it ... [1972:71]." Laslett's aims and questions extend well beyond the
boundaries of his data to the realm of kinship and the family as a social
institution. As Berkner observes, "he says that the study of kinship is
what is really important, but he does not study it. He is careful to point
out that he is talking about the family in the narrowest sense as a
residential kinship group, yet he draws conclusions about the family in
the broadest sense as a social institution [1975:724]." The confusion
that can arise from applying household data to matters of kinship and
the elementary family is all too prevalent in the literature.

Overview

This chapter has outlined some distinctive features of a perspective
on the family which represents its course of development in historical
context, a perspective that is focused on the process of status change,
and thus on the task of explicating such change. Differences in the
timing, duration, and arrangement of events across career lines generate patterns of asynchrony, relative to action sequences and normative
pressures, and problems of adaptation, as expressed in strategies of
life-course management. These strategies entail ways of coping with
demand–supply imbalances within the course of family life (that is,
patterns of resource development, time, income, and energy allocation), and on the individual level with problems of role overload and
loss.

In addition to the contingent careers of an individual, three general
modes of temporal interdependence are important aspects of life course
analysis: the intersection between life or family history and social history, between the life course of the family unit and that of individual
members, and between the course of events in the family and other
institutional sectors—the economy, polity. Formation of the marital
relationship is viewed in terms of the joining of life histories, each
characterized by a distinctive pattern of kin relations and culture, material assets and socialization. The configuration formed by these patterns has consequences for intergenerational ties with parents and in-
laws, and for the course of marriage generally: the sharing of interests
and activities, mutuality in support and understanding, the division of
labor and power. The family unit is portrayed as a set of contingent

career lines which vary in synchronization and problems of resource management; its social stage at any point in time thus acquires historical definition within the course of family events and activities.

As a concept, the family cycle offers a distinctive analytical contribution to the study of family change when it makes explicit reference to cyclical intergenerational processes: (a) generational succession through childbearing and socialization of the young to maturity; and (b) the intergenerational flow of resources—material, etc. The latter includes both the exchange of resources over the life course and inheritance. In research, the family cycle is generally indexed by a typology of stages which are defined by change in social composition and size. As we have noted, this measurement presents a number of limitations in relation to studies of the family life course.

Stage typologies of the family cycle tell us very little about the course of family history. Families with an identical history, as defined by a sequence of stages, vary markedly in their respective life course. Much of this variation is due to the differential timing and arrangement of events, variables typically excluded from studies that employ a stage classification of the family cycle. Composition models of the family cycle primarily represent stages of parenthood such as before the birth of children, the childbearing and rearing years, and the postparental phase that begins when the last child has left home. Though seemingly obvious, this observation has not been applied in the development of theory on the relation between family stages and behavior. A rationale for research on marital interaction by stage in the family cycle may be found in the literature on entry into parenthood, on the relation between parent–child and conjugal patterns, and on the effects of number and age of children. The focus on stages of parenthood suggests another limitation: Stage models of the family cycle neither represent nor sensitize researchers to the multiple, interlocking career lines of a couple and the family unit as a whole. These stages are merely one part in a more general socioeconomic model that has informed research on correlated change in family composition and the family economy. A final restriction also applies to the emphasis on parenthood: Most stage models of the family cycle are based on the conventional script of a marriage that bears children and survives to old age.

In family cycle and life-course studies, observed variation in family patterns by stage (whether defined by role structure, age of marriage partners, or both) are subject to interpretations that are based on historical context and change. Stage differences in marital behavior may be due to historical trends and unique events, as well as to the constraints and requirements of particular role systems. With the emergence of a cohort–historical approach in life-course analysis, we have become more aware of the complex meanings associated with age differentiation; in particular, that age locates individuals and family units in historical context by defining their cohort membership, and also places them in the social structure by indicating their career stage. To understand the impact of historical change on family life, we must know something of the process by which this effect occurred, a process which varies according to family stage and situation at the point of change. Such knowledge warrants priority on the agenda of family studies.

References

Aldous, Joan, and Reuben Hill
   1969   "Breaking the poverty cycle: strategic points for intervention." Social Work 14:3–12.
Balan, J., H. L. Browning, E. Jelin, and L. Letzler
   1969   "A computerized approach to the processing and analysis of life histories obtained in sample surveys." Behavioral Science 14:105–120.
Baltes, Paul B., and K. Warner Schaie (eds.)
   1973   Life-span Developmental Psychology: Personality and Socialization. New York: Academic Press.
Bailyn, Lotte
   1970   "Career and family orientations of husbands and wives in relation to marital happiness." Human Relations 23:97–113.
Becker, Howard S.
   1960   "Notes on the concept of commitment." American Journal of Sociology 66:32–40.
Bengtson, Vern L., and M. C. Lovejoy
   1973   "Values, personality, and social structure: an intergenerational analysis." American Behavioral Scientist 16:880–912.
Berkner, Lutz K.
   1972   "The stem family and the developmental cycle of the peasant household: an eighteenth-century Austrian example." American Historical Review 77:398–418.
   1975   "The use and misuse of census data for the historical analysis of family structure: a review of Household and Family in Past Time." Journal of Interdisciplinary History 4:721–738.
Bernard, Jessie
   1971   Women and the Public Interest. Chicago: Aldine.
Block, Jack
   1971   Lives Through Time. Berkeley, California: Bancroft.
Blum, Zahava D., Nancy Karweit, and A. G. Sorenson
   1969   "A method for the collection and analysis of retrospective life histories." The Johns Hopkins University Center for the Study of Social Organization of Schools, Report No. 48.
Bogue, Donald J. (ed.)
   1974   The Basic Writings of Ernest W. Burgess. Chicago: University of Chicago Community and Family Study Center.

Bronfenbrenner, Urie
1958   "Socialization and social class through time and space." In E. Maccoby, T. Newcomb, and E. Hartley (eds.), Readings in Social Psychology. New York: Holt.
Burr, Wesley R.
1973   Theory Construction and the Sociology of the Family. New York: Wiley.
Carp, Francis M. (ed.)
1972   Retirement. New York: Behavioral Publications.
Carr-Hill, R. A., and K. I. Macdonald
1973   "Problems in the analysis of life histories." The Sociological Review Monograph 19:57–59.
Carter, Hugh, and Paul C. Glick
1970   Marriage and Divorce. Cambridge, Massachusetts: Harvard University Press.
Clausen, John A.
1972   "The life course of individuals." Chapter 11 in Matilda White Riley, Marilyn Johnson, and Anne Foner (eds.), Aging and Society. Volume 3. New York: Russell Sage Foundation.
Cottrell, Leonard S.
1942   "The adjustment of the individual to his age and sex roles." American Sociological Review 7:617–620.
Cuisinier, Jean
1977   Le Cycle de la Vie Familiale dans les Sociétés Européenes. Paris: Mouton.
Cutright, Phillips
1971   "Income and family events: marital stability." Journal of Marriage and the Family 33:291–305.
1973   "Timing the first birth: does it matter?" Journal of Marriage and the Family 35:585–595.
Dailey, Charles A.
1971   Assessment of Lives. San Francisco: Jossey-Bass.
Davis, Kingsley
1940   "The sociology of parent–youth conflict." American Sociological Review 5:523–535.
Dizard, Jan
1968   Social Change in the Family. Chicago: University of Chicago Community and Family Study Center.
Dollard, John
1949   Criteria for the Life History. New York: Smith.
Duvall, Evelyn M.
1977   Marriage and Family Development (5th edition). Philadelphia: Lippincott.
Eisenstadt, S. N.
1956   From Generation to Generation: Age Groups and Social Structure. Glencoe, Illinois: Free Press.
Elder, Glen H., Jr.
1974   Children of the Great Depression. Chicago: University of Chicago Press.
1975a   "Age differentiation and the life course." Chapter 2 in Alex Inkeles, James Coleman, and Neil Smelser (eds.), Annual Review of Sociology. Volume 1. Palo Alto: Annual Reviews.
1975b   "Adolescence in the life cycle." Chapter 1 in S. Dragastin and Glen H. Elder,

Jr. (eds.), Adolescence in the Life Cycle. Washington, D.C.: Hemisphere/ Halstead.

Forth- "Approaches to social change and the family." American Journal of Sociol-
coming ogy.

Elder, Glen H., Jr., and Richard C. Rockwell
  1976 "Marital timing in women's life patterns." Journal of Family History 1:34–53.
  1978 "Economic depression and postwar opportunity in men's lives: a study of life patterns and health." In Roberta G. Simmons (ed.), Research in Community and Mental Health. Greenwich, Connecticut: JAI Press.

Erlanger, Howard S.
  1974 "Social class and corporal punishment in childrearing: a reassessment." American Sociological Review 39:68–85.

Farber, Bernard
  1961 "The family as a set of mutually contingent careers." Pp. 276–297 in Nelson N. Foote (ed.), Household Decision-Making. New York: New York University Press.

Faris, Robert E. L.
  1967 Chicago Sociology, 1920–1932. San Francisco: Chandler.

Filene, Peter Gabriel
  1974 Him/Her/Self: Sex Roles in Modern America. New York: Harcourt.

Freedman, Ronald, and L. Coombs
  1966 "Childspacing and family economic position." American Sociological Review 31:631–648.

Fortes, Meyer
  1970 Time and Social Structure and Other Essays. London: Athlone Press.

Furstenberg, Frank F., Jr.
  1976 Unplanned Parenthood: The Social Consequences of Teenage Childbearing. New York: Free Press.

Glaser, Barney G., and Anslem L. Strauss
  1971 The Theory of Status Passage. Chicago: Aldine.

Glick, Paul C.
  1947 "The family cycle." American Sociological Review 12:164–174.
  1977 "Updating the life cycle of the family." Journal of Marriage and the Family 39:5–13.

Glick, Paul C., and Robert Parke, Jr.
  1965 "New approaches in studying the life cycle of family." Demography 2:187–202.

Goffman, Erving
  1961 Asylums. Chicago: Aldine-Atherton.

Goode, William J.
  1956 After Divorce. Glencoe: Free Press, 1956.
  1960 "A theory of role strain." American Sociological Review 25:483–496.

Goody, Jack (ed.)
  1958 The Developmental Cycle in Domestic Groups. London: Cambridge University Press.

Goulet, L. R., and P. B. Baltes (eds.)
  1970 Life-span Developmental Psychology: Research and Theory. New York: Academic Press.

Gove, Walter, James W. Grimm, Susan C. Motz, and James D. Thompson
- 1973   "The family life cycle: internal dynamics and social consequences." Sociology and Social Research 57:182–195.

Granovetter, Mark S.
- 1974   Getting a Job: A Study of Contacts and Careers. Cambridge, Massachusetts: Harvard University Press.

Greven, Philip J., Jr.
- 1970   Four Generations: Population, Land, and Family in Colonial Andover, Massachusetts. Ithaca, New York: Cornell University Press.

Haller, A. O., and O. Portes
- 1973   "Status attainment processes." Sociology of Education 46:51–91.

Hanson, Robert C., and Ozzie G. Simmons
- 1968   "The role path: a concept and procedure for studying migration to urban communities." Human Organization 27:152–158.

Hareven, Tamara K.
- 1974   "The family as process: the historical study of the family cycle." Journal of Social History 7:322–329.
- 1975   "Family time and industrial time: family and work in a planned corporation town, 1900–1924." Journal of Urban History 1:365–389.
- 1976   "The last stage: historical adulthood and old age." Daedalus 105:13–28.
- 1977   "Family time and historical time." Daedalus 106:57–70.

Hill, Reuben
- 1964   "Methodological issues in family development research." Family Process 3:186–206.
- 1970   Family Development in Three Generations. Cambridge, Massachusetts: Schenkman.
- Unpublished   "Social theory and family development." Paper prepared for the 18th International Research Seminar, Committee on Family Research, International Sociological Association, Paris, September 24–28, 1973.

Hoffman, Lois W., and F. Ivan Nye
- 1974   Working Mothers. San Francisco: Jossey-Bass.

Hughes, Everett
- 1971   The Sociological Eye. Volume 1. Chicago: Aldine-Atherton.

Jaccoby, A. P.
- 1969   "Transition to parenthood: a reassessment." Journal of Marriage and the Family 31:720–727.

Jackman, Mary R., and Robert W. Jackman
- 1973   "An interpretation of the relation between objective and subjective social status." American Sociological Review 38:569–582.

Kagan, Jerome, and Howard A. Moss
- 1962   Birth to Maturity. New York: Wiley.

Kahl, Joseph A., and James A. Davis
- 1955   "A comparison of indexes of socio-economic status." American Sociological Review 20:317–325.

Kanter, Rosabeth Moss
- 1977   Work and Family in the United States: A Critical Review and Agenda for Research and Policy. New York: Russell Sage Foundation.

Karweit, Nancy
- 1973   "Storage and retrieval of life history data." Social Science Research 2:41–50.

Lane, Jonathan P., and James N. Morgan
1975 "Patterns of change in economic status and family structure." Chapter 1 in Greg J. Duncan and James N. Morgan (eds.), Five Thousand American Families: Patterns of Economic Progress. Volume III. Ann Arbor: Institute for Social Research.
Lansing, J. B., and Leslie Kish
1957 "Family life cycle as an independent variable." American Sociological Review 22:512–519.
Laslett, Peter (ed.)
1972 Household and Family in Past Time. Cambridge, England: Cambridge University Press.
Lieberman, M. A., and Jacqueline M. Falk
1971 "The remembered past as a source of data for research on the life cycle." Human Development 14:132–141.
Loomis, Charles P.
1936 "Study of the life cycle of families." Rural Sociology 1:180–199.
Lopata, Helena Znaniecki
1971 Occupation: Housewife. New York: Oxford University Press.
Lowenthal, Marjorie Fiske, and David Chiriboga
1972 "Transition to the empty nest: crisis, challenge, or relief?" Archives of General Psychology 26:8–14.
1973 "Social stress and adaptation: toward a life course perspective." Pp. 281–310 in M. P. Lawton and C. Eisdorfer (eds.), Psychology of Adult Development and Aging. New York: American Psychological Association.
Mannheim, Karl
1928/ "The problem of generations." Pp. 276–322 in Essays on the Sociology of
1952 Knowledge, tr. Paul Kecskemeti. New York: Oxford University Press.
Mills, C. Wright
1959 The Sociological Imagination. New York: Oxford University Press.
Miner, Horace
1939 St. Denis: A French-Canadian Parish. Chicago: University of Chicago Press.
Modell, John
Forth- "Patterns of consumption, acculturation, and family income strategy in late
coming nineteenth-century America." In Tamara K. Hareven and Maris Vinovskis (eds.), Family and Population in Nineteenth-Century America. Princeton: Princeton University Press.
Modell, John, Frank F. Furstenberg, Jr., and Theodore Hershberg
1976 "Social change and transitions to adulthood in historical perspective." Journal of Family History 1:7–32.
Modell, John, and Tamara K. Hareven
1973 "Urbanization and the malleable household: an examination of boarding and lodging in American families." Journal of Marriage and the Family 35:467–479.
Namboodiri, N. K.
1972 "The integrative potential of a fertility model: an analytical test." Population Studies 26:465–485.
Nesselroade, John R., and H. W. Reese (eds.)
1973 Life-span Developmental Psychology: Methodological Issues. New York: Academic Press.

Neugarten, Bernice L., and Nancy Datan

1973 "Sociological perspectives on the life cycle." Pp. 53–69 in Paul B. Baltes and K. Warner Schaie (eds.), Life-span Developmental Psychology: Personality and Socialization. New York: Academic Press.

Oppenheimer, Valerie Kincade

1974 "The life-cycle squeeze: the interaction of men's occupational and family life cycles." Demography 11:227–245.

Pahl, J. M., and R. E. Pahl

1971 Managers and Their Wives: A Study of Career and Family Relationships in the Middle Class. London: Allen Lane.

Pearlin, Leonard I.

1972 Class Context and Family Relations: A Cross-National Study. Boston: Little, Brown.

1975 "Status inequality and stress in marriage." American Sociological Review 40:334–357.

Rains, Prudence M.

1971 Becoming an Unwed Mother. Chicago: Aldine.

Ramsøy, Natalie Rogoff

1973 The Norwegian Occupational Life History Study: Design, Purpose, and a Few Preliminary Results. Oslo, Norway: Institute of Applied Social Research.

Rapoport, Rhona, and Robert Rapoport

1969 "The dual-career family: a variant pattern and social change." Human Relations 22:3–30.

Rausch, R., Wells Goodrich, and J. D. Campbell

1963 "Adaptation to the first years of marriage." Psychiatry 26:265–380.

Riley, M. W., M. E. Johnson, and A. Foner (eds.)

1972 Aging and Society: A Sociology of Age Stratification. Volume 3. New York: Russell Sage Foundation.

Ritchey, P. Neal, and C. Shannon Stokes

1974 "Correlates of childlessness and expectations to remain childless: U.S. 1967." Social Forces 52:349–356.

Robinson, John P.

1977 How Americans Use Their Time. New York: Praeger.

Rodgers, Roy H.

Unpub- "Improvements in the construction and analysis of family life cycle
lished categories." Unpublished doctoral dissertation, University of Minnesota, 1962.

1973 Family Interaction and Transaction: The Developmental Approach. Englewood Cliffs, New Jersey: Prentice-Hall.

Roff, Merrill, and David F. Ricks (eds.)

1970 Life History Research in Psychopathology. Volume 1. Minneapolis: University of Minnesota Press.

Roff, Merrill, Lee N. Robins, and Max Pollack (eds.)

1972 Life History Research in Psychopathology. Volume 2. Minneapolis: University of Minnesota Press.

Rollins, Boyd C., and Kenneth L. Cannon

1974 "Marital satisfaction over the family life cycle: a re-evaluation." Journal of Marriage and the Family 36:271–282.

Rollins, Boyd C., and Harold Feldman
>   1970   "Marital satisfaction over the family life cycle." Journal of Marriage and the Family 32:20–28.

Rossi, Alice S.
>   1968   "Transition to parenthood." Journal of Marriage and the Family 30:26–39.

Rowntree, B. S.
>   1901   Poverty: A Study of Town Life. London: Macmillan.

Rubinow, I. M.
>   1916   Social Insurance, With Special Reference to American Conditions. New York: Holt.

Ryder, Norman B.
>   1965   "The cohort as a concept in the study of social change." American Sociological Review 30:843–861.
>   1974   "Comment on Robert Willis' 'economic theory of fertility behavior.'" Pp. 76–80 in Theodore W. Schultz (ed.), Economics for the Family: Marriage, Children, and Human Capital. Chicago: University of Chicago Press.

Ryder, Robert G.
>   1973   "Longitudinal data relating marriage satisfaction and having a child." Journal of Marriage and the Family 35:604–606.

Schorr, Alvin L.
>   1966   "The family cycle and income development." Social Security Bulletin 29:14–25.

Spanier, Graham B., Robert A. Lewis, and Charles L. Cole
>   1975   "Marital adjustment over the family life cycle: the issue of curvilinearity." Journal of Marriage and the Family 37:263–275.

Spitzer, Alan B.
>   1973   "The historical problem of generations." American Historical Review 78:1353–1385.

Sweet, James A.
>   1973   Women in the Labor Force. New York: Seminar Press.

Szalai, Alexander (ed.)
>   1972   The Use of Time. The Hague: Mouton.

Terman, Lewis M.
>   1938   Psychological Factors in Marital Happiness. New York: McGraw-Hill.

Thernstrom, Stephan
>   1973   The Other Bostonians: Class and Mobility in the American Metropolis, 1880–1970. Cambridge, Massachusetts: Harvard University Press.

Thomas, William I. with F. Znaniecki
>   1918–   The Polish Peasant in Europe and America. Chicago: University of Chicago
>   1920   Press.

Tuma, Elias H.
>   1971   Economic History and the Social Sciences: Problems of Methodology. Berkeley and Los Angeles: University of California.

Turner, Christopher
>   1969   Family and Kinship in Modern Britain. London: Routledge and Kegan Paul.

Uhlenberg, Peter
>   1974   "Cohort variations in family life cycle experiences of U.S. females." Journal of Marriage and the Family 36:284–292.

Vinovskis, Maris A.

    1977   "From household size to the life course: some observations on recent trends in family history." American Behavioral Scientist 27:263–287.

Wilensky, Harold L.

    1960   "Work, careers, and social integration." International Social Science Journal 12:534–560.

    1961   "Orderly careers and social participation in the middle mass." American Sociological Review 26:521–539.

    1963   "The moonlighter: a product of relative deprivation." Industrial Relations 3:105–124.

Young, Michael, and Peter Wilmott

    1973   The Symmetrical Family. New York: Pantheon.

Zimmerman, Carle C.

    1936   Consumption and Standards of Living. New York: Van Nostrand.

2
Changing Configurations of the Life Course

PETER UHLENBERG

Analysis of life-course patterns of successive birth cohorts provides a straightforward method for quantifying historical changes in the family. To the extent that data allow, the family-related experiences of a cohort during particular age strata of the life course can be measured, and compared with the experiences of preceding and subsequent cohorts as they pass through the same ages. Such comparisons enable one to specify the kinds of changes that are occurring and to assess the rate at which the changes are occurring during different historical periods. Furthermore, this analysis explicates how societal trends in demographic behavior produce specific types of changes in family structure, changes that are experienced differentially by cohorts beginning the life course at different points in time. Once a clear description is available of the types and amounts of historical change in different aspects of the family, we will be in a better position to proceed with the task of relating family change to specific social, economic, and political changes in society.

How has the configuration of the life course changed for successive birth cohorts in the United States since 1870? How have declining mortality, declining fertility, changing marriage and divorce patterns, and changing migration rates during the past 100 years affected the American family? This chapter examines these questions by focusing

TRANSITIONS
The Family and the Life Course in
Historical Perspective

upon the experiences of several cohorts as they move through child-hood, adulthood, and old age. Using available census and vital statistics data, distributions of cohort members by type of family structure experienced during different age strata of the life course are calculated. Because of the unique experience of blacks, this study is limited to the white population of the United States. What emerges from this examination of aggregate life-course patterns is an overview of some major historical trends in family structure, and the relationship of these trends to demographic changes. The work of historians examining nineteenth-century census manuscripts for local areas, aided by additional cohort data from other sources, provides the necessary complement to this aggregate demographic approach. Together, these various studies offer us a richer and more accurate understanding of the social history of the family than has heretofore been available.

At the outset it should be noted that while the goal of this study is to provide a more accurate description of family change, great precision in measurement is not possible. There are problems with the quality of the data used, and there are methodological complications in trying to fit the data into a conceptual framework of cohort life-course patterns. Some of these difficulties are briefly discussed as they arise later in the chapter. The primary interest, however, is to uncover major shifts in life-course experiences related to the family, and for this purpose the data and techniques available are generally satisfactory.

Conceptual Framework

As individuals age through the life course from birth to death, they pass through an ordered series of more or less well-defined age strata or categories. Such categories as infancy, childhood, adolescence, young adulthood, middle age, and elderly are not rigidly defined, but they are socially recognized divisions of the life course. Thus the various age grades "are defined by norms that constitute a basis for self-definition and specify appropriate behavior, roles, and time schedules [Elder, 1975b:168]." In addition to sharing socially defined behavioral expectations, members of an age strata also share certain age-related biological characteristics, such as level of motor skills and sexual development. These biological facts impose constraints upon the range of social expectations that can apply to any particular strata. Within these limits, the particular age strata that are distinguished, as well as the expected behavior within these strata, vary across societies and vary over time and among subgroups in a society. Indeed, the age divisions recognized as discrete and socially meaningful reveal much about the social organization of a population.

In this chapter three broad age strata are distinguished: childhood (0–15); adulthood (15–60); and elderly (60+). In the United States, the social definitions of these strata have changed somewhat during the past century, and there has been a trend toward clearer differentiation of various categories within each of these strata. Nevertheless, much of the content of each age category has persisted over this period: Children are expected to live with parents, attend school, and be socialized into the culture; young adults are expected to establish families and take on adult work responsibilities; middle-aged adults are expected to complete the rearing of their children and maintain stability in their occupations; and the elderly are expected to progressively relinquish various roles and complete the life course by dying.

Obviously not all individuals conform to all societal norms, and there is, in reality, great variation in the actual behavior of individuals within each age category. Thus social history must be concerned not only with social definitions of age strata, but also with the actual behavior and characteristics of the population occupying the age strata. Over time the composition of each stratum changes continuously as one cohort moves out and another one moves in. If the new occupants of a stratum have the same distribution of characteristics, are equal in number, and behave in identical ways as the previous occupants, no social change occurs. Social change occurs to the extent that successive cohorts in each age stratum differ in composition and behavior from previous ones (Ryder, 1964).

By comparing successive cohorts as they occupy specific age strata, one has a mechanism for studying social change. If the concern is to simply describe change between two periods, the characteristics and behavior of the relevant cohorts occupying the age strata at each period can be compared. Comparing the distribution of successive cohorts on specific life-course variables (school attendance, marital status, migration experience, etc.) allows a quantitative assessment of change over time. This procedure encourages clarity in specification, but it does not differ in methodology from a simple comparison of age-specific factors at two periods. However, by conceptualizing the comparison in a cohort–historical perspective, a procedure for further explanation of the change is explicated.

What determines the type and extent of differences between cohorts as they occupy the same age stratum of the life course? To answer this, attention is directed toward two aspects of the historical context in which the various cohorts aged (see Mason et al., 1973;

Riley, 1973). First are the factors that determine the composition and characteristics of each particular birth cohort. Cohorts are initially differentiated because they enter the system differing in size and in composition of ascribed statuses. They are further differentiated as intracohort change up to an age stratum is affected by changes in the historical context during the aging process. Fertility changes affect the initial composition. Mortality changes over time affect the number of survivors in a cohort, and may differentially affect the composition if rate of change varies among subgroups (for example, if there is greater change for one sex, or for one social class). Likewise changes in immigration affect the number in the cohort and, if it is selective, the distribution of characteristics; changing educational institutions affect educational characteristics, etc. Changes in cohort composition that produce social change in particular age strata are referred to as *cohort effects*.

The second aspect of the historical context is the period at which the cohorts reach an age stratum. The social, economic, and political milieu during occupancy of an age stratum affects the behavior of the cohort. A robust economy, compared to a depression, may encourage shifts in timing and prevalence of marriage, amount of childbearing, and rate of employment. Level of contraceptive technology and norms regarding the role of women may influence the rate of childbearing and female participation in the labor force. Social welfare policies and norms related to retirement may influence the life style of the elderly. Sociohistorical conditions, such as those mentioned here, are important determinants of cohort behavior during any particular segment of the life course, and are referred to as the *period effects*.

A cohort–historical perspective focusing upon age strata, and transitions between strata in society is an appropriate framework for investigating a wide range of topics. In this chapter it is used to examine changes in family structure since 1870, and to relate these to demographic changes. This is largely a descriptive task, and a great deal of work remains to be done before the value of this approach for studying social change has been fully exploited. Related to studying the family, the next steps are to explore the impact of other types of social change (specific changes in technology, laws, or political structures) upon various aspects of the family, and to carefully assess the social significance of the family changes described here (perhaps in a perspective of societal evolution).

Before beginning to examine cohort life-course changes, two background topics need to be covered. First is a discussion of the data used in making the various calculations, and second is a brief overview of demographic change in the United States.

Data Available from Census and Vital Statistics Reports

Decennial census reports and annual vital statistics reports are basic sources for constructing the life-course experiences of various United States birth cohorts since 1870. The variables in these reports that are cross-classified by detailed age categories can be related to the appropriate birth cohort, and hence used to describe its experience. The birth cohort is specified when the age and census date are given, and age stratum in the life course is indexed by age. Table 2.1 indicates the census data at which the five cohorts examined in this study arrived, or will arrive, at selected age strata.

For convenience, in the remainder of this paper the 1870–1874 cohort is referred to as the 1870 cohort, the 1890–1894 one as the 1890 cohort, etc. A summary of the available census and vital statistics data for these cohort is presented in this section.

Cohort Mortality

Because age-specific death rates change over time, the mortality experience of a cohort cannot be captured by a period life table that is based on the age specific rates at one point in time. To follow the pattern of attrition due to death for a cohort, a long series of age-specific death rates is needed, so that the force of mortality at each age can be assessed. The National Center for Health Statistics (NCHS, 1972) has used the available death and population data for the United States since 1900 to construct cohort mortality and survivorship tables for the birth cohorts of 1901, 1910, 1920, and 1930. These tables, by sex and color, provide precisely the mortality information needed to construct cohort life-course patterns, but the data do not go back into the nineteenth century. Jacobson (1964), however, has calculated life tables for the

TABLE 2.1
Years in which Cohorts Occupied Selected Age Categories

	Census date at age				
Birth cohort	5–9	15–19	25–29	45–49	65–69
1870–1874	1880	1890	1900	1920	1940
1890–1894	1900	1910	1920	1940	1960
1910–1914	1920	1930	1940	1960	1980
1930–1934	1940	1950	1960	1980	2000
1950–1954	1960	1970	1980	2000	2020

white cohorts born at 10-year intervals, 1840–1960. These tables, for males and females, draw upon the limited mortality data available from the nineteenth century, and make prospective estimates of mortality for more recent cohorts that still have part of their life spans remaining. Since the earlier data are of unknown quality and rely heavily upon the experience of one state, Massachusetts, one should not exaggerate the precision that they allow. Nevertheless, these are the best indicators of cohort mortality available, and comparisons with concurrent mortality patterns in England, where better data exist, suggests that they are close to what would be expected.

Cohort Fertility

Two sources are available for obtaining cohort fertility information on United States females. The first is the annual age-specific fertility data provided from vital-statistics records. Relating the number of births in each year to women in the appropriate cohorts allows the calculation of cohort birth rates, and completed family size is obtained by summing the annual experiences of cohorts as they age from 15 through 44. Tables giving this type of information have been prepared for birth cohorts from 1876 to 1943 (NCHS, 1960).

The second source is published census data reporting on women by the number of children they have ever born. These data, by age of women, are available from the 1910 census, and each decennial census since 1940. As with all historical data, there are certain weaknesses that should be recognized. The reported children ever born may be biased by the usual census limitations (such as recall error, uneven coverage of various groups, age misreporting, etc.). Also, the data are only for survivors of the cohort, so the experience of women in the cohort who died before the census date is missed. Within these limits, however, the census material allows one to examine the distribution of women by number of children they have born, and to trace the changes for 5-year birth cohorts from 1855–1859 (aged 50–54 in 1910) through the most recent ones in their childbearing years.

Marital Status

As with fertility, annual changes in marital status for a cohort can be calculated from age-specific vital event records (marriages and divorces), while cohort composition by marital status at points in time can be obtained from census data. To compare marital behavior of cohorts since 1870, census data are more useful because they go back further and are more complete. (As late as 1967, national divorce statistics were based on reports from only 22 states.) Information on marital status of the population, by age and sex, is included in each United States census since 1890, with the following four categories distinguished: single, married, widowed, and divorced. More recent censuses offer greater detail; for example, if married, whether it is the first marriage, and whether the spouse is present. For earlier censuses there appears to be serious underreporting of the divorced status (Shyrock et al., 1971:286), perhaps because of social stigma attached to this status. Another weakness of census data is that the number recorded as widowed or divorced at any particular moment does not indicate the number in the cohort who have been in these states, since all who remarry and have their latest marriage intact are recorded as married.

Estimates of the prevalence of bachelorhood and spinsterhood can be obtained directly from census data on number single. Patterns of widowhood, divorce, and remarriage are more difficult to obtain, except in 1970 when a question on how the first marriage ended was included. For earlier time periods, analytical methods employing a combination of vital statistics and census data can be used to estimate prevalence of divorce and widowhood. Glick and Norton (1973) have carefully estimated the percentage of first marriages ending in divorce for cohorts of women since 1900, and estimates of marital disruption up to age 50 for cohorts since 1870 are included in this chapter.

Nativity

The historically strong interest in nationality and nativity of the U.S. population is reflected by the inclusion of questions on country of birth in each census since 1850, and on country of birth of parents for each native born person since 1870. As a result, from 1870 to the present, the white population, by 5-year age intervals, can be divided into the following nativity categories: native of native parentage, native of foreign or mixed parentage (one or both parents foreign born), and foreign born. Furthermore, detailed country of origin information is available. Various questions on mother tongue or language spoken in the home have been asked since 1910, but the lack of uniformity in the specific questions asked makes comparisons across time problematic.

Rural–Urban Residence

A distinction between the rural and the urban population is useful for many purposes, but such statistics, by age, are available only since the 1910 census. The current census practice of dividing the population into three categories—urban, rural nonfarm, and rural farm—dates back to 1920. However, one must be somewhat cautious in comparing across censuses since the definitions of urban and farm have changed several times (see U.S. Bureau of the Census, 1949). The 1960 census reports (U.S. Bureau of the Census, 1961: Tables 7 and 8), extend back to 1790 calculations of the urban and rural population according to the 1940 definition of urban, but unfortunately these are not available by age.

Education

Two primary measures of education are available from the United States censuses: school enrollment and educational attainment. School enrollment questions, included since 1840, report the number of persons who attended school at some time during the past year. The lack of cross-classification by age, however, makes the data from censuses prior to 1910 of little value in studying cohort educational experiences. Since 1910, percentages enrolled among those aged 14–15 and 16–17 are available, so an indication of cohort change in school attendance at these ages is available for birth cohorts since about 1890.

The second source of information, years of school completed by age, is available for each census since 1940. This measure, of course, gives no indication of quality of education, but it permits a more careful assessment of the distribution of cohort members by exposure to formal education. The 1940 census reports educational attainment for 5-year age categories up to age 70–74, thus allowing an estimate for the 1870 cohort. Differential mortality by educational attainment and misreporting both tend to produce an upward bias in the reported distribution, compared with the actual cohort experience. Responding to this problem, Gustavus and Nam (1968) have published an adjusted series of data on years of school completed, in which they attempt to eliminate this bias of overreporting level of attainment.

The discussion in this chapter of life-course changes draws upon the data just described. While attention is not directed toward the limitations of the data each time they are used, the limitations should be kept in mind. Furthermore, it is necessary at various places to make estimates or approximations of the actual cohort experience, since direct information is not available. The intention of these various calculations is not to produce precise percentage distributions, but rather to convey approximate quantitative figures. These estimates are sufficiently accurate to permit an assessment of the direction of change and the approximate rate of change between cohorts. A goal of future research should be to improve these estimates, as well as to use other data sources to add new types of information to the life-course experiences of these cohorts.

Major Demographic Trends in the United States Since 1870

Changes in mortality, fertility, nuptiality, divorce, and migration since 1870 have led to successive birth cohorts living out their life courses under markedly different demographic conditions. The changing demographic forces produced significant differences in cohort experiences, including the structure of families in which they lived. Before measuring the changes in specific aspects of family structure, it is useful to have an overview of the major long-term demographic trends during this historical period. Since these trends are well described elsewhere (e.g., see Taeuber and Taeuber, 1958), only a brief description is included here.

Almost every aspect of American society has been affected in some way by the dramatic decline of mortality rates during the last century. Between 1850 and 1950 expectation of life at birth for the United States white population rose from 42 to 69 years. Of this 27-year increase in life expectancy, about 7 years were added by mortality declines between 1850 and 1900, and the remaining 20 years were the result of declines over the subsequent half century (see Rao, 1973). From 1950 to 1970 another 3 years were added, bringing expectation of life up to about 72 years. Thus the greatest changes occurred in the first half of the twentieth century. But improvements between 1850 and 1900 should not be minimized; they were probably greater than during any previous 50-year period in the history of the human population. The most significant component of mortality declines since 1850 was the change in infant mortality (a 75% drop occurred between 1900 and 1950), but death rates at all ages fell substantially during this 100-year period of unprecedented improvement in the control of deaths.

As predicted by the theory of demographic transition, a movement from high birth rates to low birth rates accompanied the fall in death rates in the United States. However, the trend is slightly more complicated than this model indicates because of the unanticipated rise in birth rates after World War II. The crude birth rate in colonial America exceeded 50 per 1000 population, but a decline from this high level began sometime around 1800. A steadily downward trend in the birth rate persisted from this time until the late 1930s, when it reached a low of 18. In terms of average number of children ever born per mother surviving to age 40, this meant a decline from about eight to slightly less than three. The upswing in fertility following the war increased the crude birth rate to 26.6 in 1947 (the same level as in 1920–1924), and a resumption of the downward trend did not occur until 1958. By the early 1970s the birth rate declined to a level below the Depression low. Overall, from 1870 to 1970 there was a large and continuous fertility decline, with the exception of a small reversal during the decade following World War II.

Frequency and timing of marriages and divorces directly affect family structure. From 1870 to 1960 the median age at marriage in the United States declined (from 26.1 to 22.3 for males; from 22.0 to 20.0 for females), marriages were increasingly concentrated within a narrow range of ages, and the percentage who never married declined (see Rele, 1965; Uhlenberg, 1974). Since 1960 there has been a slight reversal of each of these trends. The divorce rate over this period increased up to 1947, then declined for a decade, and more recently has turned upward again. The magnitude of the change is indicated by the ratio of divorces to marriages; which was 1:32 in 1870, 1:12.7 in 1900; and 1:3.7 in 1967 (NCHS, 1973). Tracing the effect upon cohorts shows that the percentage of women whose first marriage eventually ends in divorce increased continuously, going from 12% of women born in 1900–1914 to about 29% for women born in 1940–1944 (Glick and Norton, 1973).

Two types of migration significantly changed American society after 1870: immigration from Europe and rural–urban movement. Large-scale immigration to the United States occurred from 1870 to 1930, during which time a total of 30 million immigrants arrived. The peak of this immigration was reached in 1907 when 1.3 million arrived in a single year—more than double the number of immigrants who came during the entire decade of 1930–1939. Since World War II the rate of immigration has increased from the Depression low, but it remains at a level much below the average for the period 1880–1930.

The population movement from rural to urban areas within the United States has greatly altered the environmental surroundings of most people. In 1790 only 5% of the population was urban, and the overwhelming majority of children were reared on farms. By 1970, 75% of the population lived in urban areas, and less than 5% of the population lived on farms. During the period from 1850 to 1950, the urban population increased from 25 to 60% of the total. It was during this period that the transformation from a predominantly rural to a predominately urban society occurred.

The impact upon individuals of the major demographic changes described is, to a large extent, mediated through the family. As family structure changes in response to changes in nuptiality, fertility, mortality, and migration, successive cohorts experience significantly altered life courses. The beginning point for each cohort is childhood, so changes in this segment of the life course for cohorts from 1870 to 1950 are examined first.

Successive Cohorts during Childhood

Childhood, as used in this paper, consists of that segment of the life course lasting from birth up to age 16. Any definition of childhood is somewhat arbitrary since the concept of childhood varies greatly among different cultures and among different historical eras. In medieval Europe the infant was regarded with considerable indifference, and somewhere between the ages of 5 and 7 the child was absorbed into the world of adults (Aries, 1962:329). With the development of schools and other age-specific institutions for youths, childhood became increasingly a well-defined age stratum with a distinctive cluster of normative expectations regarding behavior and roles. During the past century the duration of the childhood phase increased and several more specific categories within childhood emerged, such as preschool and adolescence (Elder, 1975a). Currently accepted images of the child were shaped by a complex set of social changes, including the structural changes in the family resulting from recent demographic events.

Size of Family of Orientation

Perhaps the most obvious structural variable affecting the family environment of children is the size of the unit. In a straightforward way, increasing the number of children within a family decreases the per-capita income of the family members. A lower per-capita income, in turn, may affect the future life-course chances of children through its effect on such things as nutrition, health care, travel experiences, and educational opportunities. Beyond economics, family size may affect child development by influencing the type and amount of interaction with parents and with siblings. A number of later studies have concluded that family size is inversely related to the intelligence and welfare of children, even when social class of parents is controlled (Wray, 1971; Belmont and Marolla, 1973).

Data necessary for calculating the distribution of persons in birth cohorts by the size of families of orientation do not exist for the United States. A complete population register would contain the necessary information, but in the United States one must estimate the distribution from census data on women by number of children ever born and from vital registration data on childhood mortality. The major difficulty in identifying the mothers of any particular 5-year birth cohort is that the mothers' ages span approximately 30 years, and that mothers within these age brackets contribute children to 10 or more different 5-year birth cohorts. Several methods of approximating the desired distribution are possible, but if the purpose is to derive crude approximations for comparisons over time, the simple approach described below appears adequate.

The distribution of infants born during a 5-year period by number of children ever born to their mothers is approximated by the distribution characteristic of all children born to women aged 20–24 at the beginning of the 5-year period (25–29 at the end of the period). For example, the experience of the cohort born in 1890–1894 is approximated by the experience of children born to the cohort of women aged 20–24 in 1890. For each cohort included here, the cohort of mothers used for the approximation bore a larger proportion of the children during the 5-year period than did any other. Furthermore, this cohort of mothers bore a larger proportion of their children during this period than during any other period. Finally, approximately 75% of the infants born during the 5-year period had mothers either from the specified cohort or from the immediately preceding or subsequent cohort of mothers. Thus, unless dramatic shifts in distribution of completed family size occurred between adjacent cohorts, this method gives a reasonably good approximation of the actual experience of members of the various cohorts, and provides a basis for examining change over time.

The striking effect of declining fertility upon the number of siblings for members of various cohorts is shown in Table 2.2. Whereas 565 of 1000 persons in the 1870 cohort were born into families in which the mother bore seven or more children, less than 150 per 1000 in the 1950 cohort were in this category. Balancing this decline, the proportion born into small- and medium-size families rose sharply over time, peaking with the 1930 cohort where 30% had either no sibling or only one.

Due to high infant mortality, the number of children who survived through childhood, and hence affected actual family size during those years, historically was much lower than the number born. For the 1870 cohort, only about 70% of the children born survived to age 10. Nevertheless, a child born in 1870 to a mother who gave birth to seven

TABLE 2.2

Distribution of Children by Number of Children Ever Born to Their Mothers, White U.S. Birth Cohorts From 1870 to 1950

Birth cohort	Total	Number whose mother bore X children			
		$X = 1-2$	3–4	5–6	7+
1870	1000	70	160	205	565
1890	1000	105	205	220	470
1910	1000	180	280	225	315
1930	1000	300	335	170	195
1950	1000	205	425	225	145

Sources: Calculated from U.S. Bureau of the Census, 1944: Tables 1 and 4; U.S. Bureau of the Census, 1955: Table 2; U.S. Bureau of the Census, 1964b: Table 2; U.S. Bureau of the Census, 1973b: Table 2.

children (the mean number of siblings for a person in this cohort was over six), would be expected to have at least four siblings survive past age 15.

The larger families of orientation for individuals in earlier cohorts meant not only that they tended to have more siblings, but also that they experienced greater changes in family structure as they moved through childhood. Consider, for example, children in a family in which eight children are born, compared with those in a two-child family. In the larger family, the first born enters a family with 3 members, but as he ages it keeps expanding up to a maximum of 10. The youngest child in this family enters a very large unit, which then contracts in size as he ages until finally he or she is the only remaining child. Furthermore, the ages of parents and ages and numbers of siblings present at different childhood stages will vary considerably for the various children in the large family, depending upon their birth order. In the small family, in contrast, the two siblings may be born a few years apart, and throughout their childhood no additional changes occur. Another change with declining family size is a decrease in the variability of birth order for cohort members. For example, 61% of the 1930 birth cohort were either first or second in birth order, compared to only 41% of the 1890 cohort and 36% of the 1870 one.

In summary, declining fertility has radically reduced the number of persons with more than three siblings, has reduced structural change in the family during childhood, and has sharply increased the number who have a low-order birth position. As number of children per mother declined, the variability in age of parents was reduced. The social, psychological, and economic consequences of these major structural changes in childhood experiences has received almost no attention.

Mortality in Family of Orientation

In addition to increasing the probability of survival for a child, changing mortality has directly affected the family structure of children who do survive by reducing the proportion who are orphaned or who have siblings die. The probability of a child having a mother or father die can be calculated if the ages of parents at the time of birth are known and an appropriate cohort life table is available. United States vital statistics have reported the age distribution of those bearing children since 1917, so it is necessary to estimate the age distribution of the parents of earlier cohorts. Fortunately the probability of losing a parent during the first 15 years of life is not very sensitive to the parents' age, so the need to estimate this in Table 2.3 does not seriously affect the accuracy of the calculated extent of orphanhood. Using cohort life tables for the entire white population, rather than one specific to parents, does not introduce a serious bias since the total adult population is composed primarily of parents. In estimating the probability of one or more sibling dying before they reach age 15, one needs to have the distribution of children by number of children born to their mothers.

The impact of declining mortality upon the childhood experience of various cohorts is indicated by the data in Table 2.3. The extent of change during the century covered by these data is impressive. Of 1000 infants born around 1870, only 515 survived to age 15 and had both parents still alive, while 925 of 1000 born around 1950 had this experience. This alteration in the childhood experience of cohorts is due to an 88% decline in the number of children who die during childhood, and an 85% decline in orphanhood among those who do survive. The changed probability of a child's mother dying before the child reaches age 15 is even greater; it is 11 times greater for the 1870 cohort than for the 1950 cohort. The greater probability of a father dying than a mother reflects the substantial sex differential in mortality during the adult years and, to a much lesser extent, the tendency for the father to be a few years older than the mother. The increase in the ratio of paternal orphans to maternal orphans reflects the increase in the sex differential in mortality over this period. Overall, these data indicate that the necessity of coping with the economic, social, and psychological problems associated with orphanhood moved from a fairly common childhood experience to a rare one.

Another consequence of declining mortality is the reduction in the

TABLE 2.3

Distribution of Children out of 1000 by Type of Mortality Experience to Their Family, White U.S. Birth Cohorts From 1870 to 1950[a]

Birth cohort	Type 1[b]	Type 2[c]	Type 2a[d]	Type 2b[e]	Type 3[f]	Type 4[g]
1870	295	190	80	130	515	90
1890	260	160	60	110	580	165
1910	155	125	35	95	720	385
1930	85	60	15	45	855	655
1950	35	40	10	30	925	825
Children surviving to age 15						
1870		275	110	180	725	130
1890		220	80	150	780	220
1910		150	40	115	850	455
1930		65	20	45	935	715
1950		40	10	30	960	855

[a] To calculate this it was assumed that the age distribution of the parents for members of the 1870, 1890, and 1910 cohorts was similar to that of the 1920 cohort.

[b] Child dies before reaching age 15.

[c] Child survives, but one or both parents dies before the child reaches age 15.

[d] Mother dies before the child reaches age 15.

[e] Father dies before the child reaches age 15.

[f] Child survives and is not orphaned by age 15.

[g] Child survives, is not orphaned, and no sibling dies before the child reaches age 15.

Sources: Jacobson, 1964; NCHS, 1972: U.S. Bureau of the Census, 1917, 1930; U.S. Department of Health, Education, and Welfare, 1950. NCHS, 1969: Table 1-53.

probability that one has a sibling die during childhood (Table 2.3). For those born prior to the twentieth century, few grew up without having a death occur to some member of their family of orientation. Less than 10% of those born around 1870 survived to age 15, with both parents alive, and had all of their brothers and sisters also survive to age 15. This does not mean that all who had a sibling die were alive at the time of the death, since many later-order births occurred after earlier siblings had died. Also, some of these deaths to siblings occurred while the child from this cohort was very young, or after he had left his family of orientation. Nevertheless, a clear picture emerges of how few families in the nineteenth and early twentieth centuries were unaffected by death during the childbearing and childrearing years. In less than 100 years the milieu shifted from one in which death within the family was the usual childhood experience to one in which it was the exception.

Other Cohort Changes

Heavy immigration up to 1925 brought a large number of foreign-born young adults to the United States, and these immigrants tended to have larger families than the native born. As a result, about 30% of the children in each of the first three cohorts had foreign-born parents (Table 2.4). With the decline in immigration, the percentage of children with native-born parents increased rapidly around 1930, and only 55 out of a 1000 children in the 1950 cohort were second generation. A substantial decrease in cohort diversity occurs as the members almost uniformly are socialized in native American families. The literature on assimilation suggests that it is primarily children from the second generation that are confronted with the difficult adjustment of moving from their parents' culture to that of the broader society (e.g., see Gordon, 1964). As a result of changes in immigration rates, more recent cohorts contain relatively few persons caught in this marginal position between cultures.

Another type of movement, rural to urban, has also altered the socialization experience of children in families. With urbanization comes an increase in population density and hence an increase in number of peers outside the family for possible interaction. Also, movement from farms to cities decreases opportunities for children to be usefully occupied with family chores, and increases opportunities to be involved in youth activities, such as schools, church groups, clubs, and recreational leagues. Over time an increasing proportion of individuals have lived in urban areas during their childhood—rising from 21% of the 1870 cohort to 67% of the 1950 cohort (Table 2.4). By 1950 only about 80 children out of 1000 were living on farms. The proportion of children exposed to environments where the family plays a lesser role in socialization, and peers and other agencies play a greater role, has increased rapidly among successive cohorts since 1870.

Of all the extrafamilial influences upon children, schools probably have the greatest effect. The proportion of children attending school and the number of years they spend in school have increased continuously for all cohorts since 1870 (Table 2.4). This change was facilitated by increasing population density, which increased the feasibility of constructing public schools easily accessible to children, and by declining agricultural employment of children, which is a major cause of irregular school attendance. For recent cohorts, school attendance past age 15 has become almost universal, and with few exceptions children are in classes with others of the same age throughout most of their childhood. This shifting educational experience of cohorts is both an

TABLE 2.4

Distribution of Children on Selected Characteristics, White U.S. Birth Cohorts from 1870 to 1950

| Birth cohort | Total | Nativity and parentage at ages 5–9 | | |
		Native of native parents	Native of foreign-born parents	Foreign-born
1870	1000	NA	NA	NA
1890	1000	675	305	20
1910	1000	690	290	20
1930	1000	850	150	—
1950	1000	935	55	10

| Birth cohort | Total | Rural–urban residence at ages 5–9 | | |
		Urban	Rural	Rural–farm
1870	1000	215	785	NA
1890	1000	345	655	NA
1910	1000	470	530	335
1930	1000	490	510	275
1950	1000	670	330	80

| Birth cohort | Percentage enrolled in school at ages X | | Percentage completing X years of school | | |
	14–15	16–17	Less than 8	8–11	12+
1870	NA	NA	44.2	41.9	13.9
1890	77.4	44.1	33.3	46.2	20.5
1910	90.4	58.9	16.3	44.8	38.9
1930	93.6	75.9	8.4	24.6	67.0
1950	96.2	89.9	1.7	13.3	85.0

Sources: U.S. Bureau of the Census, 1897, 1943a, 1943b, 1945, 1964a, 1965, 1973a.

important cause and an important consequence of the increasing societal complexity that has occurred over the past century.

Before proceeding to trace the life-course patterns of these cohorts as they move through subsequent age strata, a summary of the changes in their childhood experiences is useful. On a number of important variables there has been a significant trend toward increasing uniformity of experience for cohort members. The result of this trend can be seen clearly for the 1950 cohort: 93% entered families with native-born parents; 92% lived in nonfarm settings; 85% completed a high school education; 96% had both parents survive through their child-hood; and 63% had three or fewer siblings. Much of this increasing uniformity has been the result of demographic change: the decline in fertility, immigration, and urbanization. Beyond the demographic fac-tors discussed, other changes have operated to increase the homogeneity of other aspects of the childhood experience. For exam-ple, an increasing proportion of children are exposed to the same con-tent of programs on television, and they increasingly have access to standard types of toys and consumer products. Perhaps childrearing practices have also become increasingly similar among families as a re-sult of greater reliance upon "authoritative" guide books on how to rear children. It goes well beyond the scope of this chapter to assess the societal consequences of the decline in variability in those aspects of the childhood experience that have accompanied increasing societal complexity, but surely these consequences are not trivial.

Life-Course Patterns during Adult Years

The transition from childhood to adulthood involves potential changes in several dimensions of the life course, such as employment status, marital status, parental status, and residential location. There are alternative courses that an individual may take on each of these variables, and hence within a population we observe variability. But it should not be assumed that each individual is faced with a "free choice" in deciding which direction to go. As Ryder states, on impor-tant life-course variables "the society intervenes, in obvious and in subtle ways, to ensure that the outcomes, at least in the aggregate, make sense on society's behalf. These constraints on choice are what sociologists call norms [1974:77]." These norms that regulate behavior may take the form of laws, kinship rules, religious injunctions, etc., and with each norm is associated sanctions to encourage compliance. In addition to normative controls, choices are also restricted by economic constraints (e.g., limited income, opportunity costs), biological con-straints (e.g., physical appearance, fecundity), demographic constraints (e.g., sex ratio), or various other factors which either limit the alterna-tives or impose varying rewards for different choices.

Since norms, as well as the other constraints upon behavior, change over time, the behavior of cohorts entering the adult years of life during different historical periods should be expected to vary. Census and vital statistic data allow us to examine changes in several family-related areas for the birth cohorts of 1870, 1890, 1910, and 1930 as they move through the adult years. (The 1950 birth cohort did not enter adulthood until the 1970s, so cannot yet be studied.) Since sex differentiation is of such importance throughout the adult years of life, the experiences of females and males are examined separately. As with childhood in the preceding section, attention here is directed toward measuring the distribution of cohort members according to life-course types, and toward relating the changes in distribution over time to demographic changes.

Changing Patterns of Females

Is there a socially prescribed family course for females to follow as they age through the adult years, and, if so, has it changed over the last century? This question regarding norms affecting the family needs to be critically examined, but goes beyond the scope of this chapter. For the purposes of this study, it is assumed that Blake (1972) and others are correct in stating that the normatively preferred role for females has been one in which marriage, childbearing, and childrearing are of paramount importance. However, even if this norm has remained constant over this time period, sanctions for violation of the norm may have changed, and other factors leading to nonconformance may have changed. Thus it is reasonable to expect that if we follow the life-course experience of actual cohorts of women as they move through the adult years, a variety of nonconforming patterns will emerge. Further, the proportion of women in each of the nonconforming patterns may change among cohorts. A typology describing alternative possibilities was developed in an earlier paper (Uhlenberg, 1974), and the distribution of women in various cohorts by type experienced was estimated. This section summarizes the findings of that paper.

The typology distinguishes five different possible life courses that females might follow as they age through the adult years from 15 to 50. Each women in the cohort can be located in one, and only one, of the types specified.

1. Normatively expected. This is the life course that involves marrying, bearing children, and surviving to age 50 with the first marriage still intact. Women in this category have conformed to the societal expectation that all females should become wives and mothers, and to the preference that their marriages be stable.
2. Early death. The first exception to the above pattern is death occurring to women before they reach age 50. This category includes women who married, as well as those who were single at the time of death.

3. Spinster. This category includes all women who survive to age 50, and have never married. Very few of those who are spinsters at age 50 subsequently marry, and, if they do, they are obviously excluded from marital childbearing.
4. Childless. Females in this category survive and marry, but do not have any children.
5. Unstable marriage—with children. The final category consists of women who conform to the norms of marriage and childbearing, but who have their first marriage broken by divorce or death of husband before they reach age 50. Most of these women have dependent children at the time of marital disruption, and a large percent remarry. By remarrying, women are able to once again live within the normatively preferred family structure.

The distribution of white women in cohorts from 1870 to 1930 who experienced each of these types is given in Table 2.5. Several major shifts over time in American family structure are revealed by these data. The largest change has been in the proportion of the cohort which arrives at age 50 in the "normatively expected" category. Of 1000 females in the 1870 cohort who survived to age 15, only 440 followed the socially expected life course. The number who deviated from this category declined for each successive cohort, so that 600 of 1000 in the 1930 cohort were in conformance.

TABLE 2.5
Distribution of 1000 White Females in the U.S. by Type of Life-Course Experiences, Birth Cohorts From 1870 to 1930

Birth cohort	Early death	Spinster	Childless	Unstable marriage with children	Normatively expected
			Those surviving to age 15		
1870	235	80	70	175	440
1890	170	85	115	170	460
1910	90	60	145	185	520
1930	50	45	40	265	600
			Those surviving to age 50		
1870		105	90	230	575
1890		100	140	205	555
1910		65	160	200	575
1930		45	45	280	630

Sources: Jacobson, 1964; NCHS, 1972; and U.S. Bureau of the Census, 1944, 1955, 1964, 1973b.

By distinguishing life-course patterns in this way, the influence of changing demographic behavior upon family structure for adults is explicated. Declining mortality has had a marked effect upon female cohort life-course experiences in two ways. First, it has drastically reduced the proportion of women who fail to survive to age 50. As the number of survivors has increased for each successive cohort, the opportunity to conform to societal expectations has increased. The second effect of declining mortality has been a reduction in the proportion of women who have their marriage broken by the death of their husband before reaching the end of the childbearing stage. The number of women who have their husband die before they reach age 50 declined by about 60% between the 1870 and the 1930 cohorts. Clearly changing mortality has had the effect of increasing family stability among adults as well as among children.

A second trend has been a declining rate of spinsterhood among females who survive. The proportion still single at age 50 declined from over 10% of the 1870 cohort to about 4.5% for the 1930 cohort. Along with the increase in proportion marrying, the age at which females marry has declined. Assuming that there is a hardcore of "unmarriageable" females, the number who follow this nonconforming pattern must have reached a near minimum with the 1930 cohort.

A third demographic variable affecting family structure, childlessness, has not changed in a consistent direction. Up to the 1910 cohort an increasing proportion of women followed the childless pattern, and then an extremely sharp reduction occurred between the 1910 and 1930 cohort. The 1910 cohort, with the high rate of childlessness, also had an overall fertility rate so low that it was below the replacement level. This cohort, it should be noted, entered its prime childbearing years during the Depression. The 1930 cohort, by contrast, reached its peak childbearing years during a period of strong economic expansion, and had a level of reproduction higher than that of the 1890 cohort. (For a more detailed discussion of these fertility patterns, see Easterlin, 1962; Campbell, 1973.) Unless significant advances are made in reducing sterility, the number of childless women in a cohort cannot be reduced much below the level reached by the 1930 cohort.

Finally, the fourth trend influencing the distribution of women in Table 2.5 is the increasing rate of marital dissolutionment due to divorce and separation. During this century, the substantial decline in widowhood before age 50 has been approximately equalled by the increase in voluntary marital disruption, so that the proportion of women in successive cohorts whose marriage is broken by the end of the childrearing state remained fairly constant up to the 1930 cohort. However, the proportion who remarry after their first marriage is broken has increased (Glick and Norton, 1973), so the proportion of ever-married women who are living in a family with a husband at age 50 has increased substantially.

In summary, demographic trends between 1890 and 1960 led to increasing conformance with a traditional family structure for adult females that involves marriage and motherhood. This increase, to a large extent, was a result of reductions in involuntary factors that blocked conformance—specifically mortality and infecundity. The trend toward increasing uniformity of females in life-course experience probably reached a peak with the 1930 cohort, for which very low levels of nonmarriage and childlessness combined with low mortality to produce an exceptionally high rate of conformance to the expected pattern. As more recent cohorts experience higher rates of voluntary marital disruption, and perhaps more childlessness and nonmarriage, uniformity in experience will decline (Uhlenberg, 1974).

Changing Family Patterns of Males

A typology of family-related life-course patterns for males, similar to that developed for females, is given in Table 2.6. However, since information on paternity status of males is not available from censuses, the distribution of men by whether they are fathers cannot be calculated. The typology follows male cohorts as they age from 20 to 50, and distinguishes five categories, depending upon the male's status at age 50: die before age 50, bachelor, marriage broken by death of wife, marriage broken by other cause, and married once with spouse present at age 50.

Cohort life tables are used to estimate the number of men out of 1000 alive at age 20 who die before reaching age 50 for successive cohorts. The percentage of men surviving to age 50 without having married is estimated from various censuses, using data on percentage single at ages 45–49. The probability of a man having his first wife die before he reaches age 50 is calculated from female cohort life tables, using the formula: $1 - l(y + x)/lx$; where x is the mean age at first marriage for wives of men in the cohort, and y is $50 -$ mean age at first marriage of men. (l_a is the life table function giving the number in the cohort who survive to exact age a.)

The probability of the first marriage being disrupted by other causes cannot be calculated directly for males because the necessary census data do not exist. Rather, the fate of the first marriage (when the wife does not die) for males is estimated from the experience of females

TABLE 2.6

Distribution of 1000 White Males in the U.S. by Type of Life-Course Experiences, Birth Cohorts from 1870 to 1930

Birth cohort	Die between 20 and 50	Bachelor	Wife died	Other broken marriage	Spouse present
		Those surviving to age 20			
1870	245	95	110	60	490
1890	190	90	90	85	545
1910	115	60	50	145	630
1930	75	55	25	210	635
		Those surviving to age 50			
1870		125	150	75	650
1890		110	110	100	680
1910		70	60	165	705
1930		55	30	230	685

Sources: Jacobson, 1964; NCHS, 1972: Rele, 1965; U.S. Bureau of the Census, 1922: Table 2; 1943b. Table 6; 1963: Table 177; 1972: Table 1.

in first marriages not ended by the death of the husband before age 50. The following formula is used to estimate the probability of a marriage being dissolved by a cause other than the wife's death, for ever-married men aged 50:

$$1 - (F_1/F_3) - F_2$$

where

F_1 = females 45–49, married once with spouse present.
F_2 = females 45–49, first marriage ended in widowhood.
F_3 = females 45–49, ever married.

The results of using these formulae to calculate the experience of white males from 1870 to 1930 are given in Table 2.6. As with females, changing mortality has led to a large reduction in the number of males who die during this stage of life, and an even greater percentage reduction in the number who have a spouse die. Also parallel to females, the proportion of males who never marry declined sharply over time. The declining number of men having their first marriage broken by the death of their wives was almost equally matched by the increasing number whose marriage was broken by other causes for the 1870–1910 cohorts. Between the 1910 and 1930 cohorts, the increase in voluntarily broken marriages greatly exceeded the decline in marriages broken by death, so the total number of broken marriages rose over 15%. The overall effect of the various changes has resulted in surprisingly little change in the number of men who arrive at age 50 with their first marriage intact.

Due to high rates of remarriage, the number of men who are married at age 50 substantially exceeds the number who are living with their first wife. At age 50, 820 of 1000 men in the 1870 cohort were married, and this increased to 890 of 1000 for both the 1910 and 1930 cohorts. This indicates a high and increasing degree of uniformity in family structure for adult males. Thus, for males, as well as for females, extrafamilial activities have not been a substitute for family involvement, but are in addition to the normatively defined family role.

Cohorts as They Enter Old Age

It was noted earlier in this chapter that the transition from childhood to adulthood involves changes in employment status, marital status, and parental status. It is interesting that the transition to old age involves changes in these same life-course variables. Perhaps the most salient characteristics of old age are loss of dependent children, birth of grandchildren, retirement, and widowhood. While in the normal course of aging these four events may be expected, and in this ordered sequence, there is, of course, diversity in the actual experiences of members of a cohort. In this section, two aspects of entering into old age are examined, one applying primarily to females and the other primarily to males. The distribution of females at age 60 according to family structure is calculated, and a measure of the proportion of females living in an empty-nest situation at this point in their life course is obtained. Then the duration of empty-nest marriages beyond age 60 is estimated for various cohorts. For males, a cluster of cohort characteristics having some bearing upon retirement from the labor force are calculated. In looking at the transition into old age, attention is focused upon birth cohorts from 1830 to 1910. (The 1910 birth cohort reached age 60 in 1970.)

Females at Age 60

In a typical life course, a female marries, bears children, rears children, and survives to see her children marry and bear children. The segment of the life course between the time the last child leaves home and the marriage is disrupted by death is popularly referred to as the empty-nest phase. Glick and Parke (1965), in studying the life cycle of the family, called attention to this phase by calculating the median age of females at the marriage of their last child and at the death of one spouse. For cohorts born between 1880 and 1889, they found that the median age to disruption of the marriage due to death exceeded the age at marriage of last child by less than 1 year, while for the 1920–1929 cohort this difference was about 12.5 years. The implication of this large change is that the empty-nest phenomenon has increased greatly in significance as a part of the life course.

The approach of Glick and Parke, calculating median ages at occurrence of selected events for those who follow a typical course, leaves unanswered the question of how many actually experience the empty-nest phenomenon. Women who die early, never marry, bear no children, or have their marriage disrupted early, never enter an empty-nest phase. Because of substantial variability in age at birth of last child and in age at which the last child leaves home, it is difficult to estimate how many women experience this aspect of the life course. However, we can look at the distribution of women in a cohort at age 60, as they are making the transition into old age, and estimate how many are in an empty-nest situation at that time. Also, we can compute the number of these marriages that endure for specified periods of time past age 60.

The distribution of white women by type of family status at age 60 for birth cohorts from 1830 to 1910 is given in Table 2.7. Despite changing mortality, nuptiality, and childbearing patterns over this 80-year period, the proportion of women in the cohort who were living in an empty-nest family at age 60 changed remarkably little. In fact, the proportion in the 1910 cohort in this category is virtually identical to that in the 1830 cohort. Decreases in the widowed or divorced category have been roughly countered by increases in the childless category for women.

TABLE 2.7

Percentage Distribution of White Females by Family Status at Age 60, U.S. Birth Cohorts 1830 to 1910

Birth cohort	Single	Widowed or divorced	Married and childless	Married with children	Birth cohort in empty nest[a]
1830	5.9	32.8	5.4	55.9	21.6
1850	7.3	29.7	5.6	57.4	24.0
1870	9.3	27.8	10.1	52.8	25.0
1890	8.2	26.0	11.5	54.3	30.8
1910	6.8	24.2	13.5	55.5	36.4

[a] Percentage who survive from birth to age 60, and at age 60 are married and have given birth to one or more child.

Sources: U.S. Bureau of the Census, 1913, 1933, 1963, 1972.

TABLE 2.8
Percentage of Empty Nest Marriages Among Females Aged 60 That are Intact After X Years

Birth cohort	X = 0	5	10	15	20
1830	100.0	70.0	41.5	19.6	6.7
1850	100.0	71.6	44.3	21.3	6.7
1870	100.0	73.2	46.4	24.6	9.9
1890	100.0	77.8	54.0	32.4	15.2
1910	100.0	83.3	64.2	42.8	22.2

Despite this apparent stability, declining mortality has substantially altered the empty-nest phase of the life course in two ways. First, declining mortality has resulted in a much greater proportion of women surviving to age 60, and hence the likelihood of a female eventually entering into this category has increased over time. As shown in Table 2.7, the percentage of females who survive to age 60, and at that age are married and not childless, increased continuously from 21.6% for the 1830 cohort to 36.4% for the 1910 cohort. It is interesting to note that even for this most recent cohort only about one-third of the females born into the cohort experienced this "typical" aspect of the life course at age 60.

The second change resulting from mortality declines is an increase in the duration of the empty nest past age 60 for those who enter into this category. Table 2.8 indicates attrition patterns from empty-nest marriages by age of females. Among women in empty-nest marriages at age 60, the median duration of this condition has increased from 8.5 to 13.3 years. Also due to a decrease in age at birth of last child, women in more recent cohorts have entered into this status at somewhat earlier ages. Thus the empty-nest phenomenon has in some ways increased in significance, although the percentage of females aged 60 who are in this category has changed little. Since expectation of life at age 60 has increased more than the expected duration of marriages past age 60, and since an increasing proportion of marriages are disrupted by the death of the male, the duration and significance of widowhood as a segment of the female life course has also increased over time.

Males at Ages 55–59

An important transition for many males as they enter the terminal phase of the life course is retirement from the labor force. In some ways this loss of major occupational activity for males parallels the loss of

TABLE 2.9
Selected Characteristics of White Males in the Age Category 55–59, U.S. Birth Cohorts from 1830 to 1910

Birth cohort	Sex ratio[a]	Percentage married	Ratio to cohort 10 years earlier	Percentage foreign born	Percentage urban	Percentage rural– farm	Percentage in agriculture[b]
1830	107.4	84.0	1.30	35.1	NA	NA	49.6
1850	113.6	80.7	1.31	27.9	47.9	NA	NA
1870	107.6	79.7	1.28	24.9	55.9	24.8	27.4
1890	98.0	83.3	1.18	21.5	66.1	15.9	15.8
1910	92.0	87.3	1.15	6.5	71.0	6.7	6.2

[a] White males aged 55–59 per 100 white females aged 55–59.
[b] Percentage of labor force engaged in agriculture.
Sources: U.S. Bureau of the Census, 1897, 1913, 1933, 1955, 1963, 1972, 1973a.

the mothering role by females as they enter an empty-nest family. But the increase in proportion of males entering the retired category has been much more marked than the increase of females entering empty-nest families. Not only do more males survive to old age, but also an increasing proportion of older men now retire. The labor-force participation rate by white males aged 65 and over dropped from about 67% in 1890 to 41.3% in 1950, and continued to drop to a low of 24.9% in 1970. A look at characteristics of males aged 55–59, as they begin the transition into old age, for successive cohorts shows a variety of changes that accompanied this reduction in labor force activity (see Table 2.9).

The ratios of each cohort at age 55–59 with the cohort at this same age 10 years earlier shows that the absolute number of males entering old age has increased substantially over time. Since this trend has occurred concurrently with the trend toward a larger proportion of males retiring from the labor force, the increase in number of males in the category retired has been very rapid between adjacent cohorts. Furthermore, the increasing concentration of these males in urban areas has produced an exceedingly sharp increase in the number of urban, retired older males. Such a rapid shift between cohorts can have interesting social implications because it leads to an imbalance between the number of role spaces available and the actual number of persons in the age stratum (see Waring, unpublished). In particular, as these cohorts of males have entered old age in urban areas, a mismatch has occurred between cohort size and facilities available for retired persons.

Two additional demographic changes have produced further changes in cohort composition of males as they enter into old age. The 1910 cohort is sharply differentiated from the earlier cohorts in percentage foreign born. The contraction of immigration to the United States after 1920 resulted in a much larger proportion of recent cohorts being native born. If being native born gives a person advantages in knowing how to cope with the social system during old age, then the 1910 cohort is clearly in a superior position relative to earlier ones. The other demographic change, greater reduction in female than male mortality, has resulted in an increasing proportion of older males entering old age with a surviving wife present. Further, the decreasing sex ratio of men to women in old age increases the opportunity for widowed or divorced older men to remarry. As a consequence, an increasing proportion of men who enter retirement are married, and have a spouse present as they live out the last years of the life course.

Conclusion

Time, in its December 28, 1970 issue, had a cover article titled, "The U.S. Family: Help!" The article, which attempts to summarize current thinking about changes in the family, begins as follows:

America's families are in trouble—trouble so deep and pervasive as to threaten the future of our nation," declared a major report to last week's White House Conference on Children. "Can the family survive?" asks Anthropologist Margaret Mead rhetorically. "Students in rebellion, the young people living in communes, unmarried couples living together call into question the very meaning and structure of the stable family unit as our society has known it." The family, says California Psychologist Richard Farson, "is now often without function. It is not longer necessarily the basic unit in our society."

The data of doom—many familiar, some still startling—consistently seem to support this concern [1970:34].

This view, which sees the American family as undergoing profound change, is currently widespread, but it is not new. In 1949 the sociologist Carle Zimmerman wrote:

The influence of these gradual developments during several centuries, and the recent upheavals, have given us a plethora of unusual family behavior in recent years. Some persons see these changes as "progress," or the breaking through toward a new and more interesting family system. Others, including the writer, look upon it as a polarization of values typical of the breakdown of a family system [1949:200].

A similar theme was presented even earlier by William Ogburn, who in 1938 wrote:

Prior to modern times the power and prestige of the family was due to seven functions it performed. . . . The dilemma of the modern family is caused by the loss of many of these functions in recent times [1938:139–140].

These sweeping observations on the demise of the family as an institution are presented with vivid and persuasive language, but how accurate are they?

Social historians can make a major contribution to discussions of family change by carefully describing what the family of the past was actually like (in contrast to popular and romantic views of the past). Historical research can clarify such issues as: What has changed? In what direction did the change occur? At what time did specific changes occur? This chapter was directed toward answering some of these questions as it compared family-related behavior of various cohorts as they enter or pass through particular segments of the life course.

A wide array of profound changes affecting American society occurred between 1870 and 1970. There was a major shift in the population from rural, agricultural settings to urban, industrial environments. Advances in medicine and public health produced sharp declines in mortality and introduced modern, efficient contraceptives. Forms of mass communication and travel underwent radical alterations. Immigration changed from a large, unregulated flow into a much smaller, carefully regulated one. The federal government expanded rapidly in size and influence, and a broad system of social welfare developed. There was a vast expansion in the formal educational system. During this era of dramatic and unprecedented change in the social system, what occurred to the traditional institution of the family?

Clearly, the family could not remain unaffected by all of the social, economic, and political changes occurring during this century. For children, the family became a smaller, urban unit with less pervasive control over childhood behavior. But almost universally, children continued to be reared and socialized in families, and the proportion who have this unit disrupted by the death of a parent has declined by over sixfold.

For adult females, the average number of children born has declined, the segment of the life span spent rearing children has become shorter, and the probability of divorce has increased. But the proportion of women who reach age 50 having experienced a "normatively expected" life course has increased. Over this time span, an increasing proportion of women entered marriage, an increasing proportion bore children, and many fewer had their marriage disrupted by death before the childrearing years were completed. For males, also, the changes over this century did not reduce participation in family roles. More males from the 1930 cohort will be married and living with their first wife at age 50 than was true for the 1870 cohort, and the percentage who never marry among the more recent cohort will be less than half that of the earlier one.

With the changing marriage, divorce, and mortality patterns, a larger percentage of those in more recent cohorts have been divorced by the time they reach old age, but a lower percentage have been widowed and a lower percentage have never married. The net result of these trends upon cohorts as they enter into old age has been an increase in the proportion who are married, for both males and females. Further, the duration of these marriages into old age has increased over time.

Thus, the American family has changed over the past 100 years, but quantitative evidence does not support the notion of family disorganization and disintegration. An increasing proportion of the population lives out the life course almost wholly within a family context. In speculating on the family of the future, one should not ignore the remarkable stability and adaptability of the American family during the past century of vast social change.

References

Aries, Philippe
    1962   Centuries of Childhood. Tr. Robert Baldick. New York: Vintage.
Belmont, Lillian, and Francis A. Marolla
    1973   "Birth order, family size, and intelligence." Science 182:1096–1101.
Blake, Judith
    1972   "Coercive pronatalism and American population policy." Pp. 85–109 in Robert Parke, Jr. and Charles F. Westoff (eds.), U.S. Commission on Population Growth and The American Future, Aspects of Population Growth Policy. Volume VI. Washington, D.C.: U.S. Government Printing Office.
Campbell, Arthur A.
    1973   "Three generations of parents." Family Planning Perspectives 5:106–112.
Easterlin, Richard A.
    1962   "The American baby boom in historical perspective." Occasional paper No. 79, National Bureau of Economic Research.
Elder, Glen H., Jr.
    1975a   "Age differentiation and the life course." Annual Review of Sociology 1:165–190.
    1975b   "Adolescence in the life cycle: an introduction." Chapter 1 in Alex Inkeles, James Coleman, and Neil Smelser (eds.), Adolescence in The Life Cycle. Washington, D.C.: Winston.
Glick, Paul C., and Arthur J. Norton
    1973   "Perspectives on the recent upturn in divorce and remarriage." Demography 10:301–314.
Glick, Paul C., and Robert Parke, Jr.
    1965   "New approaches in studying the life cycle of the family." Demography 2:187–202.
Gordon, Milton M.
    1964   Assimilation in American Life. New York: Oxford University Press.
Gustavus, Susan O., and Charles B. Nam
    1968   "Estimates of the 'true' educational distribution of the adult population of the United States from 1910 to 1960." Demography 5:410–421.
Jacobson, Paul H.
    1964   "Cohort survival for generations since 1840." Milbank Memorial Fund Quarterly 42:36–53.
Lee, Everett S., Simon Thomas, and Dorothy Swayne Thomas
    1957   Population Redistribution and Economic Growth: United States, 1870–1950. Volume 1. Philadelphia: American Philosophical Society.

Mason, Karen Oppenheim, William M. Mason, H. H. Winsborough, and W. Kenneth Poole
  1973   "Some methodological issues in cohort analysis of archival data." American Sociological Review 38:242–258.
National Center For Health Statistics
  1960   "Fertility Tables for Birth Cohorts of American Women." Vital and Health Statistics, Special Reports, Selected Studies. Vol. 51—No. 1.
  1969   Vital Statistics of The U.S., 1969, Vol. I.
  1970   Vital Statistics of The U.S., 1970, Vol. II—Section 5, Life Tables.
  1972   "Cohort Mortality and Survivership: United States Death-Registration States: 1900–1968." Vital and Health Statistics. Series 3—No. 16.
  1973   "100 Years of Marriage and Divorce Statistics, United States, 1867–1967." Vital and Health Statistics. Series 21—No. 24.
Ogburn, William F.
  1938   "The changing family." The Family 19:139–143.
Rao, S. L. N.
  1973   "On long-term mortality trends in the United States, 1850–1968." Demography 10:405–419.
Rele, J. R.
  1965   "Trends and differentials in the American age at marriage." Milbank Memorial Fund Quarterly 43:219–234.
Riley, Mathilda White
  1973   "Aging and cohort succession: interpretations and misinterpretations." Public Opinion Quarterly 37:35–49.
Ryder, Norman B.
  1964   "Notes on the concept of a population." American Journal of Sociology 69:447–463.
  1974   "Comment on 'economic theory of fertility behavior'." Pp. 76–80 in Theodore W. Schultz (ed.), Economics of The Family. Chicago: University of Chicago Press.
Shryock, Henry, Jacob S. Siegel, and associates
  1971   The Methods and Materials of Demography. Volumes 1 and 2. Washington: U.S. Government Printing Office.
Taeuber, Conrad, and Irene B. Taeuber
  1958   The Changing Population of The United States. New York: Wiley.
Uhlenberg, Peter
  1974   "Cohort variations in family life cycle experiences of U.S. females." Journal of Marriage and the Family 36:284–292.
U.S. Bureau of the Census
  1897   U.S. Census of Population: 1890. Part II. Washington, D.C.: U.S. Government Printing Office.
  1913   U.S. Census of Population: 1910. Volume I. Washington, D.C.: U.S. Government Printing Office.
  1917   Birth Statistics, 1917. Washington, D.C.: U.S. Government Printing Office.
  1922   U.S. Census of Population: 1920. Chapter 4 in Volume 2. Washington, D.C.: U.S. Government Printing Office.
  1930   Births, Stillbirths, and Infant Mortality Statistics, 1930. Washington, D.C.: U.S. Government Printing Office.
  1933   U.S. Census of Population: 1930, Volumes II and IV. Washington, D.C.: U.S. Government Printing Office.

1943a   U.S. Census of Population: 1940. Part I in Volume II. Washington, D.C.: U.S. Government Printing Office.

1943b   U.S. Census of Population: 1940. Vol. IV, Part I: Characteristics by Age, U.S., Summary. Washington, D.C.: U.S. Government Printing Office.

1944   U.S. Census of Population: 1940. Differential Fertility: 1940 and 1910. Women by Number of Children Ever Born. Washington, D.C.: U.S. Government Printing Office.

1945   U.S. Census of Population: 1940. Nativity and Parentage of The White Population. Washington, D.C.: U.S. Government Printing Office.

1949   Current Population Reports, Series P-23, No. 1, "The Development of The Urban-Rural Classification in The United States" (by Leon F. Truesdell).

1955   U.S. Census of Population: 1950. Volumes II and IV, Special Reports, Part 5, Ch. C, Fertility. Washington, D.C.: U.S. Government Printing Office.

1961   U.S. Census of Population: 1960, Vol. I, Characteristics of the Population. Washington, D.C.: U.S. Government Printing Office.

1963   U.S. Census of Population: 1960. Detailed Characteristics. U.S. Summary. Final Report PC91)-ID. Washington, D.C.: U.S. Government Printing Office.

1964a   U.S. Census of Population: 1960. Vol. II, Part I, Characteristics of The Population. Washington, D.C.: U.S. Government Printing Office.

1964b   U.S. Census of Population: 1960. Subject Reports, Women by Number of Children Ever Born, Final Report PC (2)-3A. Washington, D.C.: U.S. Government Printing Office.

1965   U.S. Census of Population: 1960. Subject Reports. Nativity and Percentage, Final Report PC(2)-1A. Washington, D.C.: U.S. Government Printing Office.

1972   U.S. Census of Population: 1970. Subject Reports, Marital Status, Final Report PC(2)-4C. Washington, D.C.: U.S. Government Printing Office.

1973a   U.S. Census of Population: 1970. Detailed Characteristics, U.S. Summary. Washington. D.C.: U.S. Government Printing Office.

1973b   U.S. Census of Population: 1970. Subject Reports, Women by Number of Children Ever Born, Final Report PC(2)-3A. Washington, D.C.: U.S. Government Printing Office.

U.S. Department of Health, Education, and Welfare
  1950   Vital Statistics of The U.S., 1950. Volume 2. Washington, D.C.: U.S. Government Printing Office.

Waring, Joan
  Unpub-   "Disordered cohort flow: a concept for the interpretation of social change."
  lished   Paper presented at the Annual Meeting of the American Sociological Association, New York, August 28, 1973.

Wray, Joe
  1971   "Population pressure on families: family size and child spacing." Pp. 403–461 in Roger Revelle (ed.), Rapid Population Growth: Consequences and Policy Implications. Volume 2. Baltimore: Johns Hopkins Press.

Zimmerman, Carle C.
  1949   The Family of Tomorrow. New York: Harper.

3

The Setting:
The Essex County Context

JOHN MODELL
HOWARD P. CHUDACOFF

Essex County, Massachusetts, the arena for the intensive studies reported in this volume, was one of the four original counties of Massachusetts and one of the earliest counties in the United States. Stretching from Massachusetts Bay to the New Hampshire border, the county underwent many of the social and economic changes that the American Northeast experienced in the seventeenth, eighteenth, and nineteenth centuries. By the end of the nineteenth century, Essex County was a region of contrasts, anchored by Salem, the old port city, in the southeast, and by Lawrence, a new manufacturing community, in the northwest. Between the old fishing and shipping towns along the Atlantic coast and the younger industrial towns along the Merrimac River Valley was a varied landscape, sometimes scenic and arid, sometimes sandy and forlorn, where residents of some two dozen towns earned their livelihoods on small farms and in small factories.

This chapter and the six that follow focus on Essex County in the late nineteenth century and, more particularly, on 8 of its 35 communities: the cities of Salem, Lawrence, and Lynn; and the towns of Boxford, Hamilton, Lynnfield, Topsfield, and Wenham. These 8, although not a microcosm of the whole county, represent varying community types whose social, demographic, and economic patterns resembled those of many places in the Northeast.

TRANSITIONS
The Family and the Life Course in
Historical Perspective

In population growth, for example, Essex County experienced two trends common to many similar regions: rural stagnation and depopulation on one hand and urban expansion on the other. As Table 3.1 indicates, the county's population grew at a somewhat moderate rate after 1850, approximately doubling between 1850 and 1885. The state's population grew at about the same pace. But within Essex County, there was great variation. The populations of the five smaller and more rural communities hardly changed at all; indeed, with the exception of Topsfield, they generally declined. This stagnation and decline occurred principally because a new outflow (more out-migration than in-migration) carried people and families to the West and to the growing cities. Between 1850 and 1885, Lawrence's population grew to five times its 1850 level; Lynn's tripled. Both of these cities underwent rapid industrial expansion in this period: Lawrence in textile manufacturing and Lynn in shoe production. Salem, which had shifted from its early nineteenth-century function as a major shipping center to a less successful local center with a mixed commercial and industrial economy, experienced much more modest population growth.

In Massachusetts, generally, and in Essex County, particularly, foreign immigration as well as native movements accounted for much of the population growth (see Table 3.2). Between 1860 and 1885, the proportion of foreign-born among Essex County's inhabitants grew from just over one of six to one of four. Mostly Irish, English, and Canadian, the immigrants pushed into the cities where they often joined the industrial workforce. Although on a percentage basis the foreign born in the rural towns increased quite rapidly, they still comprised very small proportions of the populations and rarely totaled over 100 in any of the five communities. Foreign-born proportions in middle-sized Essex towns such as Amesbury, Andover, Gloucester, and Peabody matched those of Salem and Lynn, 20–25%, and generally the smaller and less industrialized communities in the county contained proportionately fewer immigrants than larger towns and cities. Lawrence, an archtypical immigrant city, grew so rapidly because of a heavy influx of foreigners. By the 1860s, nearly four-fifths of Lawrence's population was of foreign stock (either foreign born or native born of foreign or mixed parentage).

Age distributions (presented in Table 3.3) reflect the migration statuses of the various communities. Generally, the three cities contained higher proportions of children and young adults, while the five towns contained relatively more old people. The concentration of young people in cities and the greater incidence of older people in rural areas mostly derive from migration differentials: Young families and

TABLE 3.1
Population by Year

Year	U.S.	Massachusetts	Essex County	Lawrence	Lynn	Salem	Boxford	Hamilton	Lynnfield	Topsfield	Wenham
1840	17,069,453	737,700	94,987	—	9,367	15,082	942	818	707	1,059	689
1850	23,191,876	994,514	131,300	8,282	14,257	20,264	982	889	1,723	1,170	977
1855		1,132,369	151,018	16,114	15,713	20,934	1,034	896	883	1,250	1,073
1860	31,443,321	1,231,066	165,611	17,639	19,083	22,252	1,020	789	866	1,292	1,105
1865		1,267,031	171,034	21,698	20,747	21,189	868	799	725	1,212	918
1870	38,558,371	1,457,351	200,843	28,921	28,233	24,117	847	790	818	1,213	985
1875		1,651,912	223,342	34,916	32,660	25,958	834	797	769	1,221	911
1880	50,155,183	1,783,085	244,535	39,151	38,274	27,563	824	935	686	889	1,141
1885		1,942,141	263,727	38,862	45,867	28,090	840	851	766	1,658	871

TABLE 3.2
Nativity and Birthplace

	1860	1875	1880	1885
Percentage foreign born in:				
U.S.	15.0		13.3	
Massachusetts	21.1		28.0	27.1
Essex County	17.8	22.7	23.2	24.8
Lawrence		44.5	44.1	44.0
Lynn		17.4	18.4	21.3
Salem		24.7	27.0	27.1
Boxford		6.2		10.0
Hamilton		8.3		9.4
Lynnfield		8.3		11.4
Topsfield		5.2		9.3
Wenham		5.9		7.1
Percentage of native-born born in state of residence in:				
U.S.			77.9	
Massachusetts			81.3	
Essex County		80.1		78.7
Lawrence		69.1	70.2	72.1
Lynn		77.6	76.2	73.5
Salem		87.0		87.5
Boxford		87.3		83.2
Hamilton		89.3		88.1
Lynnfield		86.7		84.5
Topsfield		87.3		87.1
Wenham		88.2		86.8

individuals moved to urban areas in greater numbers than older people. As Table 3.3 suggests, Essex County in general and the five smaller communities in particular seem to have had unusually heavy concentrations of older age cohorts compared with the total United States figures. In an era of rapid territorial expansion, heavy immigration, and higher fertility in areas where cheap land was available, this contrast highlights the longer duration of settlement in the New England states.

Unusual sex ratios also skew the age distributions of Salem, Lawrence, and Lynn in this period. Table 3.3 reveals that compared with the five smaller communities and with the U.S. as a whole, the three cities had high proportions of females concentrated in the 10–19, 20–29, and 30–39 age cohorts. In fact, in almost every age category these cities contained more females than males. In part, the excesses result from the process of nineteenth-century urbanization which usually left Eastern cities with larger numbers of women, as men left to seek fortunes in newer communities or in the West. But also, especially among the ages 10 to 29, heavy factory employment of females accounts for the higher proportions of women.

During the period under study in this volume, the American economy was in the middle of a half century of ebullient growth. Nationally, as Table 3.4 indicates, the number of farms doubled between 1860 and 1880, and the number of manufacturing firms grew at about the same rate. Per-farm value grew somewhat more slowly, as rapid expansion onto potentially but not yet valuable new land outpaced increases in worth of older farms. By contrast, capitalization of manufacturing quadrupled nationally. Although in 1880 the United States was still an agrarian country, the balance was shifting rapidly toward industry; in just two decades the ratio of manufacturing capitalization to farm values doubled, from one-sixth to one-third.

In Massachusetts, the industrial transformation was more highly advanced than for the nation as a whole. Between 1860 and 1880, the number of farms in Massachusetts increased, but not by very much (see Table 3.4). Farm value also increased, but at a rate much slower than the national one. Massachusetts manufacturing, measured both by numbers of companies and by value of output, grew at about the same rate as the country as a whole. While in 1860 the Massachusetts ratio between manufacturing capitalization and farm value was about equal, by 1880 it was 2.5:1 in both instances considerably higher than national ratios. Essex County followed the same pattern as Massachusetts in these indexes, only the county's trends were more extreme. In 1860 in Essex County, manufacturing capitalization already was twice as high as farm values, and by 1880 the ratio increased to 4.5:1.

Table 3.5 suggests that most Essex County farms were small and intensively used. Although average number of improved acres per farm was smaller than state and national figures and percentage of small holdings (3 to 19 acres) was larger, average values of Essex County farms were higher than comparable state and national values. This pattern occurred because the ratio of improved to unimproved land in Essex County was so high. In some places, such as around Hamilton and Wenham, the soil was quite fertile, and the topography was level enough for intensive farming.

Yet even in Essex County's most heavily farmed areas, only a small minority of the population was engaged in agrarian pursuits (Table 3.6). The five rural areas under study in this volume ranked among the eight Essex communities with the highest proportions engaged in farm-

TABLE 3.3
Age and Sex Structures

	U.S. 1860	U.S. 1880	Massa-chu-setts 1860	Massa-chu-setts 1875	Massa-chu-setts 1880	Massa-chu-setts 1885	Essex 1860	Essex 1875
Male								
0–4	7.8%	7.0%	6.2%	5.3%	5.1%	4.6%	6.4%	5.0%
5–9	6.7	6.5	5.2	5.1	4.8	4.7	5.3	5.0
10–19	11.3	10.7	9.3	9.5	9.1	9.2	9.4	9.2
20–29	9.3	9.3	9.1	8.9	9.5	9.2	9.9	8.6
30–39	6.8	6.5	7.3	7.0	7.1	7.1	7.5	7.2
40–49	4.4	4.6	5.1	5.4	5.5	5.2	5.1	5.4
50–59	2.7	3.3	3.2	3.9	3.8	3.8	3.4	3.7
60–69	1.5	1.9	1.8	2.2	2.5	2.5	2.2	2.3
70+	.7	1.0	1.1	1.3	1.4	1.4	1.5	1.2
Total	51.1	50.8	48.4	48.5	48.8	47.8	46.2	47.6
Female								
0–4	7.6	6.8	6.1	5.4	5.0	4.6	6.3	5.1
5–9	6.6	6.4	5.2	5.0	4.8	4.7	5.3	4.9
10–19	11.3	10.7	9.8	9.9	9.4	9.5	10.0	9.8
20–29	9.0	9.0	10.7	9.3	10.3	10.7	11.6	10.4
30–39	6.0	6.2	7.6	7.9	7.7	7.7	7.7	8.0
40–49	3.9	4.5	5.0	5.9	5.9	6.0	5.2	5.9
50–59	2.4	2.9	3.4	3.9	4.1	4.3	3.7	3.8
60–69	1.4	1.7	2.2	2.5	2.7	2.8	2.4	2.7
70+	.8	1.0	1.5	1.8	1.9	1.9	1.6	1.8
Total	48.9	49.2	51.6	51.5	51.8	52.2	53.8	52.4

ing in 1875. Only one town in the county, Newbury, had a higher percentage engaged in agricultural occupations than Boxford's 20.1%. Moreover, in Lynnfield, Topsfield, and Wenham, the proportion employed in manufacturing (mostly shoemaking) nearly equaled or surpassed that employed in agriculture. Even Boxford and Hamilton contained clothmaking and shoemaking establishments. In all eight communities, proportions involved in domestic service and in trade and transportation were more evenly distributed. Thus generalizations drawn from analyses of Essex County and its eight target communities have kept this context in mind. Some urban–rural contrasts are possible, but community size, town function, population composition, and other factors besides those of an agrarian–industrial dichotomy weigh in the analyses as well.

Essex 1885	Law-rence 1885	Lynn 1885	Salem 1885	Box-ford 1885	Ham-ilton 1885	Lynn-field 1885	Tops-field 1885	Wen-ham 1885
4.4%	4.7%	4.3%	4.3%	4.5%	3.8%	4.4%	3.8%	2.9%
4.5	4.8	4.3	4.6	4.8	2.8	4.2	3.7	3.0
8.9	9.5	6.0	9.0	8.7	7.9	7.7	9.1	9.3
9.4	8.7	10.0	8.4	6.7	9.0	7.7	8.7	7.3
7.3	6.7	8.0	6.4	5.8	6.9	7.0	6.4	5.6
5.7	5.3	6.3	5.1	4.9	5.1	6.3	5.9	6.4
3.9	3.2	3.6	3.8	3.7	6.6	5.1	5.2	5.9
2.4	1.8	1.8	2.4	5.0	3.8	3.3	3.7	4.4
1.4	0.7	1.0	1.4	4.4	3.5	3.0	2.9	4.0
47.8	45.5	45.3	45.5	48.5	49.4	48.7	49.4	48.8
4.5	4.9	4.4	4.2	5.1	3.8	2.7	2.7	3.3
4.5	4.8	4.3	4.7	5.5	4.2	3.9	4.0	3.9
9.3	10.3	8.8	9.5	7.6	7.4	10.4	7.0	9.2
10.6	12.4	11.9	10.9	7.4	8.2	6.0	9.2	8.0
7.9	8.3	8.8	7.9	7.9	7.9	7.2	7.8	6.5
6.2	6.2	6.5	6.4	4.4	4.6	7.4	8.2	6.7
4.5	4.3	4.2	4.9	5.2	6.2	6.0	4.3	5.5
2.8	2.1	2.3	3.3	4.6	3.9	4.2	3.8	3.7
2.1	1.1	1.5	2.6	3.8	3.6	3.4	3.7	4.4
52.2	54.5	54.7	54.5	51.5	50.6	51.3	50.6	51.2

As Table 3.6 reveals, the cities of Salem, Lawrence, and Lynn did have relatively high proportions of inhabitants engaged in manufacturing, a trend that reflected the concentration of industrialization in Essex County, in Massachusetts, and in the United States during this period. Between 1860 and 1880, the importance of manufacturing rose considerably, as the analysis of Table 3.4 already has indicated and as the rise in manufacturing value per capita substantiates in Table 3.7. In addition, productivity increased, measured by value-added (in current dollars) per manufacturing hand; in turn, this increase partially resulted from increased capitalization (per establishment and per hand).

At the same time, wages rose—although the trend in Essex County was somewhat remarkable. In 1860, Essex industrial workers had been considerably less productive than Massachusetts workers (measured by

TABLE 3.4
Essex County Agriculture and Manufacturing

	Number of establishments		Capitalization or value		Ratio of manufacturing to agriculture	
	Agriculture (farms)	Manufacturing (firms)	Agriculture	Manufacturing	Number of establishments	Capitalization-value
U.S.						
1860	2,044,077	140,433	$6,645,045,000	$1,009,056,000	.069	.152
1880	4,008,907	253,852	$10,197,097,000	$3,396,824,000	.063	.333
Massachusetts						
1860	35,556	8,176	$123,256,000	$132,792,000	.230	1.074
1880	38,406	14,352	$146,197,000	$386,972,000	.374	2.647
Essex County						
1860	2,695	1,119	$10,331,000	$20,856,000	.415	2.022
1880	2,847	1,971	$14,202,000	$64,822,000	.692	4.564

TABLE 3.5
Characteristics of Agriculture

	Improved acres per farm	Cash value per farm	Cash value per total acres	Ratio of improved land to unimproved
U.S.				
1860	66.7	$2719	$16	.668
1880	62.8	$2544	$19	1.132
Massachusetts				
1860	60.6	$3467	$31	1.822
1880	55.4	$3807	$44	1.729
Essex County				
1860	52.5	$3833	$56	3.360
1880	49.7	$4988	$76	3.084

Size of farms (in percentages)

	Number of acres					
	3–10	10–19	20–49	50–99	100–499	500+
U.S.						
1860	2.8	8.3	31.5	31.1	24.9	1.3
1880	3.5	6.5	20.0	26.4	41.0	2.6
Massachusetts						
1860	5.7	11.8	33.1	30.5	18.9	0
1880	6.2	10.1	25.1	27.6	30.2	.7
Essex County						
1860	8.0	13.8	35.2	29.5	13.5	0
1880	8.1	13.6	30.5	28.0	19.3	.4

value-added per manufacturing hand), and Massachusetts workers in turn were less productive than those of the United States in general (see Table 3.7). Wages per hand followed the same pattern. By 1880, however, the productivity patterns of Essex County, of Massachusetts, and of the United States had become more consistent. The change suggests that in 1860 Essex County had been characterized by low-paid workers (often female), and other data in Table 3.7 suggest that they were employed in relatively large establishments. By 1880, Essex County workers had improved their average wages while the heavy incidence of large companies seems to have abated somewhat.

Individually, the three main cities differed in their industrial indexes. Lawrence in 1880 was dominated by quite large concerns whose average number of workers tripled the state average and whose average

TABLE 3.6

Proportion of Population Engaged in Selected Occupational Categories[a] 1875

	Manufacturing	Domestic	Trade and transport	Agriculture
Essex County	19.3	26.9	4.8	8.7
Lawrence	36.1	20.3	4.2	0.6
Lynn	27.0	26.4	6.4	1.0
Salem	20.6	27.4	7.6	1.0
Boxford	11.9	29.4	2.5	20.1
Hamilton	6.9	30.0	4.1	18.4
Lynnfield	11.3	27.8	4.6	12.6
Topsfield	17.0	29.2	3.6	13.5
Wenham	12.8	28.0	4.0	15.1

[a] Proportions do not add to 100 because insignificant categories and dependents have been omitted.

capitalization quadrupled the state average (see Table 3.7). Nearly half of Lawrence's factory hands were female, and average wages per worker were considerably lower than in other communities, although they were not much below the national average. The relatively low value-added per hand in Lawrence reflected the large and unskilled nature of its industrial sector. The relatively high value-added per capita, however, meant that a large proportion of the population worked in the factories; in fact, 36.1% of Lawrence's 1875 population was engaged in manufacturing, compared with the county average of 19.3% (see Table 3.6). Lynn, while still heavily involved in manufacturing, had smaller and less elaborately capitalized companies, higher per-hand productivity, fewer female workers, and higher average wages. About 27% of Lynn's 1875 population worked in factories. Within an even smaller manufacturing sector, Salem factory hands worked in concerns of average size but less than average capitalization with high productivity and high wages. Some 20.6% of Salem's inhabitants were employed in manufacturing, slightly above the county average.

Figures on housing and family patterns complement the foregoing observations about economic change. Table 3.8 reveals that multifamily living (families per dwelling) was becoming more common statewide and nationally and had been quite high in Essex County. This increase in family density resulted, at least in part, from the growth of cities, where expanding populations strained housing supplies and pushed housing costs upward. Also, it appears that average family size bore an inverse relationship to multifamily housing; as doubling up

TABLE 3.7
Characteristics of Manufacturing

	Value added per capita	Value added per manufacturing hand	Percentage of manufacturing hands female	Wages per hand	Average number of workers per establishment	Capitalization per establishment
U.S.						
1860	$7.41	$651	20.7	$289	9.3	$7,191
1880	$10.02	$722	19.5	$347	10.8	$10,992
Massachusetts						
1860	$97.87	$554	32.7	$262	26.6	$16,242
1880	$332.25	$693	30.1	$364	24.5	$21,168
Essex County						
1860	$118.03	$421	33.1	$231	41.4	$18,665
1880	$157.87	$645	32.7	$365	30.4	$21,166
Lawrence						
1880	$286	$666	47.3	$330	73.0	$81,654
Lynn						
1880	$245	$756	28.1	$470	10.3	$17,185
Salem						
1880	$166	$873	20.9	$431	21.7	$15,114

TABLE 3.8
Families per Dwelling

	1860	1875	1880	1885
U.S.	1.06		1.11	
Massachusetts	1.22		1.35	1.37
Essex County		1.43		1.38
Lawrence		1.62	1.63	1.51
Lynn		1.37	1.30	1.40
Salem		1.56	1.45	1.60
Boxford		1.20		1.12
Hamilton		1.14		1.14
Lynnfield		1.17		1.16
Topsfield		1.22		1.20
Wenham		1.22		1.20

was increasing, family size was decreasing. The trend does not suggest a direct relationship—that doubling up caused decreased family size or vice versa. Rather, it reflects the younger age structure and the increased cohabitation that were general concomitants of urbanization.

Certainly among the eight target Essex County communities, the cities had a much higher incidence of multifamily residence than did the rural places. Yet data show that the housing issue was not one dimensional. By 1885, Salem, the least industrialized city with the slowest growth rate, had an average of families per dwelling that exceeded that of Lawrence or Lynn. Explanations for variations in how crowded houses were involve many economic and social factors that are too complex (and often not ascertainable) to analyze here. For the time being, we can merely suggest that lack of growth probably accounted for lower densities in the rural places and that housing supplies were much more erratic in the cities.

Table 3.9 indicates that the sizes of household aggregations remained fairly stable and similar from place to place. Single-person households were quite rare, although the proportionately larger number of widows in the five smaller towns seem to have raised the percentages of isolated individuals slightly. In addition, higher incidences of old people in the smaller towns probably account for the somewhat higher proportions of two-person households—that is, childless couples or widowed parent with one coresident child. Nearly everywhere, the majority lived in moderate-sized households of three to five persons, a trend that complements the fact that the vast majority (80%) of residents in all eight communities lived in nuclear households with no extended kin present.

The foregoing paragraphs portray a quintessential Massachusetts county, located in a region that spearheaded the transformation to an urbanized, industrialized society in the mid-to-late nineteenth century. It would be possible to present an endless array of tables and descriptions of Essex County during this period; we have selected only a few

TABLE 3.9
Percentage Distribution of Household Sizes

	Persons per household				
	1	2	3–5	6–9	10+
U.S.					
1890	3.6	13.2	48.6	29.7	4.9
Massachusetts					
1875	3.3	15.9	52.7	24.6	3.5
1885	4.0	16.6	51.5	24.2	3.6
Essex County					
1875	3.4	16.5	54.3	22.8	2.9
1885	4.3	17.3	52.8	22.6	3.0
Lawrence					
1875	1.4	13.8	51.6	27.9	5.3
1885	4.0	14.4	51.7	26.1	3.8
Lynn					
1875	3.0	16.6	56.1	21.6	2.7
1885	2.8	16.3	54.6	23.0	3.3
Salem					
1875	4.8	16.3	52.8	23.4	2.7
1885	5.2	17.4	52.4	22.2	2.8
Boxford					
1875	7.1	21.7	47.6	22.6	.9
1885	7.0	20.9	48.8	20.9	2.5
Hamilton					
1875	5.0	12.6	58.2	21.4	2.8
1885	4.0	15.0	58.0	21.0	2.0
Lynnfield					
1875	6.3	17.4	59.5	14.7	2.1
1885	2.7	21.1	51.9	23.2	1.1
Topsfield					
1875	5.3	16.9	49.7	25.0	3.2
1885	7.0	18.2	51.9	19.3	3.7
Wenham					
1875	4.1	18.7	53.0	22.3	1.8
1885	3.7	25.1	50.2	19.6	1.4

details that should enable the reader to comprehend some of the county's characteristics and nuances. Behind the macrolevel factors of economic organization, demographic structure, and household density, complex patterns of behavior were occurring as individuals and families adjusted to and influenced the course of history. The six chapters that follow examine some of those patterns.

4

Marriage and Family Formation

BENGT ANKARLOO

The decision to marry is influenced by several elements, including mate selection, timing, residential arrangements, and reproduction. The degree of freedom connected with each of these decisions is determined by material conditions and the normative prescriptions. Legal and cultural norms prohibit or disapprove of incest and certain types of racial, ethnic, and religious intermarriages. Such restrictions tend to limit the availability of eligible partners. The timing of marriage is also restricted by legal and cultural definitions of a minimum age and a proper one, and sometimes by sanctions against late marriages. The feasible age for marriage, on the other hand, is determined by economic resources, career stage, and income. The norms, finally, may tolerate early marriages but punish early childbearing, thereby either encouraging the introduction of contraceptive methods, or, indirectly, influencing a delay in marriage.

In marriage research these larger material and normative categories are usually considered in terms of sex ratios and ethnic, religious, and socioeconomic groups. While taking all these into account, the purpose of this chapter is to see what further insight can be gained by using the concept of a family life course. The discussion will deal, therefore, not only with the individual characteristics of the spouses such as age, group affiliation, and status, but also with the possible significance of

113

TRANSITIONS
The Family and the Life Course in
Historical Perspective

their interaction with their families, and other groups, at different points in the age and career hierarchy.

It has been a common assumption that the rapid growth of urban–industrial areas, such as the New England cities, had profound effects on social interaction, including patterns of marriage. The coming together of young people from different backgrounds in an environment largely beyond the control of the family of orientation changed the old rigid rules of mate selection and social advancement. The new system of easy access to both partners and careers was sometimes eulogized as "the melting pot."

One of the observations supporting this theory was that the population, and in particular the marrying population, of the cities, as opposed to that of the rural areas, would be born in distant, even foreign places. Thus, the emerging urban pattern should offer sharp contrast to the traditional one still prevalent in the countryside (Ogburn, 1955:99–100; Barron, 1972:43). In the Essex County sample under study at least the migration part of this theory stands up. Of those marrying in 1879–1881, about two-thirds in the rural areas were born within the county. In contrast, less than half of those marrying in the cities were born in Massachusetts; in Lawrence, less than a third.

Premarital coresidence of parents with marriageable children must be regarded as one of the major preconditions for the continuation of kin control. The absence of such patterns can serve as an index of a marriage market that is free from parental interference. In the Essex sample the percentage of unmarried young adults (age 20–29) living with parents or close kin is in fact somewhat higher in the urban areas than in the rural (86 versus 78%).[1] Among those actually marrying the rate of persistence in the parental household was lower, that is, marriage was immediately preceded by residential change, particularly in the cities. But even then, the most important conclusion for the purposes of this study must be that marriage in the urban–industrial environment was hardly less subject to parental influence than in the traditional, rural areas (Anderson, 1971:86).

This is neither surprising nor new. Several studies have pointed out that kinship as a resource for immigrant and lower-class groups is relatively more important because these groups have less access to other forms of organization and fewer channels for contact than other members of society (Komarovsky, 1962:37; Young and Wilmott, 1957:189). This does not mean that nothing has changed over time. The

---

[1]Lower rates, but the same urban–rural proportions were found by Anderson (1971:85).

family and kin group in industrial populations, while obviously of greater importance than previously assumed, may well be functionally different from their preindustrial counterparts. The organization of work and its close relation to the family estate in a farm community is consistent with specific patterns of succession, intermarriage, and parental authority. Access to property as a means of production can in fact be used to control family members. This is, at least in theory, not the case in wage-earning families. But to the extent that the nineteenth-century industrial labor market was not "free" (and the traditional, paternalistic organization of the early mill towns seems to indicate such conditions), the family, and particularly the father in midcareer, may have been instrumental in supplying work for his children, even where the capital means of production were in the hands of others (Smelser, 1959:Chapters 9–11; Anderson, 1971:114; Hareven, 1975:369).

Apart from this, the fact that the working-class interaction has been based on mutual assistance and exchange of favors rather than on tangible material goods has made it less visible in historical records. The precarious balance between household size and number of breadwinners can be seriously upset if a productive member moves out or if unproductive members, such as a daughter-in-law with an infant child, move in. From the point of view of working-class families, the timing of marriage for the children can have serious economic consequences, particularly in the short run. The advantages of regrouping inherent in marriage are also often different for the parents and the marrying children. The structure and earning power of the household unit at any given time can help to determine the bargaining position of parents and children when such regrouping is decided upon. The complex relation between individual age and the developmental stage of the family life cycle is therefore of crucial importance for the understanding both of differences and changes in marriage patterns (Rodgers, 1964:262–270; Rowe, 1966:216–217).

The ethnic, cultural, and religious identity of the group, so often held to be the major reason for the rigid intermarriage patterns found in immigrant areas, can be properly understood only when analyzed in conjunction with other variables such as social class, age, timing, and stage in the family cycle (Barron, 1972:44). An Irish in-marriage, for instance, may be not only a Catholic marriage, but also in most cases a late, lower-class marriage with the parents of the spouses in their late fifties or early sixties. Other working-class people, and other Catholics, such as French-Canadians, mostly marry early. Others who marry late are predominantly from higher classes. Therefore, the mixing of patterns through class and ethnic intermarriage is also the merging of different family life cycles. The parents of the spouses may be worlds apart, not only socioculturally, but simply in terms of age.

The Essex Sample

Economic and demographic conditions vary considerably with the sample. The occupational spectrum in the cities, particularly Lawrence, favored female labor-force participation, whereas the rural areas had a predominantly male labor force. This is indicated by different sex ratios and by the relative proportions married among males and females in the various communities. Among the unmarried in the age group 20–29, the number of males to 1000 females ranges from 475 in Lawrence to 706 in Salem, to 996 in Lynn, and to 1437 in the countryside. In Lawrence and Salem, by the same token, the relative number of married males exceeds that of females by 9 and 1% respectively. In Lynn and the townships the female proportion exceeds that of males by 8 and 17%. In short, there is one pattern of female competition and male opportunities (Lawrence–Salem), and one of male competition and female opportunities (Lynn–rural).

When examining the marriage rates as the number of marriages per 1000 women in certain age groups we find them higher in Lynn than in Salem and Lawrence (see Table 4.1). We must be careful when interpreting these differences. It may be argued, on the one hand, that Lawrence more often offered the young woman an independent existence as an alternative to the dependent life of a housewife with small children. On the other hand, it must be recognized that a young woman had fewer opportunities to marry, even if she so desired. A comparison between the female age cohort 20–24 in 1875 and 30–34 in 1885 suggests that the net out-migration of women in their late twenties and early thirties was considerably larger in Lawrence, and somewhat

TABLE 4.1
Marriage Rates 1876–1885 (80% Marriages per 1000 Women Aged 15–29)

Area	1876	1877	1878	1879	1880	1881	1882	1883	1884	1885
Salem	33.0	31.3	33.7	39.4	41.8	39.0	41.3	45.1	41.2	45.5
Lawrence	37.6	37.7	38.0	40.2	47.4	44.8	53.6	48.5	45.5	41.4
Lynn	42.6	46.2	39.6	48.9	58.6	55.2	55.5	60.5	51.8	56.5

TABLE 4.2
Percentage Unmarried at Age 35–39

Area	Males	Females
Salem	14.3	31.3
Lawrence	15.5	31.0
Lynn	23.8	25.2
Rural	29.2	23.3

larger in Salem, than in Lynn (38, 25, and 22%, respectively, if mortality equals zero). For many of these women marriage and family formation, if any, took place elsewhere.

In four of five marriages in Massachusetts around 1880 the bride was under 30 years of age. An artificial but much more refined marriage rate can thus be obtained by relating 80% of all marriages to the number of women aged 15–29. The rates in the three cities suggest that the incidence of marriage around 1880 was rising from a low point in 1877–1878, probably an indication of recovery from economic depression. The upward trend is checked somewhat in 1881, possibly because the higher rates in the preceding years included marriages which were postponed in the depression. If this is so, the age at marriage in 1879 and in 1880 will be slightly above average. These marriage rates are clearly in line with the previous observation that in Lawrence and in Salem more women could be expected to remain unmarried in their late thirties, their higher rates of out-migration notwithstanding (see Table 4.2). In the rural areas, consistently, where the sex ratios are reversed, so also are the proportions of unmarried males and females. About 70% more males than females married more than once. Remarrying males were consequently competing with the first-marrying males for the never-married women. In part this problem was solved by the fact that women were legally permitted to marry 3 years earlier than men, thus increasing the number of available women. In most areas this was not enough, because as we have noted, more women than men remained unmarried. If the sex ratios were balanced or nearly balanced, more men had to seek their brides from outside or remain unmarried, and fewer could remarry (Kramm and Thomas, 1942). These conditions, combined with the sheer size of the communities, tended to make the marriage markets in the cities more self-sufficient. More than half of all rural marriages included one partner from outside the sampling area compared with only 25% in the cities.

Residence after Marriage

The static, cross-sectional information derived from an analysis of census material is of somewhat limited value in the study of marriage, where movement both in time and space obviously plays a decisive role. To compensate for this weakness of the material two separate samples were collected from the marriage records of Essex County in 1879–1881, and linked to the census. The census date is the dividing line between the samples. Those marrying after June 1, 1880 constitute a premarital group, while those marrying before that date were found in the census as a postmarital group. Both the antecedents and the consequences of marriage are thus to some extent covered.

The object of the tracing from marriage record to the census was to obtain information about the marrying individuals and their families of orientation. In the rural part of the sample, the tracing was performed by direct search in the census manuscripts, in the urban part, city directories were used as an intermediate step. Altogether 501 couples were sampled: all couples from the rural area, 10% at random from the cities.[2] Of these, 246 couples, or 49%, were located. This is slightly less than in comparable studies dealing only with postmarital couples in the census (Chudacoff, forthcoming). One reason for this may be that the city directories in Salem and Lawrence were compiled only in 1881. Another, and perhaps more important reason, is that the present sample includes a majority of couples with a premarital position in the census. In order to find them two separate households had to be traced, instead of one. Until methods and resources for the tracing of the moving population, and the moving couples, have been found, conclusions must be based on the persistent minority.

Since coresidence of marriageable children with their parents was used as an index of parental control in connection with marriage, this issue will be dealt with first. It is straightforward enough: Either they lived with their parents, or they did not (see Table 4.3). At the same time the importance of rural–urban, sex, and class differences will be considered.[3]

In the cities, the proportion living with parents is clearly smaller than it is among all unmarried individuals aged 20–29. Perhaps urban marriages were more often immediately preceded by residential change. Still the urban–rural differences are hardly significant. A clear

[2]Random number tables were used.

[3]The social strata were classified as follows: upper—professionals, semiprofessionals, merchants, manufacturers, and farmers; middle—white collar and skilled blue collar workers; lower—semiskilled and unskilled blue collar workers.

TABLE 4.3
Percentage of Premarital Coresidence with Parents

	Class origin				
	Upper	Middle	Lower	All	N
Rural	84	100	56	75	(65)
Urban	82	77	56	67	(94)
Males	96	80	51	72	(83)
Females	70	83	60	71	(76)
All	84	81	56	71	
N	(31)	(44)	(74)		(159)

decline in those living with parents can be seen from upper to lower class. The rural middle class is so small as to be negligible, but the higher incidence of female, middle-class coresidence will be discussed further.

The postmarital location of the newly married couples is somewhat more complicated, since three options were available to them. They could remain with the parents of either spouse (see Table 4.4), or set up an independent household. Full information about each marriage as listed in the marriage record includes census data on both spouses and their respective families of orientation. This additional tracing was, of course, even less successful. But even when we have data only on the spouses or on only one of their families, valuable information is provided. In the case, for instance, of finding only the bride's parents, we can at least be sure that the couple does not have a matrilocal postmarital residence. Such partial information was available in 30% of the cases. By combining complete with partial information we can make fairly informed guesses about the residential patterns among individuals marrying shortly before the census date in 1880.

If we assume that the nonpatrilocal and the nonmatrilocal couples are distributed as in the cases where full information is available, we arrive at the proportions seen in Table 4.4. By subtracting the percentage still at home in the postmarital sample from those living with parents before marriage we can compute the relative importance of residential change immediately connected with marriage. In other words we are treating the two samples as one (Table 4.5). The urban, female, and lower-class groups are least affected by change at marriage. This is in all three cases the combined result of high premarital independence and postmarital dependence. Middle-class women, the

TABLE 4.4
Percentage of Postmarital Coresidence with Parents

	Class origin			All	N
	Upper	Middle	Lower		
Rural	19	8	30	20	(59)
Urban	6	28	26	23	(90)
Males	14	12	26	18	(96)
Females	15	50	29	30	(53)
All	14	22	27	22	
N	(42)	(45)	(72)		(149)

daughters of clerical and skilled workers, constitute in this respect an exceptional group: Their low mobility at marriage is connected with high dependence both before and after.

It can be assumed that the postmarital location to some extent will depend on the duration of marriage. The chances of finding the couple in a parental household will be greater among those who are recently married. The average duration in our sample ranges from 9.6 months for those living independently to 7.4 and 6.5 months respectively for the patrilocal and matrilocal couples.

But another factor seems to be even more important. Among the couples already with a child the average duration of the marriage at the time of the child's birth was computed. Where it was 7 months, the conception was regarded as marital, when less as premarital. In those cases where the child was conceived before marriage half of the

TABLE 4.5
Percentage of Residential Change at Marriage

	Class origin			All	N
	Upper	Middle	Lower		
Rural	65	92	26	55	(124)
Urban	76	49	30	44	(184)
Males	82	68	25	54	(179)
Females	55	33	31	41	(129)
All	70	59	29	49	
N	(73)	(89)	(146)		(308)

TABLE 4.6
Percentage of Dependent Members of Household N = 90

	Chosen	Not chosen
Native	15.6	32.6
Foreign	23.7	30.9

couples were living with parents (21% with his parents, 29% with hers) as against only 18% of those with marital conception. Of course, not all the marriages involving premarital conceptions must be emergency measures, but the chances certainly are greater that they are. In addition, among the childless couples with an average marital duration of 6 months, there may be a fair number of similar cases with the bride pregnant at marriage. Only by linking marriage to birth records can this assumption be tested; it has not been done as yet. In couples unable to establish their own households at once, a pregnant bride would probably prefer to live with her mother rather than her mother-in-law. This would account for the larger proportion of matrilocal couples both in our sample and in other investigations (Young and Wilmott, 1957:31; Komarovsky, 1962:242; Anderson, 1971:56; Chudacoff, 1975:17).

Choice of residence is clearly determined by other considerations, too. In order to test the impact of the presence or absence of the newlywed couples in their parental households the following assumptions were made.[4] A male 15–65 equals 1 production unit, a female in that age range .8, unless she is the mother of a child below 5. Such women, and household members above 65, are considered as .8 consumption units, and children .5 consumption units. It was also assumed that 50% of the newlyweds had a child. Then, the mean percentage of dependent members was computed both in the household chosen by the couple and in the one abandoned (see Table 4.6). The households actually chosen were, on the average, those which best could afford it in terms of consumption–production ratios.

But these differences are based on rather abstract assumptions. In a smaller number of cases (N = 22) we have full information about the couples and their parental households and can make a more realistic evaluation of the alternatives in each individual case. The actual choice–nonchoice percentages are 21.0 and 25.0. It would seem that if

[4]This is a somewhat simplified version of an analytical model introduced by A. V. Chayanov in 1925/1966; see Kerblay (1971) and Berkner (1972). For a more sophisticated elaboration of this model see Lorimer (1965).

the residence of a newlywed couple in one of the parental households would raise the proportion of dependent members to one-fourth, such residence was avoided.

Marriage, Age, and the Family Cycle

Average age at marriage hardly changed at all in Massachusetts during the nineteenth century (Monahan, 1951:541). Considering the fact that the state in the last half of the century received huge numbers of immigrants with possibly different marriage patterns, this is somewhat surprising. Either the immigrants adapted to the American custom of marrying early, or the different immigrant groups averaged on both sides of the mean so as to offset the deviations. In other words, the later age at marriage among European immigrants could be counterbalanced by immigrant Canadian couples, who married earlier than native Americans. If this is the case the apparent absence of change can very well hide important emerging differences.

Marital age in Western Europe had long been significantly higher than in other parts of the world, including the United States (Hajnal, 1965:101–140; Goode, 1963:41–42). European immigrants could therefore be expected to introduce their pattern to the American scene. Median age at first marriage among first- and second-generation Irish immigrants in our sample is in fact between 3 and 4 years higher than among native and Canadian spouses. Whatever the reasons for these differences, they will have profound effects on the life-course experience of successive generations. To conceptualize the age differences we define the reproductive span as the age of the father or mother at the birth of his or her first grandchild. If age at marriage in successive generations is 22 and a child is born within 2 years, the span will be 48 years.

To compare two extremes from the Essex data: In Lawrence one-fourth of the marrying Irish males were 29.5 years or more, with a reproductive cycle of at least 63 years. Equally, one-fourth of the Canadian males were 21 years or less at marriage, with a cycle of, at most, 46 years. The formation of such a Canadian family occurs in a two-generational setting, which is quite different from that of an Irish family. The likelihood, for instance, of a Canadian child having age peers among his aunts and uncles is considerably higher. And his grandfather will still be in midcareer.

Age at marriage, to some extent, can be used as a predictor of the structural characteristics of the parental household (see Table 4.7). Those marrying late will more often have obligations to support a

TABLE 4.7
Age at Marriage and Family Variables[a] (N = 210)

	Males		Females	
	Young	Old	Young	Old
Size of parental household	6.1	4.5	5.2	4.4
Same, kin only	5.4	4.2	4.6	4.1
Percentage of widowed mother or father past 60	35	67	38	60
Percentage of siblings 15 or older in parental household	78	79	62	81
Percentage of postmarital coresidence with parent(s)	30	9	15	5

[a] The broad categories used here for classifying age at marriage are based on median age and quartile ranges of all first marriages in the sampling area in 1879–1880 (N = 4219). Median age for males was 24.0 (q.-range 5.7), and for females 22.0 (q.-range 5.2). Accordingly, the following age categories were selected:

	males	females
young	0–21	0–19
average	22–26	20–24
old	27+	25+

Although there are considerable variations in median age at marriage, particularly between Irish and other groups, the transitional period of the central 50%, i.e. the range from first to third quartiles, is surprisingly stable.

widowed mother or a retired father. The absence of such constraints, or even the prospect of support from parents, are connected with marriage at an earlier age, when one's work career only recently has begun.

Insofar as the direction of support and favors in the kin network is structurally based, the family of orientation seems to be in a position to give when children marry young, and in need of help when they marry at an older age. When marriage is postponed the filial responsibilities are shared by a constant or even increasing number of siblings in breadwinning ages. The marriage of a child, at any age, will have quite different implications both to himself and to his parents depending on whether he is first, subsequent, or last in the birth order (Table 4.8). The obligations of unmarried children will increase as their parents grow older and their siblings move out to marry. The launching stage, when children leave the family, can be dangerously contracted if birth order and marriage order is confused or even reversed, that is, if the oldest

TABLE 4.8
Position in Family Cycle and Family Variables[a] (N = 210)

	Males		Females	
	Early	Late	Early	Late
Size of parental household	6.1	5.8	5.7	5.3
Same, kin only	5.5	4.9	5.3	4.8
Percentage of widowed mother or father past 60	12	68	36	82
Percentage of siblings 15 or older in parental household	85	72	75	70
Percentage of postmarital coresidence with parents	37	64	31	40
Mean age	23.5	23.9	22.1	22.3

[a] Position in family cycle is measured as age of mother at birth of self, i.e. seniority of mother. The categories are, for both sexes: early 0–24, intermediate 25–34, and late 35+. Consequently, only those are included in tables dealing with position in the cycle whose mother was located in the census.

child marries late, and the youngest early. The disadvantages of deviant timing of marriage are enhanced or reduced depending on the child's position in the parental family cycle.

Since those late in the cycle are more likely to have lost both parents, their timing of marriage can take place with less consideration of the family of orientation, particularly since they will have no minor siblings to take care of. Only if one is the last remaining child living with a widowed mother or father will familial constraint have a large influence on the decision to marry. Those born early in the cycle will seldom be in that situation. But as long as the parental family is intact, familial sanctions against early marriage will be imposed by parents in their midcareer as a precaution against an uncontrolled transition to the empty-nest stage. Age at marriage of the early children therefore tends to be less deviant than among the late children, as shown in Table 4.9. The intermediate children have a fairly high degree of conformity, but their deviation is strongly on the old side.

This pattern is further complicated by class conditions. It is known from more recent data that age at marriage differs by social class (Cavan, 1953:Chapters 5–7). Since marriage is the only form of sexual interaction approved by society, physical urges would encourage early marriages. Late marriage is in this respect unnatural. From a social and economic point of view, early marriage is, on the other hand, difficult, even dangerous, since the spouses are not yet fully socialized and integrated in the production system, and, in most cases, are not even in a

TABLE 4.9
Percentage of Timing by Position in the Family Cycle (Both Sexes)

	Early	Intermediate	Late	All	N
Young	20	15	31	21	(45)
Average	59	54	43	52	(108)
Old	21	31	26	27	(57)
	100	100	100	100	(210)
N	(59)	(97)	(54)	(210)	

position to support themselves and their children. The timing of marriage, therefore, is a compromise between the social and economic demands of society, and the basic urges of the partners. "The young couple cannot be extremely young, since they have to take care of themselves; on the other hand they do not have to be very old, because they can be independent [Goode, 1963:43]." Where full or sufficient access to the production system is given early, as in unskilled industrial occupations, marriage can be expected to be early. When access is given late, as in the cases of property succession and extended education, marriage will be late. Finally, where intergenerational social mobility is low, children will marry at about the same time as their parents (Table 4.10).

Class origin refers to the stratification of the parental generation. The chances of social advancement may of course influence the decision to marry. The importance of actual, anticipated, and illusory social mobility can be established only in a longitudinal or panel study.[5] Furthermore, the class position, as opposed to the class origin, of the marrying females can be found but very rarely. We must, therefore, content ourselves in Table 4.11 with comparing the status of fathers with that of their marrying sons. What looks like downward generational mobility may be a reflection of different career stages, that is, some of the sons have not yet reached the social position of their fathers (Table 4.12). Consequently, those marrying late can be expected to have reached a higher position in the occupational hierarchy. Not only do members of higher strata marry later, they may also in some cases have had time to reach these positions before marrying.

When marrying at an older age the males have almost the same occupational distribution as their fathers. But, to what extent is this

[5]The interrelation between marriage and career mobility is briefly discussed in Eriksson and Akerman (1974).

TABLE 4.10
Percentage of Age at Marriage and Class Origin (Both Sexes)

	Upper	Middle	Lower	All	N
Young	15	17	19	17	(66)
Average	38	^8	56	49	(190)
Old	47	35	25	34	(132)
	100	100	100	100	(388)
N	(102)	(126)	(160)	(388)	

TABLE 4.11
Percentage Marrying Males by Class and Class Origin

	Upper	Middle	Lower	All	N
Class	20	38	42	100	(246)
Class origin	28	38	34	100	(246)

TABLE 4.12
Ratio of Class to Class Origin by Position in Family Cycle (Males)

	Upper	Middle	Lower	N
Early	.62	1.08	1.18	(30)
Intermediate	.67	1.67	1.00	(43)
Late	.50	.89	1.50	(27)
				(100)

TABLE 4.13
Percentage of Class Intermarriage by Position in Family Family Cycle (Both Sexes)

	Up	In	Down	All	N
Early	25	54	21	100	(44)
Intermediate	26	62	12	100	(68)
Late	6	78	16	100	(37)
All	21	64	15	100	(149)
N	(31)	(95)	(23)	(149)	

career pattern related to position in the family cycle? If the family, as has been suggested, is instrumental in supplying work for the children, those born late in the cycle would be at a disadvantage compared with their older siblings, who are starting their careers and marrying when most of them have a father still alive, and presumably, in better control of the market. The late children are more often orphaned, or have a father close to or in retirement (see Table 4.12).

To be born at the right time in the family cycle and not marry too young is clearly the best combination for upward social mobility, or at least for retaining the class position of father. If parental control and protection is important in this differentiation process, it must be most visible in the upper and middle strata. The parents in lower-class families have less to offer, and almost half of their children have left the household before marrying. But selfmade careers and interaction outside class, ethnic group, and family tend to make this picture less clear-cut. The mixing of patterns, the intermarriage between children of different social origin, ethnicity, age, and family cycle position ought to present options even for the most disadvantaged.

When first looking at class interaction, the previous impression of reduced chances for those born late in the cycle is further strengthened. As Table 4.13 shows, while almost half of the early children marry outside their class, only one in five among the late children do.

Both class and ethnic intermarriage are possible only in heterogeneous communities. As a result, it has long been observed that the larger the group the lower the rate of intermarriage. To overcome this problem, a method was introduced by Glick (1960:31–38) and further explained by Bencanceney (1965:717–721). By computing an intermarriage rate to be expected if the members of each group had married randomly and comparing it with the actual rate, a ratio of actual to expected intermarriage is determined. Without this control the ethnic intermarriage rates in Lawrence and Salem would exceed those in Lynn simply because the former cities had a larger proportion of foreign born in their populations, as shown in Table 4.14.

Of all marriages 40% were class intermarriages. Of these in turn three out of four were hypergameous, that is, the groom was from a higher stratum than the bride. The reluctance of women to marry men of lower status indicates the class status was transmitted by males (Merton, 1972:30). This would to some degree compensate for balanced sex ratios restricting the market for men. Where class and ethnicity are correlated by prevalence, in Lynn, matches of native males to foreign females are even more predictable.

Because only the upper and middle groups can marry down, and

TABLE 4.14
Ratio of Actual to Expected Intermarriage Rates

	Class (N = 149)			Nativity (N = 2251)			
	Upper	Middle	Lower	Native	Canadian	Irish	All foreign
Marriage sample	.63	.78	.79				
Salem				.49	.31	.51	.29
Lawrence				.61	.59	.52	.59
Lynn				.70	.84	.60	.71
All urban				.62	.66	.53	.61

only the lower and middle up, out-class marriage must be measured as the proportion of those in a position to marry up or down actually doing it (Table 4.15). Because there are considerably more women than men in the lower-class group, the direction of female out-class marriage more often will be upward. Even so, the importance of status transmission by males is clearly visible.

Native and rural males are less willing than foreign and urban ones to choose their brides in a lower stratum. This exclusiveness is also shown in the proportions of females marrying up, where the rank order is reversed. This suggests that ethnic and class endogamy tends to coincide. Nevertheless, class intermarriage is far more common than marriage between ethnic groups. While the number of out-class marriages is virtually the same among native and foreign females, the proportions of ethnic intermarriages are highly differentiated (native

TABLE 4.15
Direction of Outclass Marriage: Percentage of Those in a Position to Marry Up or Down Who Do

	Males		Females	
	Up	Down	Up	Down
Rural	30	35	50	23
Urban	9	48	45	17
Native	17	41	47	21
Foreign	20	61	40	33
All	14	44	46	22
N	(106)	(97)	(108)	(67)

8%, foreign 38%). The transmission of status by the male seems to be even more important in the ethnic dimension.

Definitions of ethnicity vary. The simplest one is place of birth. But it has long been realized that ethnocultural socialization patterns extend over at least two generations, and that consequently, the second-generation immigrants should be classified with their parents rather than with their places of birth. A distinction will therefore be made between nativity, which relates to place of birth, and ethnicity, which includes the nativity of the parents. In the few cases of mixed foreign parentage the nativity of the father will be assigned arbitrarily as the ethnicity of the individual.

It is, however, only in the separate marriage sample where the couples are traced to the census that this procedure can be followed. The marriage records include information only about the nativity of the spouses, not of their parents. The higher incidence of intermarriage by nativity in Lynn as indicated by Table 4.15 may therefore simply be the result of numerous marriages between first- and second-generation immigrants.

To test the extent of the difference between nativity and ethnicity, as defined here, a large sample was drawn from the census manuscripts from Salem, Lawrence, and Lynn, including married couples where both spouses were present and the wife was below 30 years of age, that is, where the marriage was fairly recent. The rate of intermarriage was measured according to both nativity and ethnicity (Table 4.16).

Not surprisingly, the native marriages turn out to be less frequent and the foreign more so when using the ethnicity classification. Most important, however, is the fact that the mixed marriages vary in different directions. In Lawrence and Salem they are less than apparent from the nativity index, but in Lynn they are somewhat more common. With this method the ratio of actual to expected intermarriage rates is roughly the same in Lynn as previously measured; in Salem and Law-

TABLE 4.16

Type of Marriage: Percentage of Married Women Under 30 with Husband Present in 1880 Census N = 1779

	Nativity				Ethnicity			
	Native	Mixed	Foreign	All	Native	Mixed	Foreign	All
Lawrence	38	18	44	100	26	9	65	100
Lynn	73	17	10	100	63	21	16	100
Salem	61	18	21	100	50	12	38	100

rence it is reduced to below .40. It is not surprising to note that about 6 out of 10 of these hidden mixed marriages in Lynn were contracted between a native male and a second-generation foreign female, as against only 4 in Salem and Lawrence. The male competition in Lynn would tend to encourage this type of match. When studying the official data on intermarriage, based on nativity, it is worth remembering that the data can overstate the rates in one community and understate them in another.

Ethnic and class differences in the timing of marriage, ranging from young in native and working class to old in (European) immigrant and upper class present something of an enigma. Since immigrants mostly are lower-class members, and the upper class almost entirely is native American, it should be the other way around. The explanation is of course that when class differences are controlled, immigrants tend to marry later than natives (and Canadians); and when ethnicity, on the other hand, is controlled, upper-class marry later than lower-class members.

Whatever ethnocultural or socioeconomic factors are at work, the timing of marriage in successive generations had a highly differentiating effect on family interaction (Table 4.18). First, upper-class children were more often socialized, as infants, by parents in their mid-thirties, whereas middle- and lower-class children had younger parents. Second, since property succession and extended education in the late nineteenth century mostly were the prerogatives of males, and since females were free to marry earlier, the age differences between spouses would be larger in upper-class families of successive generations. In most cases an upper-class father was clearly older than the mother, as shown in Table 4.17. In middle and lower strata the parents more often will be age peers. If age differences are associated with a continuum ranging from authority to equality, the lower-class family interaction

TABLE 4.17
Mean Seniority by Class Origin, Where Groom Is Older or Same Age

Groom	Bride			N	Percentage older than bride
	Upper	Middle	Lower		
Upper	6.7	6.0	6.8	(36)	13
Middle	2.4	4.7	3.6	(61)	14
Lower	2.0	5.0	3.1	(45)	15

will be more egalitarian, both in its interspouse and parent–child relations.

Status was more strongly associated with the males. They were more often marrying down from a higher position in terms of class, ethnicity, and age. Given the contemporary attitudes towards the sexes, males were in such cases superior on all counts. The marriage exchange between higher and lower strata, and between native and foreign groups, would rather tend to enhance these differences.

In some respects the working-class marriages were more in conformity with the ideal conjugal or nuclear family types of modern times. A larger proportion of them were contracted only after the spouses had left their parental households, and male authority based on age and class position was less significant. On the other hand, family interaction, the exchange of support and favors among the generations, appears, when analyzed within the framework of the family life course, to be of instrumental importance for the work careers, for residential options, and generally for the decision to marry among young adults.

The material presented here deals only with those who actually married in Essex County around 1880. Their options were limited by the local context, and by structural conditions such as the demographic, socioeconomic, and ethnic composition of the population in the eight communities. But they married. Hundreds of others in roughly the same circumstances did not marry right then; some never did. We shall never know exactly why.

Some of the major issues on the marriage market are easily demonstrable. Different age-specific sex ratios caused by occupational opportunities and selective migration enhanced the male's chances in some areas, the female's in others. Although it is doubtful if the actual behavior can be used to make assumptions about norms, some inference can be made from the intermarriage patterns emerging in our sample. A man could choose his partner more easily in groups regarded as inferior by his own group. To transgress the boundaries set by group affiliation, be it class or ethnicity, was much harder for underprivileged males and overprivileged females.

The importance of marriage as the final step toward independence, at least as measured by residential change, varied by socioeconomic groups. The transition seemed much more casual in lower strata, partly because independence before marriage was fairly common, but also because of a higher incidence of postmarital coresidence with parents. An analysis of this family interaction suggested that residential arrangements could be interpreted in terms of economic rationality: The production–consumption ratios were rarely permitted to decrease below a certain level in two-generational households.

This implies that the several decisions taken in connection with marriage were influenced not only by the general normative and material context, but also by conditions within the individual families. Age at marriage, and, perhaps even more, position in the parental family cycle, could help to explain individual variations in career development, familial obligations, and mate selection.

Certainly, the melting pot did not offer an unlimited range of options. The access to careers and partners was far from free. But even if the rules of social reproduction were set, they were not so rigid as to prevent manipulation. The new material conditions changed the nature of family formation, but that change was affected by the conditions within the existing families of Essex County.

References

Anderson, Michael
    1971   Family Structure in Nineteenth Century Lancashire. Cambridge, England: Cambridge University Press.

Barron, M. L.
    1972   "Intergroup aspects of choosing a mate." Pp. 36–48 in M. L. Barron (ed.), The Blending American; Patterns of Intermarriage. Chicago: Quadrangle Books.

Bencanceney, Paul H.
    1965   "On reporting rates of intermarriage." American Journal of Sociology 70(May):717–721.

Berkner, Lutz K.
    1972   "The stem family and the developmental cycle of the peasant household: an eighteenth-century Austrian example." American Historical Review 77(April):398–418.

Cavan, Ruth
    1953   The Family. New York: Crowell.

Chayanov, A. V.
    1925/   The Theory of Peasant Economy. Tr. D. Thorner, R. E. F. Smith, and B.
    1966   Kerblay. Homewood, Illinois: Irwin Press.

Chudacoff, Howard
    1975   The Evolution of American Urban Society. Englewood Cliffs, New Jersey: Prentice-Hall.
    Forth-   "Newlyweds and family extension: the first stage of the family cycle in
    coming   Providence, Rhode Island, 1864–65 and 1879–80." In Tamara K. Hareven and Maris Vinovskis (eds.), Family and Population in Nineteenth-Century America. Princeton: Princeton University Press.

Eriksson, M., and S. Akerman
    1974   "Migration, social mobility and social change." Scandia 40 (Fall):299–306.

Glick, Paul
    1960   "Intermarriage and fertility patterns among persons in major religious groups." Eugenics Quarterly VII:31–38.
Goode, William J.
    1963   World Revolution and Family Patterns. Glencoe, Illinois: Free Press.
Hajnal, J.
    1965   "European marriage patterns in perspective." Pp. 101–140 in D. V. Glass and D. E. C. Eversley (eds.), Population in History. London: Arnold.
Hareven, Tamara K.
    1975   "Family time and industrial time: family and work in a planned corporation town." Journal of Urban History 1 (May):365–389.
Kerblay, Basile
    1971   "Chayanov and the theory of peasantry as a specific type of economy." Pp. 150–160 in Teodor Shanin (ed.), Peasants and Peasant Societies. London: Hammondsworth.
Komarovsky, Mirra
    1962   Blue-Collar Marriage. New York: Random House.
Kramm, Elizabeth, and Dorothy Thomas
    1942   "Rural and urban marriage in relation to the sex ratio." Rural Sociology 7 (March):33–39.
Lorimer, Frank
    1965   The Economics of Family Formation Under Different Conditions. Belgrade: World Population Conference. Volume II.
Merton, Robert K.
    1972   "Intermarriage and the social structure: fact and theory." In M. L. Barron (ed.), The Blending American; Patterns of Intermarriage. Chicago: Quadrange Books.
Monahan, Thomas P.
    1951   "One hundred years of marriage in Massachusetts." American Journal of Sociology 51 (May):534–545.
Ogburn, William F.
    1955   Technology and the Changing Family. Chicago: University of Chicago Press.
Rodgers, Roy H.
    1964   "Toward a theory of family development." Journal of Marriage and the Family 26(August):262–270.
Rowe, George P.
    1966   "The developmental conceptual frameworks to the study of the family." In F. Ivan Nye and Felix M. Berardo (eds.), Emerging Conceptual Frameworks in Family Analysis. New York: Macmillan.
Smelser, Neil
    1959   Social Change in the Industrial Revolution. Chicago: University of Chicago Press.
Young, Michael, and Peter Wilmott
    1957   Family and Kinship in East London. London: Routledge and Kegan Paul.

5

From Fireside to Factory: School Entry and School Leaving in Nineteenth-Century Massachusetts

CARL F. KAESTLE
MARIS A. VINOVSKIS

Introduction

Childbearing and childrearing are important features of the typical family life course. Indeed, sociologists often define family stages in terms of childrearing because children impose many responsibilities upon parents. The commitment to childrearing is not only economic; it involves a loss of freedom for the parents (or at least the mother) and an affective commitment to the child, both of which are of greatest import in the case of the first child. The family's childrearing experience is substantially affected by external institutions, most notably in modern societies by the school and the workplace, which provide custody and training for the child and offer the possibility of the child's earning an income. The child's experience can in turn be affected by other shifts associated with family life course such as the mother's going (or returning) to work.

As children get older, they not only offer the potential of additional family income, but also perform nonrenumerated tasks within the family. They also insure the future possibility of caring for their parents in old age. The balance between burden and benefit shifts toward the plus side as children grow up even though most children never become a net lifetime benefit to their parents. Childrearing is a continuing pro-

135

TRANSITIONS
The Family and the Life Course in
Historical Perspective

cess moving toward the independence of the children, which varies widely by historical period, type of community, ethnic and economic characteristics of the family, and composition of the family and household.

The family life-course concept considers childrearing as both a transition and a portion of a continuum in a family's history. Family life-course stages may be defined demographically, economically, and in other ways. For example, parents who begin childrearing when they are older may be able to provide children with more education than parents who are at an early stage in their economic career. In other words, using a one-dimensional family cycle concept is not as helpful as studying the different dimensions of a family's life-course experience.

The research reported in this chapter was designed to investigate certain aspects of childhood in eight Essex County towns in 1860 and 1880, keeping in mind these life-course concepts. Although the study is not longitudinal, the large sample sizes and the possibility of comparing two different periods should give us some insight into the different varieties of family experience in late nineteenth-century Massachusetts.

The most systematic data concerning the activities of individual children in this period, available in the manuscript schedules of the federal censuses after 1850, consist of whether the child attended school during the previous year (not how long or what type of school) and whether the child was employed, and, if so, at what occupation. Our study will analyze children's differing positions by using school attendance as the dependent variable, although we shall discuss children's employment as an important alternative to school.[1]

For our younger sample, children aged 4–8, we are attempting to analyze the initial entry into school, a crucial transition in the life

[1]The census schedules for 1860 and 1880 did not ask identical questions on the occupation of individuals. In 1860, the census asked: "Profession, occupation, or trade of each person, male or female, over 15 years of age." In 1880, the trade of each person, male or female; in addition, the number of months this person has been unemployed during the census year.

Some of the census enumerators in 1860 did record the ages of working children aged 10–15 while other enumerators did not record that information. Therefore, one should be very cautious about trying to compare the rates of labor force participation for children aged 10–15 between 1860 and 1880.

Instructions for these censuses can be found in Wright and Hunt (1900). For useful discussions about the meaning of questions relating to labor-force participation in this period, see Fabricant (1949) and Whelpton (1926).

course of virtually all children when the family begins to share custody and training with a formal institution. For our samples of youths aged 13–19 we are studying the age structure of school leaving and how it is influenced by family background and family experience. It is possible, of course, that some children left and reentered school more than once in their youth, but in a large sample like ours, the census information on nonattenders should reflect the characteristics of those who have left school permanently. As for the truthfulness of the responses, there would seem to have been little pressure for false claims of school attendance in our sample of ages 4–8 and ages 13–19. The only children covered by attendance legislation in these age-groups were the 13-year-olds, and the enforcement of this law was inadequate. Secondly, even if some parents claimed school attendance for nonattenders, the converse seems unlikely. Because our data reveal substantial numbers of parents reporting nonattendance, which we have no reason to disbelieve, our multivariate analysis should reveal the relationships between the independent variables and either school entry or school leaving.

Our study uses a form of multivariate analysis called multiple classification analysis. Despite recent studies of nineteenth-century school attendance that rely on descriptive statistics as opposed to more manipulative multivariate analysis, two factors compel us to push beyond mere description and cross-tabulation of school attendance at a single urban site. First, if we seek to discover the relative statistical association of possible causal factors upon school attendance, multivariate analysis is required. Second, if we wish to study the influence not only of the child's characteristics and those of his family, but also the type of community in which the child lives, a multicommunity sample is essential.[2]

The research we report meets these two requirements. It is a study of five rural and three urban towns in Essex County, Massachusetts in 1860 and 1880 using multiple classification analysis to investigate the

[2]Studies of nineteenth-century school attendance at the individual level include Troen (1973); Katz (1972a); Denton and George (1974a). The latter prompted a debate found in Katz (1974); Denton and George (1974b); Calhoun (1974).

Studies of nineteenth-century school attendance at the aggregate level include Fishlow (1966). For comments on the Fishlow study and an analysis of Massachusetts statistics which controls for age, see Vinovskis (1972). For an analysis of the determinants of school attendance, see Kaestle and Vinovskis (1974). We are currently engaged in a multivariate analysis of education in all the towns of Massachusetts in 1840, 1860, and 1875, as part of a larger work on schooling in the nineteenth century. See also Field (unpublished).

determinants of school attendance.[3] In addition to the important and difficult question of the relative impact of cultural and economic variables, we are particularly interested in the relationship between family experience and schooling. To focus on the influence of family structure and family life course on our subjects' education, we have included many more variables regarding the family than previous studies. From our large samples—over 14,000 persons for each of our years—we created for our study of children and youth a compressed file of all individuals aged 0–19. For each of these individuals in our file detailed information was added concerning the subject's siblings, parents, and household. Before discussing our results, however, we must first turn to a description of some aspects of childhood in Essex County in 1860 and 1880.

Schooling and Child Labor in Essex County, 1860–1880

Massachusetts Laws Affecting Education and Child Labor

The legislative history of child labor and compulsory school attendance laws in Massachusetts is complicated; we shall summarize those statutes that affected our two sample years, 1860 and 1880. As of 1860, no child under 10 years of age was to be employed more than 10 hours a day (1842); children under 15 working in manufacturing establishments were to have attended school for 3 months during the preceding year and obtained a certificate proving this (1836,1838); and school committees were instructed to enforce the law (1842). Towns were permitted to make further provisions to enforce the laws (1850); truants could be incarcerated (1850); and all children, whether employed or not, were to attend school for 12 weeks each year, unless they already knew the rudiments, were physically or mentally defective, or impoverished

---

[3]Our overall sample consists of all individuals in five rural Essex County towns (Boxford, Hamilton, Lynnfield, Topsfield, and Wenham) and a sample of individuals from three cities in that county (Lawrence, Lynn, and Salem) from the manuscript federal censuses of 1860 and 1880. In order to make our urban sample roughly comparable in absolute number of individuals, for 1860 we selected individuals in every sixth urban household and for 1880 in every tenth. Since the various studies to be made of this population all deal with family history, we omitted individuals in institutions and in boarding houses (defined as households with 13 or more unrelated members).

(1852).[4] Evidence abounds to show that these laws were neither widely nor strictly enforced.[5]

During the late 1860s and the 1870s there was a flurry of legislation on these subjects, spurred in part by the studies of the newly created Massachusetts Bureau of Labor Statistics. As of 1880, the following regulations were in effect: No child under 10 was to be employed in a manufacturing, mechanical, or mercantile establishment (1876); children thus employed between the ages of 10 and 14 must have attended school for 20 weeks in the preceding year (1876) and were not to work more than 60 hours per week (1867); a Deputy Constable of the Commonwealth was assigned to enforce child labor laws (1867); towns were required to provide truant officers (1873); all children aged 8–14, with the same exceptions as in 1852, were to attend school for 20 weeks a year (1874); no child under 14 was to be employed during public school session if unable to read or write (1878); and employers were required to keep proof of their employees' birth and school attendance on file for truant officers' inspection (1878).[6]

That these laws were still controversial is suggested by the constant revision of age limits and length of schooling requirements. Despite stiff provisions for reports by truant officers and school committees, and despite requirements that employers prove both age and school attendance for employees under 14, the laws were still inadequately enforced. In the late 1860s and early 1870s, the Massachusetts Bureau of Labor Statistics collected and published voluminous evidence of abuse. Children under 10 worked in factories, children aged 10–15 had not been to school for years, and factory officials falsified records.[7]

Despite widespread complaints of noncompliance with child labor and school attendance laws, it would not be accurate to assume that there were no differences in enforcement between 1860 and 1880. In rural towns the laws were cited by school officials to reinforce their traditional pleas to parents, and sometimes they used the statutes as a stick to persuade uncooperative parents (Wenham School Committee, 1880). In the large towns, truant officers could harass and cajole, and sometimes actually compel, truants to return to school. The Lawrence

[4]Massachusetts Laws, 1836, Chapter 245; 1838, Chapter 107; 1842, Chapter 60; 1850, Chapter 294; 1852, Chapter 240.

[5]Ensign (1921), Perrin (1876). For contemporary documents on this issue, see especially Oliver (1869).

[6]Massachusetts Laws, 1867, Chapter 285; 1873, Chapter 262; 1873, Chapter 279; 1874, Chapter 233; 1876, Chapter 52; 1876, Chapter 257.

[7]Massachusetts Bureau of Labor Statistics (1870); see also McNeill (1875: 4). (This report is Senate Document #50 for 1875.)

school superintendent boasted that his truant officer had nearly eliminated truancy, and a report of the Massachusetts Bureau of Labor Statistics claimed in 1882 that Lawrence's working class was better educated
than other factory towns and that the factory laws regarding children
were generally in force (Massachusetts Bureau of Labor Statistics, 1883;
Lawrence School Committee, 1880: 39). Meanwhile Lynn's school
superintendent complained in 1880 that truancy seemed "to be a growing and, at present, an irrepressible evil [Lynn School Committee, 1880:
29]." Obviously, enforcement varied from town to town. It is important
to note that no school laws affected children under 8 or those over
14-years-old—the two major groups of children in our analysis.

The Employment of Children

Swimming, berry picking, and loitering around the wharves presented alluring alternatives to multiplication tables and hard benches.
But our statistics do not catch the occasional truants, any more than the
truant officer did. The bulk of our analysis deals with whether children
attended school at any time in the previous 12 months, and child labor
was the most common cause of sustained nonattendance among teenagers, especially males. Employment opportunities differed substantially between urban and rural towns. Most labor for children in the
rural towns was agricultural. This meant that it was more seasonal than
urban work, and to the extent that children were working on their
parents' farm, that it was nonremunerative. Of course, such work contributed directly to the family income, just as factory wages did for
urban children's families. The difference is that the manuscript census
reports only remunerated labor, so family farm work is not amenable to
study from our sources.

Urban youth employment, which in good times was year-round,
was not only recorded in the census somewhat more accurately, but
was also more in conflict with school attendance. Thus, while older
boys in rural areas commonly attended school in winter, perhaps for
lack of anything better to do, urban employers complained of the disruption caused by having to replace children who had to take time off
to complete their required schooling. This problem generated some
new forms of schooling, such as half-time and evening schools for
factory youths, which—however educationally meager—were more
compatible with full-time work.

Aggregate census data provide a profile of youth employment in
the eight towns. The 1880 federal census gives separate figures for
employees aged 10–15 but includes those over 15 with all adults. More

interesting for our purposes are the aggregate employment figures of 1885 because the largest concentration of youth workers were over 15. The number of children aged 10–13 reported as working is very small, due either to the fact that young children were not commonly employed by this date, or, more likely, to underreporting. The number of youths age 14–19 employed in each town's principal occupations are presented in Tables 5.1 and 5.2.

The Structure of School Systems in Urban and Rural Towns

Although the availability of youth employment in cities probably inhibited school attendance, the availability of the more developed and differentiated urban school systems should have enhanced it. By 1880 our three Essex County urban towns had not only the standard three-tiered system of primary, grammar, and high schools, but also various bureaucratic innovations such as intermediate, middle, mixed, evening, or upgraded schools designed largely to deal with the educational problems created by working and/or foreign children. Rural systems, in contrast, were much simpler. Each district had its district school, and sometimes there was a grammar department in the center district. Rural children who wished to attend high school had to board in one of the larger towns or commute a long distance.

Private and parochial schooling was also more available in urban areas, although data on private schooling are much less reliable than that on public schools. For example, Boxford had an academy throughout this period but reported none in the school report for 1860. Lawrence school officials reported 1200 private students in 1880. These children were all in St. Mary's parochial schools, of which the public school officials approved. The figure does not include children in French-Canadian parochial schools, of which the school board did not approve; nor did the board collect any figures on nonparochial private schooling. Salem's figures for 1880, on the other hand, seemed to be more thorough. In its returns to the state for 1879–1880, the Salem school committee reported 13 private schools and academies, enrolling 950 students during the year. In their own local school report for the following year, the figure is higher but not drastically so, and they list the categories of students. Of 1210 children of all ages then in private institutions, 67 were in college, 884 in Catholic schools, 183 under private tuition, 45 in asylums, and 31 in reformatories (Massachusetts Board of Education, 1879–80; Salem School Committee, 1881: 95).

Leaving aside for the moment the problem of private school esti-

TABLE 5.1
Principal Occupations and Total Employed Youth Ages 14–19 in Five Rural Essex County Towns, 1885

Principal occupations	Number	Percentage of all youth
Males		
Boxford		
Farm laborers	23	48.9
Farmers	1	2.1
Boot and shoemakers	2	4.3
Matchmakers	1	2.1
Carpenters	1	2.1
Sawmill employees	1	2.1
Total employed in all occupations	34	72.3
Hamilton		
Farm laborers	23	60.5
Clerks	5	13.2
Steam railroad (officials and employees)	1	2.6
Farmers	1	2.6
Total employed in all occupations	34	89.5
Lynnfield		
Farm laborers	9	22.5
Teamsters	4	10.0
Boot and shoemakers	4	10.0
Bookkeepers and clerks	3	7.5
Blacksmiths	1	2.5
Stoneworkers	1	2.5
Total employed in all occupations	27	67.5
Topsfield		
Farm laborers	26	41.9
Boot and shoemakers	3	4.8
Bookkeepers and clerks	3	4.8
Painters	1	1.6
Slaughterhouse employees	1	1.6
Total employed in all occupations	36	58.1
Wenham		
Farm laborers	24	45.3
Boot and shoemakers	5	9.4
Salesmen	4	7.6
Fishers, curers, and packers	2	3.8
Total employed in all occupations	40	75.5

TABLE 5.1 (*continued*)

Principal occupations	Number	Percentage of all youth
Females		
Boxford		
Housework	13	37.1
Servants (in families)	6	17.1
Total employed in all occupations	23	65.7
Hamilton		
Housework	12	32.4
Servants (in families)	7	18.9
Teachers	1	2.7
Total employed in all occupations	20	54.1
Lynnfield		
Housework	14	26.4
Servants (in families)	6	11.3
Boot and shoemakers	3	5.7
Total employed in all occupations	26	49.1
Topsfield		
Housework	11	23.4
Servants (in families)	4	8.5
Boot and shoemakers	4	8.5
Total employed in all occupations	21	44.7
Wenham		
Housework	14	32.6
Boot and shoemakers	2	4.7
Servants (in families)	2	4.7
Total employed in all occupations	21	48.8

Source: Massachusetts State Census of 1885.

mates, Table 5.3 presents some basic data on the public systems in our communities for 1860 and 1880.

   With some anomalies (notably, the marked decline in attendance in Hamilton and Boxford), the following generalizations can be made: Rural attendance and enrollment levels are higher than in urban towns in 1860 and 1880, even though for the state as a whole there is a tendency for urban rates to catch up with rural rates during this period; the length of the school year was much longer in the cities, so those children who did attend regularly were receiving more instruction. By

TABLE 5.2

Principal Occupations and Total Employed Youth Ages 14–19 in Three Urban Essex County Towns, 1885

Principal occupations	Number	Percentage of all youth
Males		
Lawrence		
Cotton mill operators	524	23.4
Worsted mill operators	158	7.1
Laborers	134	6.0
Apprentices	109	4.9
Bookkeepers and clerks	101	4.5
Woolen mill operators	78	3.5
Print works operators	77	3.4
Dye works operators (cotton)	34	1.5
Salesmen	26	1.2
Farm laborers	23	1.0
Total employed in all occupations	1656	73.9
Lynn		
Boot and shoemakers	786	34.3
Apprentices	143	6.2
Bookkeepers and clerks	142	6.2
Morocco workers	53	2.3
Salesmen	39	1.7
Errand boys	33	1.4
Teamsters	32	1.4
Laborers	23	1.0
Merchants and dealers	22	1.0
Machinists	18	.8
Tannery employees	18	.8
Total employed in all occupations	1576	68.7
Salem		
Boot and shoemakers	236	15.4
Cotton mill operators	141	9.2
Bookkeepers and clerks	130	8.5
Tannery employees	67	4.4
Apprentices	52	3.4
Salesmen	47	3.1
Morocco workers	38	2.5
Jute mill operators	26	1.7
Laborers	25	1.6
Errand and office boys	24	1.6
Total employed in all occupations	1021	66.7

TABLE 5.2 (continued)

Principal occupations	Number	Percentage of all youth
Females		
Lawrence		
Cotton mill operators	696	27.4
Worsted mill operators	457	18.0
Housework	272	10.7
Woolen mill operators	231	9.1
Servants (in families)	71	2.8
Bookkeepers and clerks	37	1.5
Dressmakers	23	.9
Seamstresses	12	.5
Teachers	10	.4
Paper mill operators	9	.4
Total employed in all occupations	1922	75.6
Lynn		
Boot and shoeworkers	656	26.5
Housework	383	15.4
Servants (in families)	198	8.0
Bookkeepers and clerks	61	2.5
Saleswomen	38	1.5
Dressmakers	26	1.1
Paper box makers	21	.9
Teachers	19	.8
Laundry work	14	.6
Music teachers	10	.4
Total employed in all occupations	1507	60.8
Salem		
Cotton mill operators	270	16.2
Housework	257	15.4
Boot and shoemakers	148	8.9
Servants (in families)	134	8.0
Jute mill operators	38	2.3
Bookkeepers and clerks	35	2.1
Saleswomen	17	1.0
Dressmakers	12	.7
Compositors and printers (book and job)	8	.5
Laundry work	5	.3
Total employed in all occupations	1507	60.8

Source: Massachusetts State Census of 1885.

TABLE 5.3
Public School Attendance in Eight Essex County Towns, 1860 and 1880

Town	Population		Number of children		Length of school year (in days)	
	1860	1880	1860	1880	1860	1880
Lawrence	16,114	39,178	7,420	15,638	228	220
Lynn	15,713	38,284	8,124	13,605	232	224
Salem	20,934	27,598	9,107	10,266	253	224
Topsfield	1,250	1,165	521	371	133	184
Hamilton	896	935	282	305	113	183
Wenham	1,073	889	462	299	165	184
Boxford	1,034	824	437	289	143	201
Lynnfield	883	686	335	218	183	185

Source: Calculated from Massachusetts Board of Education, Annual Reports, 1859–60 and 1879–80.
*ᵃ*Average summer attendance plus average winter attendance, divided by 2.
*ᵇ*Estimated: Winter attendance plus .25 times the summer attendance.

1880 the rural towns had increased their public school term substantially, but had not caught up with the large towns. This phenomenon makes sense in view of the seasonal nature of family work in agricultural towns. Schools were kept open longer in the urban communities because reformers and school officials desired longer school sessions for a variety of reasons, and families wanted schools, at least in part, to share the custodial functions of childrearing because more adult work was outside of the home in the cities.[8]

Trends, however, cannot be reliably discerned from only two points in time; furthermore, the data in Table 5.3 are for public school only. Using a complex set of estimates and assumptions, we have generated information on the length of the public school year (Figure 5.1) and rates of total attendance for public and private schooling combined (Figure 5.2).

Figure 5.1 confirms the impression that had been gained from our data on individual towns in 1860 and 1880: Urban schools are kept open longer than rural ones and the gap between them narrows over time. Figure 5.2 illustrates that despite the systemization of schooling and the increasing societal pressures to attend school, the rate of total attendance for all persons aged 0–19 was actually declining in Massachusetts from 1840 to 1880. Our urban and rural communities in Essex County follow this general trend throughout this period. One of

[8]These trends will be discussed at length in our forthcoming study of rural–urban differences in Massachusetts education in the period 1826–1880.

Average daily attendance				Total enrollment			
1860		1880		1860		1880	
Number[a]	Percentage of all youth 0–19	Number	Percentage of all youth 0–19	Number[b]	Percentage of all youth 0–19	Number	Percentage of all youth 0–19
1,662	22.4	4,232	27.1	2,873	38.7	5,866	37.5
2,971	36.6	4,667	34.4	4,045	49.8	6,183	45.4
2,575	28.3	2,807	27.3	4,031	44.3	3,858	37.6
141	27.1	116	31.3	231	44.3	202	66.2
107	37.9	80	26.2	182	64.5	134	43.9
168	36.4	138	46.2	275	59.5	183	61.2
181	41.4	89	30.8	294	67.2	135	46.7
127	37.9	81	37.2	188	56.1	124	56.9

the major reasons for this decline in school attendance of children under 20 is that there was a concerted and successful effort to decrease the number of very young children in schools—a subject which we will discuss in more detail later.

The result of changes in the pattern of school attendance and in the length of the school year is summarized in our estimate of the number of days in school per person under 20 between 1840 and 1880 (Tables 5.4, 5.5, and 5.6). There was a substantial rise in the number of days in school per person ages 0–19 in Massachusetts from 60.6 days in 1840 to

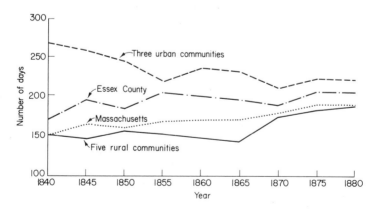

FIGURE 5.1. *Average length (in days) of public school terms in Massachusetts, 1840–1880.*

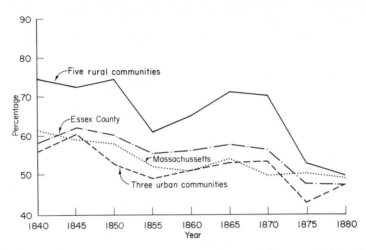

FIGURE 5.2.   *Percentage of individuals under 20 years of age enrolled in school in Massachusetts, 1840–1880.*

72.2 days in 1879. This was largely because of the increasing length of public school terms in the smaller towns. The trend in Essex County was very similar; the average number of days in school in 1840 was 63.7 days and 75.1 days in 1880. Our particular sample of towns in Essex County did not follow the pattern of either the state or Essex County. Instead, the number of school days per person under 20 declined from 92.8 days in 1840 to 74.8 days in 1880 in our three urban

TABLE 5.4
Average Length of Public School Terms (in Days) in Massachusetts, 1840–1880

	Five rural communities	Three urban communities	Essex County	Massachusetts
1839–1840	151	269	171	150
1844–1845	146	260	197	166
1849–1850	156	247	187	162
1854–1855	153	221	206	168
1859–1860	147	238	202	172
1864–1865	143	234	198	172
1869–1870	175	214	191	180
1874–1875	184	225	208	192
1879–1880	190	224	208	192

Source: Massachusetts Board of Education, Annual Reports, 1839–1840 and 1879–1880.

TABLE 5.5

Percentage of Persons Under 20-Years-Old Enrolled in School in Massachusetts, 1840–1880

	Five rural communities	Three urban communities	Essex County	Massachusetts
1839–1840	74.8	56.1	58.5	61.6
1844–1845	72.7	60.5	62.3	59.3
1849–1850	74.8	52.9	60.2	58.2
1854–1855	61.3	49.1	55.6	52.2
1859–1860	65.2	50.9	56.2	50.7
1864–1865	71.3	53.0	57.7	54.0
1869–1870	70.4	53.3	56.2	49.6
1874–1875	52.8	42.5	47.2	50.1
1879–1880	49.8	47.1	49.7	49.0

Source: Calculated from the Massachusetts Board of Education, Annual Reports, 1839–1840 and 1879–1880. (The estimation of this set of data is very difficult because the state did not provide good data on private education. Full details on our estimation procedures will be provided in our forthcoming analysis of Massachusetts education from 1826–1880.)

communities and declined from 61.7 days in 1840 to 60.1 days in the five rural towns.

Conclusion

The foregoing descriptive introduction has emphasized rural–urban differences in schooling and youth employment in order to pro-

TABLE 5.6

Annual Number of Days in School Per Person Under 20 in Massachusetts, 1840–1880

	Five rural communities	Three urban communities	Essex County	Massachusetts
1839–1840	61.7	92.8	63.7	60.6
1844–1845	62.0	95.0	72.0	62.4
1849–1850	73.0	83.9	70.6	63.0
1854–1855	56.1	73.2	71.2	60.6
1859–1860	62.3	77.7	70.3	62.3
1864–1865	64.5	76.4	73.2	66.4
1869–1870	70.1	70.5	68.8	65.7
1874–1875	64.7	67.8	70.0	68.7
1879–1880	60.1	74.8	75.1	72.2[a]

[a]Figures for 1878–1879 only.

Source: Calculated from the Massachusetts Board of Education Annual Reports, 1839–1840 and 1879–1880. (The estimation of this set of data is very difficult because the state did not provide good data on private education. Full details on our estimation procedure will be provided in our forthcoming analysis of Massachusetts education from 1826–1880.)

vide an ecological context for studying the individual choices made by, or for, children in these varied communities. In urban towns the school system was more bureaucratically differentiated; high schools and special schools were available. Truant officers attempted to insure school attendance, and schools provided supervision of young children whose parents worked. On the other hand, the cities offered more diversions and more alternatives to youth; also, to the extent that the urban population was more heterogeneous, there was more alienation and less consensus on the values promoted in schools. Most important, youth made up a substantial portion of the labor force. In the country towns schooling was more compatible with family and work and also probably had entertainment value for children of all ages since they had fewer places and occasions to congregate with their peers than their urban counterparts. To examine the effect of ethnicity, occupation, and family characteristics on the activities of youth, we now turn to our analysis of the manuscript census returns for 1860 and 1880.

Multiple Classification Analysis of School Attendance in 1860 and 1880

Introduction

School attendance in our eight Essex County towns is determined to a large degree by the age of the child (see Figures 5.3 and 5.4). Children aged 0–3 rarely attended school while almost all of the children aged 9–12 were in school at least part of the year. There was very little difference in the school attendance pattern of girls and boys in 1860 and 1880. Though the overall pattern of school attendance did not vary much by age and sex between 1860 and 1880, there was a tendency for fewer children to attend school in 1880 than in 1860, particularly at the younger ages.

Generally children in rural areas attended school in slightly higher percentages than their urban counterparts (Tables 5.7 and 5.8). However, the age and sex pattern of school attendance in both rural and urban areas are very similar.

We have separated processes of school entry and leaving in our analysis because we shall argue that they involve very different considerations. Many scholars have viewed school entry and school leaving as identical issues even though nineteenth-century educators and parents saw them as distinctly separate processes. For example, whereas most educators stressed the importance of remaining in school as long

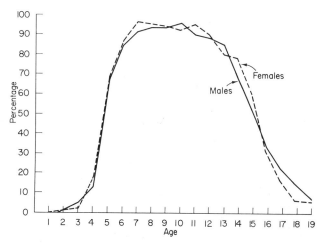

FIGURE 5.3.   *Percentage of youth ages 0–19 attending school in eight Essex County towns in 1860.*

as possible, they did not argue that children should enter school as early as possible.

Our study seeks to explain the pattern of school attendance of children on the basis of their personal characteristics, their family background, and the community in which they lived. Unfortunately, family information is not available for all of the children in our sample. For

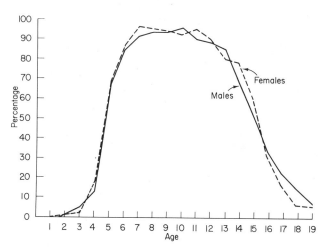

FIGURE 5.4.   *Percentage of youth attending school in eight Essex County towns in 1880.*

TABLE 5.7
Percentage of Children Aged 0–19 Attending School in Eight Essex County Towns in 1860

Age	Rural				Urban				Total			
	Male		Female		Male		Female		Male		Female	
	N	Percentage	N	Percentage	N	Percentage	N	Percentage	N	Percentage	N	Percentage
0	45	0	49	0	129	0	143	0	174	0	192	0
1	48	0	49	0	113	0	113	0	161	0	162	0
2	56	0	49	0	142	0	138	0	198	0	187	0
3	54	9.3	59	3.4	119	.8	105	0	173	3.5	164	1.2
4	48	25.0	51	23.5	157	7.6	106	14.2	205	11.7	157	17.2
5	50	72.0	56	60.7	127	64.6	110	70.0	177	66.7	166	66.9
6	57	86.0	53	92.5	97	83.5	110	84.5	154	84.4	163	87.1
7	49	87.8	44	100.0	92	93.5	106	95.3	141	91.5	150	96.7
8	52	92.3	54	94.4	107	94.4	104	96.2	159	93.7	158	95.6
9	53	96.2	43	95.3	73	91.8	100	94.0	126	93.7	143	94.4
10	40	97.5	40	100.0	84	95.2	106	89.6	124	96.0	146	92.5
11	42	95.2	45	97.8	65	93.8	79	93.7	112	94.4	124	95.2
12	42	90.5	52	92.3	90	87.8	101	90.1	132	88.6	153	90.8
13	54	92.6	46	84.8	62	79.0	83	78.3	116	85.3	129	80.6
14	62	80.6	63	82.5	79	59.5	93	75.3	141	68.8	156	78.2
15	57	71.9	50	80.0	78	38.5	92	48.9	135	52.6	142	59.9
16	44	52.3	43	67.4	84	22.6	93	14.0	128	32.8	136	30.9
17	54	42.6	41	34.1	85	8.2	84	6.0	139	21.6	125	15.2
18	54	29.6	41	14.6	83	3.6	123	2.4	137	13.9	164	5.5
19	55	12.7	52	11.5	83	2.4	107	.9	138	6.5	159	4.4

TABLE 5.8
Percentage of Children Aged 0–19 Attending School in Eight Essex County Towns in 1880

	Rural				Urban				Total			
	Male		Female		Male		Female		Male		Female	
Age	N	Percentage	N	Percentage	N	Percentage	N	Percentage	N	Percentage	N	Percentage
0	35	0	34	0	106	0	92	0	141	0	126	0
1	33	0	33	0	65	0	88	0	98	0	121	0
2	39	0	38	0	110	0	97	0	149	0	135	0
3	33	3.0	34	0	101	3.0	95	0	134	3.0	129	0
4	28	10.7	40	20.0	115	2.6	102	2.9	143	4.2	142	7.7
5	32	43.8	39	71.1	90	23.3	96	34.4	122	28.7	135	45.2
6	36	86.1	35	71.4	101	58.4	98	76.5	137	65.7	133	75.2
7	45	75.0	35	88.6	97	76.3	107	82.2	142	76.1	142	83.8
8	33	78.8	38	84.2	84	83.3	89	80.9	117	82.1	127	81.9
9	31	90.3	30	93.3	73	89.0	96	88.5	104	89.4	126	89.7
10	44	90.9	35	94.3	94	89.4	74	91.9	138	89.9	109	92.7
11	35	94.3	24	91.7	87	93.1	82	82.9	122	93.4	106	84.9
12	35	94.3	32	96.9	100	87.0	97	84.5	135	88.9	129	87.6
13	37	100.0	25	100.0	89	80.9	80	78.8	126	86.5	105	83.8
14	41	78.0	33	81.8	97	61.9	95	53.7	138	66.7	128	60.9
15	27	77.8	25	80.0	93	40.9	98	35.7	120	49.2	123	44.7
16	32	43.8	27	59.3	94	21.3	107	26.2	126	27.0	134	32.8
17	30	23.3	32	58.1	89	11.3	76	18.4	119	14.3	118	28.0
18	34	11.8	33	18.2	91	7.7	115	11.3	125	8.8	148	12.8
19	47	6.4	36	13.9	103	4.9	107	6.5	150	5.3	143	8.4

example, we do not have family background information on children who migrated without their parents to these towns to seek employment or on children whose parents have died or have abandoned them. Therefore, we decided to restrict our multiple classification analysis of school attendance to those children who were living with at least one parent. In this way we could study the relationship between the characteristics of the children's family and the likelihood of them attending school.[9]

Naturally the omission of children who were not living with their parents introduced some biases in our study. Therefore, we compared the school attendance pattern of children in our multiple classification analysis (MCA) with those who were omitted (see Tables 5.9 and 5.10). For children aged 4–8, our MCA sample included approximately 90% of the total number of children of those ages of our overall sample. However, for children aged 13–19, our MCA sample included only 72.7% of the overall sample in 1860 and 82.1% in 1880. The large difference between our overall sample and our MCA sample for children aged 13–19 is due to the large immigration of young people seeking work in Lawrence, Lynn, and Salem. As a result, it is not surprising that a considerably smaller percentage of the older children not in our MCA sample attended school than those who were living with their parents. (For a discussion of our use of MCA, see the appendix, pages 181–183.)

Our study analyzes whether children were attending school during the past year in 1860 and 1880. But what about those children who did not attend school? Can we simply assume that they had left the classroom in order to begin their careers? The data presented in Figures 5.5 and 5.6 suggest that there were many older children in our MCA sample who neither attended school nor were gainfully employed. In 1860, 17.2% of the males and 28.6% of the females were recorded in the census as being neither in school nor at work. The comparable figures for 1880 are 7.7% for males and 21.9% for females. Furthermore, if we examine the data in more detail by age and sex, we discover that the proportion of children neither at school nor at work varies inversely by age for females while the pattern for males by age is more erratic (Tables 5.11 and 5.12).[10]

[9]In addition to eliminating all children without at least one parent present, we also did not use the few children whose father's occupation was not given. The inclusion of these children in our analysis would have created statistical problems in constructing another occupational category based on so few cases.

[10]It is important to remember that the census schedules for 1860 and 1880 did not ask the same questions about occupation; it is almost certain that the percentages of

TABLE 5.9

Comparison of the Percentages of Children Attending School in Eight Essex County Towns in 1860 in the Various Samples

	Original sample		MCA sample		Non-MCA sample	
Age	N	Percentage	N	Percentage	N	Percentage
			Males			
4	205	11.7	188	12.2	17	5.9
5	177	66.7	159	66.0	18	72.2
6	154	84.4	140	85.7	14	71.4
7	141	91.5	126	91.3	15	93.3
8	159	93.7	142	95.8	17	76.5
13	116	85.3	98	88.8	18	66.7
14	141	68.8	116	69.0	25	68.0
15	135	52.6	104	52.9	31	51.6
16	128	32.8	96	34.3	32	28.1
17	139	21.6	113	23.9	26	11.5
18	137	13.9	83	14.5	54	13.0
19	138	6.5	89	7.9	49	4.1
			Females			
4	157	17.2	139	15.8	18	27.8
5	166	66.9	153	66.7	13	69.2
6	163	87.1	150	89.3	13	61.5
7	150	96.7	136	96.3	14	100.0
8	158	95.6	140	95.0	18	100.0
13	129	80.6	110	85.4	19	52.6
14	156	78.2	128	82.0	28	60.7
15	142	59.9	113	68.2	29	27.6
16	136	30.9	100	39.0	36	8.3
17	125	15.2	88	17.1	37	10.8
18	164	5.5	93	8.6	71	1.4
19	159	4.4	82	6.1	77	2.6

School Attendance of Young Children

The continual emphasis that nineteenth-century educators placed on increasing school enrollments has led most educational historians to assume that there was a steady rise in the percentage of children attending schools. This is an erroneous impression, however, of the

---

children ages 13–19 who are working was more underestimated in 1860 than in 1880 because of the differences in the census questions. See Footnote 1 for a discussion of this issue.

TABLE 5.10
Comparison of the Percentages of Children Attending School in Eight Essex County Towns in 1880 in the Various Samples

Age	Original sample		MCA sample		Non-MCA sample	
	N	Percentage	N	Percentage	N	Percentage
			Males			
4	143	4.2	126	4.8	17	0
5	122	28.7	113	29.2	9	22.2
6	137	65.7	126	65.9	11	63.6
7	142	76.1	135	74.8	7	100.0
8	117	82.1	106	83.0	11	72.7
13	126	86.5	106	89.6	20	70.0
14	138	66.7	121	67.8	17	58.8
15	120	49.2	106	51.9	14	28.6
16	126	27.0	108	27.8	18	22.2
17	119	14.3	99	16.1	20	5.0
18	125	8.8	99	11.1	26	0
19	150	5.3	111	7.2	39	0
			Females			
4	142	7.7	131	6.9	11	18.2
5	135	45.2	121	47.1	14	28.6
6	133	75.2	120	72.5	13	100.0
7	142	83.8	131	83.2	11	90.9
8	127	81.9	112	83.9	15	66.7
13	105	83.8	92	84.3	12	83.3
14	128	60.9	115	63.5	13	38.5
15	123	44.7	106	48.1	17	23.5
16	134	32.8	115	35.7	19	15.8
17	118	28.0	85	31.8	33	18.2
18	148	12.8	119	16.0	29	0
19	143	8.4	98	11.2	45	2.2

school attendance pattern of young children. Reacting to the warnings of psychiatrists and educators that the premature education of young children might cause them irreparable harm, school officials discouraged parents from sending their very young children to school and often tried to raise the school entrance age.[11] The school attendance of children aged 4–8 in our sample towns declined sharply from 69.3% in

[11]For a discussion of the reactions of educators to young children in school in the early nineteenth century, see May and Vinovskis (1976). We are currently working on a study of the transition from family to school in mid-nineteenth-century Massachusetts.

1860 to 54.6% in 1880 (see Table 5.13). Whereas most 5-year-olds in 1860 attended school, by 1880 only 38.3% of them were enrolled. Though there was a significant decline in the enrollment rates in all of these communities, the greatest decline occurred in Lawrence, Lynn, and Salem—perhaps reflecting the fact that educators, particularly in the urban communities of Massachusetts, were often concerned about the presence of very young children in classrooms.

Even though there was a decline in the percentage of children at each age attending school during this period, age was the single best predictor of school enrollment in 1860 and 1880 (Table 5.13), although the societal definition of when a child should enter school had shifted between 1860 and 1880.

Educational historians have tried to study the influence of socioeconomic factors on school attendance at both the community and household levels. At the household level, these studies seek to determine the relationship between school going and the personal characteristics of the child and his or her family, after controlling for the effects of the age of the child. Why is it that some 5-year-olds attend

TABLE 5.11
School and Work Patterns of Females Aged 13–19 in Eight Essex County Towns in 1860 and 1880 (Percentage of Each Age Group)

Age	N	School, no work	No school, no work	School and work	Work, no school
			1860		
13	110	83.6	13.6	1.8	.9
14	128	78.9	16.4	3.1	1.6
15	113	66.4	15.9	1.8	15.9
16	100	35.0	34.0	4.0	27.0
17	88	14.8	46.6	2.3	36.4
18	93	8.6	41.9	0	49.5
19	82	3.7	43.9	2.4	50.0
13–19	714	45.8	28.6	2.2	23.4
			1880		
13	92	80.4	6.5	4.3	8.7
14	115	60.0	13.9	3.5	22.6
15	106	45.3	18.9	2.8	33.0
16	115	34.8	24.3	.9	40.0
17	85	31.8	21.2	0	47.1
18	119	16.0	34.5	0	49.6
19	98	10.2	31.6	1.0	57.1
13–19	730	39.3	21.9	1.8	37.0

TABLE 5.12

School and Work Patterns of Males Aged 13–19 in Eight Essex County Towns in 1860 and 1880 (Percentage of Each Age Group)

Age	N	School, no work	No school, no work	School and work	Work, no school
			1860		
13	98	88.8	11.2	0	0
14	116	65.5	25.0	3.4	6.0
15	104	46.2	23.1	6.7	24.0
16	96	25.0	16.7	9.4	49.0
17	113	9.7	10.6	14.2	65.5
18	83	6.0	20.5	8.4	65.0
19	89	3.4	12.4	4.5	79.8
13–19	699	36.3	17.2	6.7	39.8
			1880		
13	106	81.1	5.7	8.5	4.7
14	121	58.7	5.8	9.1	26.4
15	106	43.4	4.7	8.5	43.4
16	108	25.9	9.3	1.9	63.0
17	99	13.1	13.1	3.0	70.7
18	99	7.1	5.1	4.0	83.8
19	111	6.3	10.8	.9	82.0
13–19	750	34.4	7.7	5.2	52.7

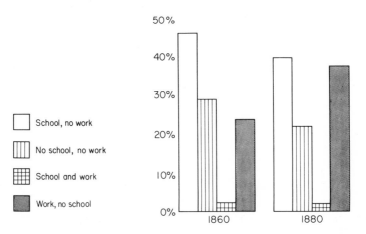

FIGURE 5.5. *School and work patterns of females ages 13–19 in eight Essex County towns in 1860 and 1880.*

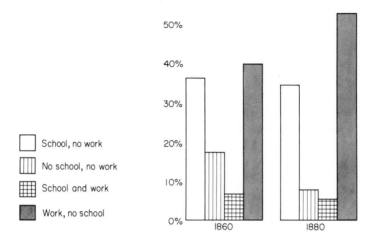

FIGURE 5.6. *School and work patterns of males ages 13–19 in eight Essex County towns in 1860 and 1880.*

school while others do not? How much of the variation in school attendance can be explained by the characteristics of the family rather than the community setting in which that family lives?

The relationship between community and attendance of small children was not dramatic. In the 1860 data it is almost nonexistent once we control for the effects of the other variables while in 1880 there was higher school attendance of young children in the rural areas (net deviation = +6.5%).

TABLE 5.13
School Enrollment in Essex County Towns of Children Aged 4–8 in 1860 and 1880[a]

	Eta^2		Beta	
	1860	1880	1860	1880
Age of child	.4642	.3494	.6588	.5966
Community	.0031	.0136	.0290	.0984
Literacy of parent	.0024	.0046	.0230	.0448
Sex of child	.0045	.0036	.0231	.0753
Work–consumption index	.0188	0	.0619	.0588
Ethnicity of child	.0106	.0070	.0452	.0862
Occupation of parent	0	.0027	.0431	.0439
Age of parent	.0348	.0172	.0930	.0460

[a]R^2s: 1860 = .4735; 1880 = .3757.

Having an illiterate parent may have imposed a double burden on children: Not only would they be less likely to learn to read at home, but they would also be less likely to attend school as young children. The negative relationship between an illiterate parent and school attendance is more pronounced in 1880 than in 1960. However, it is important to bear in mind that the literacy of the parent is not a major factor in the school attendance of young children in this sample partly because there are so few illiterate parents in the samples.

The sex of the subject has surprisingly little impact on school attendance in this age range. One might have predicted higher rates of school attendance for male children, given the prevailing attitudes about the appropriateness of education for girls, but in fact the reverse is true in our samples. In both 1860 and 1880, girls attended school in slightly larger percentages than did boys. No compelling explanation emerges from the literary evidence, except the negative finding that comports with our statistical results: School officials rarely distinguished betw een girls and boys in talking about early education needs and abilities.

So far we have focused on the community variable and the personal characteristics of the child such as sex and age. Now we shall try to analyze the effects of the economic circumstances of the family on the attendance pattern of its children.

We will focus first on the occupation of the parent. The classes under this predictor variable do not form one simple hierarchy. Farming was so common to the small towns and so unusual in the cities that this designation relates to community as well as to status. The father-absent categories are not an occupational status but rather summarize the experience of subjects without a father to bring home any income. Our three hierarchically ranked occupational categories, then, are professional and semiprofessional, white collar and skilled, and semi-skilled and unskilled.[12]

The relationship of school attendance to the occupation of the parent was not very strong compared with the other variables. The results suggest that children of parents in the higher status and better paid

[12]The categories employed for each occupation are based on Stuart Blumin's classification. We are indebted to Professor Blumin for making his classification available to us. See Blumin (1975: 293–315). We have aggregated the professional and semiprofessionals because the latter category was too small. Similarly, we have combined skilled workers, a small category, with the lower level white-collar workers.

The entire issues of categorizing occupations in the nineteenth century using census data is very complex. For a good introduction to these issues, see Blumin (1968:1–13); Griffen (1972:310–330); Katz (1972b:63–88); Hershberg et al. (1974:174–216).

occupations were being kept out of school longer—perhaps reflecting the growing concern among that segment of society about the adverse effects of sending very young children to school. But since there was not a strong relationship between the occupation of the parent and the school attendance of the child, it would seem that the age at school entry had not become a major issue among the various occupational subgroups of the population.

Although the occupation of the parent is a very useful and important indicator of the economic situation of the family, it is not the only economic datum we would like to have. Ideally, we would measure the actual income and consumption needs of the family, as several contemporary studies have done. Unfortunately, such data are unavailable to us historically. We can go beyond the occupation of the head of household, however, by considering the number of individuals in the family who are employed as well as the number of consumers within that family.

Since the earning and consuming ability of individuals varies by age and sex, we adjusted our data by a set of weights to take these factors into consideration. Our work–consumption index is therefore a crude measure of the number of working units in each family (excluding the subject) divided by the number of consuming units (including the subject). Though this index does not fully capture the individual family variations in income and consumption needs, it does provide at least a beginning toward measuring a family's economic situation.[13]

The work–consumption ratio is a measure of family members working over consumer units within that family. It is an attempt to define the income strategy of a family unit, without reference to the occupational group, which is accounted for elsewhere in the multiple classification analysis. The variable was designed with the older subjects in mind; that is, we wanted to measure whether a low (disadvantageous) work–consumption ratio was associated with a higher probability of teenagers working in our older sample (the work–consumption ratio was also used in the study of women in the labor force in Chapter 6 of this volume). We did not expect any strong or consistent relationship between the school attendance of young children and the work–consumption index since it was unlikely that any of the children aged

---

[13]Our effort to develop a work–consumption ratio for the family was greatly influenced by the use of such variables in contemporary sociological studies. For example, see Sweet (1973) and Morgan (1974).

For the numerator of the family work–consumption ratio we calculated the number of equivalent male adult workers in the family. Relying on very crude estimates based on

4–8 could be gainfully employed in Essex County at this time to supplement the family income.

The results of our MCA runs suggest that there was no consistent relationship between the school attendance of young children and the

---

various studies of wage-earners for the late nineteenth century, we used the following weights:

Age	Male	Female
10	.1	.1
11	.2	.2
12	.3	.3
13	.4	.4
14	.5	.5
15	.6	.6
16	.7	.6
17	.8	.6
18	.9	.6
19	1.0	.6
.	.	.
.	.	.
.	.	.
99	1.0	.6

The weights used in the denominator of our work–consumption index were derived after examining the consumption figures presented by Peter Lindert in his *Fertility and Scarcity in America* (1978). Lindert assembled information on consumption patterns from a variety of late nineteenth- and early twentieth-century surveys of family expenditures. The weights used were .55 for children aged 0–4, .65 for children aged 5–9, .75 for children aged 10–14, and 1.0 for everyone 15 and above.

Admittedly, our weights for both workers and consumers are very crude. Though some of these weights may be improved when more detailed studies of nineteenth-century family budgets become available to us, any weighting scheme which provides a set of weights distinguished only by sex and age for occupations and consumption patterns must of necessity be very crude. However, we do feel that these weights are reasonable and useful approximations that do provide additional data on a family's economic situation beyond knowing the occupation of the head and/or the total number of members in that family.

Since the particular computer program that we were using (OSIRIS) truncated the results of computed ratios to integers, it was necessary to multiply our work–consumption index by 100 in order to have our results accurate to at least two decimal places. Furthermore, since the OSIRIS MCA program does not allow interval independent variables, it was necessary for us to categorize our work–consumption index. As a result, though the work–consumption index in this paper is identical to the one utilized in Chapter 6 of this volume, it appears to be slightly different since the programming for the women's work did not use the OSIRIS package and therefore did not have to multiply the index by 100 or to subdivide it into categories.

work–consumption index in 1860 and 1880. There was a slight tendency for the children in families with low work–consumption indices to attend school in higher proportions, but that relationship is not consistent in both periods because in 1880 young children in families whose dependency ratio was 0–19 actually were less likely to be in school.

Since a large share of the families with the lowest work–consumption ratios are those with the father missing, one might speculate that in these families the mother is more likely to work and thus more apt to use school as a custodial institution for her young children. The attendance rates in Table 5.14 do not support this interpretation; the attendance rates of young children in our sample are slightly depressed, not inflated, for families in which the father is absent, and more important, it makes almost no difference whether the mother is working.[14]

Another very interesting factor in our analysis is the ethnicity of the child. Nineteenth-century educators were very concerned about the school attendance of the foreign-born population because they were anxious to assimilate immigrants' children into American society. The common lament among these educators was that immigrants did not realize the importance of education for their children since they were unwilling to make the necessary sacrifices to keep them in school.

Many later works on the history of education do not accept the notion that ethnicity was a major determinant of school attendance. Rather, these studies point to the importance of class rather than ethnicity in determining whether a child would attend school. They

[14]Our results are somewhat analogous to Michael Katz's for Hamilton, Ontario in 1851 and 1861. He discovered a discontinuity in the negative association between school attendance and economic status; it was reversed for the youngest children. Laborers, and families without servants, sent the fewest youngest children to school except in the youngest age categories. Schools, concluded Katz, "provided the mother with some place to send young children when she went to work [1972a:441–444]." Katz did not consider the possibility that there was a shift in attitudes toward young children being educated in Canada that might have encouraged parents in the higher status occupations to be the first to delay sending their very young children into the classroom.

In our study, very few mothers worked and therefore the custodial advantages of early childhood education were not as important to most of our population. The constraints upon present day women working if they have children are outlined in Sweet (1973: 113). These constraints are: the psychological and cultural compulsion to care for one's own children, the lower rate of return on work if one must pay for child care, and the sheer inability of some mothers to arrange child care. These factors probably operated to some degree in the nineteenth century as well, but there was a much stronger feeling that married women should not work than there is today.

TABLE 5.14

School Attendance in Essex County Towns of Children Aged 4–8 in 1860 and 1880: Class Means, Adjusted Means, and Net Deviations

	Class mean		Adjusted mean		Net deviation		Number of cases	
	1860	1880	1860	1880	1860	1880	1860	1880
Age of child								
4	13.8	5.8	15.4	5.7	−53.9	−48.9	327	257
5	66.3	38.3	67.1	37.7	−2.2	−16.9	312	235
6	87.6	69.1	87.0	69.9	+17.7	+15.3	290	246
7	93.9	78.9	93.0	78.9	+23.7	+24.3	262	266
8	95.4	83.4	94.0	83.5	+24.7	+28.9	282	218
Community								
Salem	66.8	51.0	68.1	52.3	−1.2	−2.3	352	255
Lawrence	64.7	53.5	67.7	56.1	−1.6	+1.5	312	333
Lynn	71.3	48.2	71.1	48.0	+1.8	−6.6	355	307
Rural	72.9	64.5	70.0	61.1	+.7	+6.5	454	327
Literacy of parent								
Illiterate	58.1	39.1	64.7	45.1	−4.6	−9.5	74	64
Literate	69.9	55.4	69.6	55.2	+.3	+.6	1399	1158
Sex of child								
Male	66.1	51.2	68.3	50.8	−1.0	−3.8	755	607
Female	72.7	57.9	70.4	58.3	+1.1	+3.7	718	615
Work–consumption index								
0–19	74.4	56.3	72.6	54.2	+3.3	−.4	238	144
20–24	73.5	56.9	71.8	56.2	+2.5	+1.6	272	202

25–29	62.0	52.4	67.2	54.9	−2.1	+.3	303	212
30–34	58.1	53.1	64.2	56.6	−5.1	+2.0	217	194
35–39	79.8	55.6	71.6	51.3	+2.3	−3.3	129	133
40–49	71.9	47.7	69.9	45.7	+.6	−8.9	64	86
50 and above	72.4	56.6	69.1	56.5	−.2	+1.9	250	251
Ethnicity of child								
First generation	73.2	36.5	65.4	37.4	−3.9	−17.2	41	63
Second generation Irish	62.1	51.9	66.7	55.2	−2.9	+.6	385	320
Second generation other	61.5	58.6	66.3	58.7	−3.0	+4.1	104	222
Third generation and above	73.0	56.4	70.9	54.5	+1.6	−.1	943	617
Occupation of parent								
Professional and semiprofessional	73.2	51.5	68.9	50.3	−.4	−4.3	190	136
Farmer	70.3	66.7	66.1	58.0	−3.2	+3.4	118	102
White collar and skilled	69.0	54.6	68.9	53.4	−.4	−1.2	672	317
Semiskilled and unskilled	68.3	54.0	72.3	55.9	+3.0	+1.3	375	587
Father absent, mother working	63.7	43.3	65.3	53.3	−4.0	−1.3	49	30
Father absent, mother not working	69.6	52.0	66.9	51.5	−2.4	−3.1	69	50
Age of parent								
0–29	43.0	34.7	57.5	49.5	−11.8	−5.1	142	118
30–34	67.8	51.2	69.9	54.4	+.6	−.2	363	258
35–39	73.8	59.2	73.6	57.4	+4.3	+2.8	378	294
40–44	73.2	55.8	68.6	55.3	−.7	+.7	291	265
45–49	75.4	60.5	70.3	54.4	+1.0	−.2	175	167
50 and above	72.6	59.2	68.6	51.8	−.7	−2.8	124	120
Total	69.3	54.6		54.6			1473	1222

argue that the low school–attendance rates of children of foreign-born parents really reflect the fact that most of these parents were concentrated in low-paying occupations; therefore, they were forced to send their children to work to generate sufficient income for the family's survival.[15]

The child's ethnicity is not a very important predictor of school attendance of young children. Though the beta coefficient of the ethnicity of the child variable is higher than that of parental occupation in both 1860 and 1880, neither of these variables is very strong.[16] The only striking group is the first-generation children in 1880 who were very low in their school attendance (net deviation = 17.2%). Since first-generation children were born abroad and are only aged 4–8, these 63 subjects were indeed very new to America. The disruptions of recent immigration may account in part for their depressed attendance rate. The difference between second-generation immigrant children and the third-or-more generation Americans is neither striking nor consistent from 1860 to 1880.

We included the age of the parent as a general index of family life course. Our hypothesis was that parents further along in their careers, up to a certain point, would have more resources (though we expected that this might vary according to the occupation of the parent). Thus, while controlling for the occupation of the head and the work–consumption index for that family, the age of the parent might give us additional information about the economic well-being of the family. The parent's age may also reflect attitudinal variation since younger parents may be the most likely to have adopted the increasingly popular idea that very young children should not be in the schools. The effect of a parent's age on the attendance of young children is not consistent. There is a substantial negative association between attendance and parents aged under 30 (net deviation = −11.8% in 1860 and −5.1% in 1880). For parents aged 30 and above, young children's attendance increases, controlling for the other variables, to parental age 35–39 and then generally declines. This curvilinear relationship is roughly the same for 1860 and 1880.

Summarizing our findings, we would agree with the reader who may think that the results are in several cases unpatterned or involve

[15]Katz (1972a) states "It was the poverty that accompanied laboring status and not Catholicism or Irish birth that did most to keep children out of school." Troen (1973) concludes that "class became the most important parameter." See also, Bowles and Gintes (1975).

[16]Second- and third-generation status was determined by the subject's father if present, mother if not.

relatively small differences in attendance among the different sub-groups in our towns. The main conclusion, then, is that age is by far the strongest predictor of school attendance among young children be-cause most children attended school eventually and the age at which they started was somewhat, but not drastically, affected by family characteristics. At a given age, however, the likelihood of a child's attendance was associated with other predictor variables in the follow-ing manner. Rural attendance rates were consistently the highest. In the cities attendance varied considerably although not consistently over time (most notably the strong drop in Lynn among children aged 4–8 in school between 1860 and 1880). Illiteracy of the parent had the ex-pected negative effect. Girls attended school earlier and in greater numbers than boys, but the difference was not very great. The family's work–consumption ratio had no strong, consistent relationship to school attendance. The parent's occupation was not a strong predictor of school attendance although children of semiskilled and unskilled parents were enrolled in school in higher proportions than the general population. Contrary to the argument that working mothers used schools for the custody of young children, employed mothers in households without fathers were less likely to send their children to school than were the mothers who remained at home in 1860. Ethnicity had an effect only at the extreme of the newly arrived foreign-born children in 1880 who were less likely to attend school; there was no consistent difference in school attendance by young children of foreign-born and native parents. The effect of the parent's age was not dramatic in magnitude and was curvilinearly related to school atten-dance with the peak occuring for parents aged 35–39 in both 1860 and 1880.

Despite differences associated with community and family var-iables, small children in our Essex County towns seem to have had a rather similar school experience as young children. We now turn to the experience of their teenage contemporaries.

School Attendance of Older Children

Youths in late nineteenth-century Essex County had to weigh sev-eral factors deciding whether to remain in school. They could stay in school hoping to improve future job opportunities; however, there was no consensus in the society that continued education was essential for economic success. Entry into the labor force was not only affected by the number and type of job openings in a community, but also by the economic needs of a family. These youths were beginning to face a world of economic exigencies in which career opportunities were often constrained by membership in a particular subgroup of the population. At the same time, these teenagers were entering a phase of their lives of greater personal freedom and choice—growing independence from their parents as well as independence from state regulation of schooling and work. Our data capture only a small part of this interplay between choice and constraint, but they suggest patterns of influence that may have pervaded this crucial transitional period in the life course.

To investigate the determinants of school attendance of older children, we ran multiple classification analyses in 1860 and 1880 for children aged 13–19 with at least one parent present in the household. As our predictor variables we used the same set of factors employed in our school attendance analysis of young children. The results of these MCA runs are displayed in Tables 5.15 and 5.16.

Despite the efforts of professional educators to encourage children to remain in school longer, there was a decline in the percentage of children aged 13–19 attending school from 45.6% in 1860 to 40.3% in 1880. The overall decline in school attendance was due partly to the drop in the percentage of older children enrolled in both Lawrence and the rural towns and partly to the decline in the percentage of children in our sample from rural communities, which had the highest rate of school attendance, from 35.7% of the total sample in 1860 to only 25.7% in 1880.

As in our study of younger children, age is the single best predictor of the school attendance of older children (see the beta coefficients in

TABLE 5.15

School Enrollment in Essex County Towns of Children Aged 13–19 in 1860 and 1880[a]

	Eta²		Beta	
	1860	1880	1860	1880
Age of child	.3479	.2881	.5786	.5502
Community	.0627	.0338	.1982	.1010
Literacy of parent	.0087	.0187	.0233	.0194
Sex of child	.0500	0	.0226	.0205
Work–consumption index	.0089	.0136	.0507	.0960
Ethnicity of child	.0393	.0606	.1198	.1860
Occupation of parent	.0450	.0466	.1011	.1181
Age of parent	.0227	.0037	.0812	.0540

[a]R^2s: 1860 = .4329; 1880 = .3802.

Table 5.4). Whereas most 13-year-old children are still in school, by the age of 19 the overwhelming majority have left the classroom. The decline in school attendance by age is very similar in both 1860 and 1880 and only slightly affected by adjusting the results for the effects of the other predictor variables. The finding that school leaving is largely a function of age is hardly surprising and has surely been true of all societies with voluntary educational systems. Within this context, however, how do other factors influence whether a youth of a given age will have attended school during the past year?

The effect of community on teenage attendance shows a strong, rural bias toward school going. Both young children and youths went to school at greater rates in the countryside in Essex County, demonstrating, perhaps, the school's greater communal role in rural children's lives, as well as the compatibility of schooling and agricultural labor. The greater school attendance in rural areas at the bottom and top of the school-age range accounts in large measure for the higher rural attendance rates in the percentage of persons under 20 attending school.

Comparing 1860 and 1880 figures we note a rough and imperfect convergence of rural and urban school experiences. While the rural towns in Massachusetts approached the urban towns in the length of the school year, the gap between the rates of school attendance began to narrow between rural and urban communities. The picture is more complex when we look at particular towns. For example, teenage school attendance declined in Lawrence while it increased in Lynn and Salem. In addition, attendance rates in a particular community were very age-specific; in Lynn, where the attendance of young children declined from 1860 to 1880, the school enrollment of teenagers increased during that same period.

We anticipated that illiterate parents would be less likely to keep their teenage children in school, partly because they valued education less and partly because they were more likely to be financially disadvantaged compared with literate parents, and, therefore, more dependent upon the supplementary income their children would provide. Once again, that factor is not very important compared with others in those years. In part, this is due to the small number of illiterate parents in our samples.

The three ranked categories of father's occupation display a consistent relationship to school attendance. Youths aged 13–19 whose fathers were professionals or semiprofessionals attended school at the highest rates while those whose fathers were in the semiskilled or unskilled occupations were least likely to enroll. The causes of these

TABLE 5.16
School Attendance in Essex County Towns of Children Aged 13–19 in 1860 and 1880: Class Means, Adjusted Means, and Net Deviations

	Class mean		Adjusted mean		Net deviation		Number of cases	
	1860	1880	1860	1880	1860	1880	1860	1880
Age of child								
13	87.0	87.4	84.7	86.5	+39.1	+46.2	208	198
14	75.8	65.7	75.8	68.4	+30.2	+28.1	244	236
15	60.8	50.0	60.8	49.6	+15.2	+9.3	217	212
16	36.7	31.8	38.0	32.2	−7.6	−8.1	196	223
17	20.9	23.4	21.1	23.8	−24.5	−16.5	201	184
18	11.4	13.8	13.4	12.5	−32.2	−27.8	176	218
19	7.0	9.1	6.0	7.9	−39.6	−32.4	171	209
Community								
Salem	35.3	40.8	36.3	42.7	−9.3	+2.4	317	292
Lawrence	39.6	30.0	46.2	36.9	+.6	−3.4	280	434
Lynn	34.1	37.5	34.8	35.2	−10.8	−5.1	311	373
Rural	62.4	54.6	57.7	57.5	+12.1	+7.2	505	381
Literacy of parent								
Illiterate	23.4	19.0	40.2	37.4	−5.4	−2.9	64	137
Literate	46.6	42.5	45.8	40.6	+.2	+.3	1349	1343
Sex of child								
Male	43.1	39.6	44.4	39.3	−1.2	−1.0	699	750
Female	48.0	41.1	46.7	41.3	+1.1	+1.0	714	730
Work–consumption index								
0–19	47.2	41.5	47.4	42.5	+1.8	+2.2	271	234
20–24	51.2	43.4	47.0	42.0	+1.4	+1.7	217	205

25–29	48.2	51.1	47.3	48.2	+1.7	+7.9	226	237
30–34	36.2	31.0	46.0	34.5	+.4	−5.8	174	203
35–39	56.1	45.0	48.5	32.0	+2.9	−8.3	114	131
40–49	43.3	40.0	41.8	39.2	−3.8	−1.1	120	120
50 and above	40.2	34.3	41.7	39.6	−3.9	−.7	291	350
Ethnicity of child								
First generation	22.0	17.8	31.8	24.5	−13.8	−15.8	218	258
Second generation Irish	45.3	35.7	45.9	36.3	+.3	−4.0	86	339
Second generation other	50.0	38.2	44.4	36.9	−1.2	−3.4	48	170
Third generation and above	50.2	51.2	48.4	48.8	+2.8	+8.5	1061	713
Occupation of parent								
Professional and semiprofessional	56.8	56.4	55.3	51.8	+9.7	+11.5	213	156
Farmer	63.7	56.0	49.7	41.0	+4.1	+.7	179	150
White collar and skilled	46.2	48.9	44.1	46.1	−1.5	+5.8	541	325
Semiskilled and unskilled	30.0	32.9	39.3	36.8	−6.3	−3.5	273	607
Father absent, mother working	33.0	32.2	43.1	35.7	−2.5	−4.6	97	59
Father absent, mother not working	40.9	25.7	45.2	33.0	−.4	−7.3	110	183
Age of parent								
0–34	75.0	43.8	58.7	35.8	+13.1	−4.5	32	32
35–39	60.0	47.0	46.3	35.6	+.7	−4.7	150	164
40–44	48.1	42.0	44.0	38.4	−1.6	−1.9	339	334
45–49	45.6	42.4	48.6	43.0	+3.0	+2.7	349	340
50–54	39.4	39.7	44.6	42.2	−1.0	+1.9	310	310
55–59	40.1	35.0	36.7	42.7	−8.9	+2.4	137	160
60 and above	32.3	30.7	50.5	38.4	+4.9	−1.9	96	140
Total	45.6	40.3					1413	1480

levels of school attendance by occupational status are multiple, and somewhat obvious. Higher-status families enjoyed more income on the average and could better afford the luxury of extended education for their children. It may also be that families in higher-status occupations placed a greater value on extended education. This attitudinal factor may be associated with occupational groups but may operate independently from income per se. Thus one might speculate, for example, that an ill-paid struggling doctor might press harder for extended education for his children than a relatively affluent factory foreman, simply because extended education played a larger role in the expected career pattern of the former's children than it did in the latter's. Different constructions may be put upon this attitudinal influence. Katz, for example, argues that middle- and upper-status parents were increasingly looking to secondary education in the nineteenth century as a means of transfering their status to their children in a world where such status was increasingly difficult to transfer merely by ascription.[17] It may have been, however, more than just an arbitrary credential-giving process. Secondary education may have actually transmitted skills that were more useful for children who aspired to middle- and upper-status jobs. The clearest example of this is teaching as a career goal for girls (Katz, 1968). For boys, advanced writing and reading skills might have been prerequisites for professional and white-collar occupations. For any and probably all of these reasons, children of upper-status fathers stayed in school longer as teenagers.[18]

The school attendance of farm children is not only influenced by their fathers' occupations, but also by the fact that they lived in rural communities where children remained in school longer than their urban counterparts. The overall rate of school attendance of farm children is substantially higher than that of any other occupational group in 1860 and is only slightly lower than that of children of professionals and semiprofessionals in 1880. When we control for the effects of the other variables, the school attendance of farm children is still very high but is significantly less than that of children of professionals and semiprofessionals in 1860 and 1880, and also lower than that of children of white-collar and skilled workers in 1880.

---

[17]Michael B. Katz, at the Michigan Conference on radical school reform, Ann Arbor, Michigan, March 1974. For Katz's view of the other functions of secondary education for the middle class in mid-nineteenth-century Massachusetts, see Katz (1968: 91–93).

[18]Nonetheless, it should be emphasized that even in the middle and upper groups the attendance rates for teenagers were not nearly as high as modern rates for the same groups.

In fatherless families the mother's work status, which had little impact on young children's school attendance, had a strong negative association with teenage school attendance in 1880. The net deviation for fatherless families with the mother working was −4.6% in that year whereas the net deviation for fatherless families with the mother not working was −7.3%. The effect was less pronounced in 1860 but went in the same direction. We may infer from these findings that families without fathers were more likely to send their children to work and that if the mothers in those families were not working, the teenage children would be even more likely to leave school for work.

In addition to the occupation of the parent, we also considered the family work–consumption ratio. We hypothesized that the higher, that is, the more advantageous, the work–consumption ratio of the family, the more likely the child would remain in school rather than enter the labor force to supplement the family's income. The results of our analysis indicate just the opposite: The higher the work–consumption ratio, the less likely a child is to attend school, although the overall importance of the work–consumption variable in our MCA runs is not very strong. This is a very surprising result since it implies that those families that most needed income from their teenage children allowed them to remain in school.

Since our attempt to construct a crude family work–consumption ratio is an innovation and because that ratio did not predict school attendance as we had anticipated, we devoted considerable effort to further checking our results. We reran the MCAs without the children whose fathers were absent to eliminate the possibility that our results had been distorted by the presence of fatherless families that were concentrated in the lowest categories of the work–consumption ratio. In addition, we reran our MCAs by occupation to see if the pattern of the work–consumption ratio varied by that. None of these tests explained satisfactorily the inverse relationship between the work–consumption ratio and teenage school attendance in our basic MCA runs for 1860 and 1880.

There are several possible explanations for our results using the work–consumption ratio. Since the same work–consumption ratio does correctly predict the probability of women working, it may suggest that families did not expect their teenage children to leave school prematurely simply because the family was encountering economic difficulties. Or, more likely, since not all children who left school went directly into the labor force, our measure of school leaving is not as dependent on economic considerations within the family as predicting children's entry into the labor force. Another plausible explanation is that we have not controlled adequately for the actual economic situation of the family. Therefore, if any of the other members of the family had to work besides the father, it might indicate the extent of economic distress within that family even though the family's work–consumption ratio would seem favorable. A fourth possibility is that families that sent other members besides the father into the labor force (and thereby improved their work–consumption ratio) may not have valued education very highly and therefore were willing to have their other children drop out of school. Obviously, we cannot solve this problem at this time. We do urge, however, that future studies of past family behavior try to develop indices such as our work–consumption ratio that try to measure the economic situation of the entire family rather than relying only on the occupation of the head of the household or the size of the family.

In addition to the influence of the family's economic circumstances on school attendance of older children, we anticipated that the children of foreign-born parents would be less likely to attend school than those of native parents—partly because foreign-born parents may have valued education less and partly because they may have needed the economic resources of their children's labor more. Our MCA runs indicate that ethnic status had a clear linear relationship to school attendance: The longer a child and his parents had been in America, the more likely the child would attend school as a teenager, even when controlling for occupational status and other economic variables. The results for 1860 and 1880 are consistent; the ethnicity of the child affected his or her school attendance more than the occupation of the parent.

We included the parent's age in our MCA runs in an attempt to approximate the life-course situation of the family. We anticipated a curvilinear relationship between parent's age and school enrollment of teenage children, with low attendance rates in the early and late stages of the family when the income of most families might have been the most strained. Unfortunately, the results for 1860 and 1880 did not reveal any consistent pattern.

We then speculated that the lack of any consistent pattern in the age of the parent may have resulted because income profiles of wage-earners differ by occupation. Therefore we ran separate MCAs for white-collar and skilled workers, and for semiskilled and unskilled workers. The results partly confirmed our hypothesis. The adjusted school attendance in 1880 of 13–19 year-olds whose fathers were white-collar or skilled workers was directly related to the age of the parent, a relationship that probably paralleled the earning profiles of those families. However, there was no single consistent age pattern for the white-collar and skilled workers in 1860. Similarly, the adjusted school attendance of children aged 13–19 in 1860 whose fathers were semiskilled or unskilled workers varied inversely with parental age. In 1880 school attendance patterns of older children whose parents were semiskilled or unskilled workers were not consistent. As a result, we cannot conclude that our crude measure of the life course of these families was a good predictor of the school attendance of older children. Hopefully future studies will be able to improve our estimate of the family life-course situation by obtaining more detailed information on the actual conditions and past experiences of those families than can be approximated by the age of the parent.

Interaction: Ethnicity and Occupation

A problem with multiple classification analysis, as with other forms of multiple regression, is the difficulty in analyzing the impact upon a dependent variable of two or more variables that are highly correlated. The most serious interaction problem involved in the present study is the overlap between ethnicity of the child and the occupation of the parent, both because of the degree of overlap and the importance of the question. The problem is not only statistical but conceptual and historical as well. The issue is complex, and we can only briefly state here the perspective from which we interpret our material on education.

The conceptual problem is to define the relationship between culture and class. It will not do to think of culture, including religion and ethnicity, as an isolated sphere in one's identity and motivation, independent of the social structure and the distribution of goods. Obviously, culture is related to and interacts with social structure, partly arising from it, partly acting upon and shaping it. But culture is neither the same as social structure nor a mere epiphenomenon determined by it, because there can be (and constantly are) lags, discontinuities, and diversity in the interaction of culture and social structure. Nor is culture associated only with ethnicity and religion, or simply opposed to the construct "class." However, we can and should distinguish between culture and the social structure. The language, the imagery, the prejudices, the aspirations, and the daily customs which fall under the rubric of culture, whatever their relationship to the social structure in which they arose, may stubbornly persist when transported to a new social setting, or when technology, politics, or other developments transform social structure. One of the failings of functionalist, equilibrium approaches to history is that they underestimate the "dysfunctional" relationship of culture and the social system.

In what sense, then, is economic motivation more fundamental than cultural baggage in the actions of ordinary people, who are the stuff of the "new" social history? Because life requires sustenance, the closer an individual gets to rudimentary subsistence, the more salient will become straightforward economic strategies, and the more potently these will overrule competing inclinations such as an abstract value placed on education or sanctions against women's work. Obviously, the formula is not predictive. Given the range of human diversity and the complexity of motivation, some individuals will approximate the calculating economic man while others in the same position will doggedly pursue a course opposed to their economic self-interest because they are imbued with a cultural commitment. Choices are constrained, of course. Many plain folk of the past did not have the latitude to pursue their economic wellbeing. The constraints imposed by others, once again, are themselves both economic and cultural.

In addition to this conceptual problem, ethnicity and class are related in the minds of the historical actors, and they are often mutually reinforcing. If we could go back in a time machine to interview an Irish laborer in Lawrence in 1880 and inquire why his 13-year-old son had not attended school during the previous year, he might tell us that the public schools are insulting, that they turn kids away from the church, that parochial schools cost too much, that the family needs his son's mill wages, that his son does not need extended education, and that anyway the boy prefers the factory to the school. The father might be baffled as to which reason is the most salient, or whether he and his son are more motivated by "class" or "ethnicity," since all the factors reinforce the same behavior. This is analogous on the individual level to the statisticians' advice quoted previously for the aggregate: If two factors equally predict an outcome, they both do equally well as predictors.

This returns us to the statistical problem. One approach to assessing the independent inpact of ethnicity on class (defined here by occupation) is to explore the cases or groups where the two factors do not combine in the same way. An analysis of the distribution of occupations among ethnic categories for our samples shows that there is substantial but not complete overlap. Farmers and professionals are overwhelmingly native, and immigrants are disproportionately laboring class. Is our ethnicity variable, then, simply reflecting an economic phenomenon? One technique for sorting out the interaction in MCA analysis is to combine the related variables, as we have done in the MCA analyses presented in Tables 5.17 and 5.18.

Except for the combined ethnicity–occupation variable, the analysis is the same as that presented earlier in Tables 5.4 and 5.5. By dividing our middle and lower occupational groups into native and foreign-born fathers, we can demonstrate the independent effect of ethnicity. For example, the net deviations on teenage school attendance in 1880, in rank order, are as follows: native white collar and skilled, +20.5%; native semiskilled and unskilled, +3.5%; foreign white collar and skilled, −6.7%; foreign semiskilled and unskilled, −11.2%. It may be that within each broad category foreign-born children's fathers are concentrated nearer the bottom; nevertheless, foreigh-born children of white-collar and skilled workers attended school at substantially lower rates than native children of semiskilled and unskilled workers. The same pattern prevailed in 1860. Clearly, something is operating here besides occupational status. Several factors may explain the association of immigrant status with lower attendance. For example, the level and role of schooling in the societies from which the immigrants came probably made them less oriented toward extended formal education than the native population. In addition, the public schools were biased against foreigners and Catholics. To the extent that alienation from schooling among working class Americans in the nineteenth century existed, it was probably greater among the foreign-born than the native population. Whatever the reasons, some aspects of ethnic status operated independently of occupational status in schooling decisions.

TABLE 5.17

School Attendance in Essex County Towns of Children Aged 13–19 in 1860 and 1880[a]

	Eta^2		Beta	
	1860	1880	1860	1880
Age of child	.3479	.2881	.5817	.5541
Community	.0627	.0338	.2016	.1077
Literacy of parent	.0087	.0187	.0303	.0459
Sex of child	.0018	0	.0237	.0185
Work–consumption index	.0089	.0136	.0514	.0920
Ethnicity and occupation combined	.0529	.0739	.1607	.2259
Age of parent	.0227	.0037	.0816	.0543

[a]R^2s: 1860 = .4303; 1880 = .3806.

TABLE 5.18
Școol Attendance in Essex County Towns of Children Aged 13–19 in 1860 and 1880: Class Means, Adjusted Means, and Net Deviations

	Class mean		Adjusted mean		Net deviation		Number of cases	
	1860	1880	1860	1880	1860	1880	1860	1880
Age of child								
13	87.0	87.4	85.1	87.1	+39.5	+46.8	208	198
14	75.8	65.7	76.0	68.6	+30.4	+28.3	244	236
15	60.8	50.0	60.6	49.2	+15.0	+8.9	217	212
16	36.7	31.8	37.9	31.8	-7.7	-8.5	196	223
17	20.9	23.4	21.1	23.3	-24.5	-17.0	201	184
18	11.4	13.8	13.0	12.5	-32.6	-27.8	176	218
19	7.0	9.1	6.0	8.2	-39.6	-32.1	171	209
Community								
Salem	35.3	40.8	37.1	42.4	-8.5	+2.1	317	292
Lawrence	39.6	30.0	44.2	35.3	-1.4	-5.0	280	434
Lynn	34.1	37.5	34.7	36.6	-10.9	-3.7	311	373
Rural	62.4	54.6	58.3	48.2	+12.7	+7.9	505	381
Literacy of parent								
Illiterate	23.4	19.0	38.6	33.3	-7.0	-7.0	64	137
Literate	46.6	42.5	45.9	41.1	+.3	+.8	1349	1343
Sex of child								
Male	43.1	39.6	44.4	39.4	-1.2	-.9	699	750
Female	48.0	41.1	46.7	41.3	+1.1	+1.0	714	730
Work–consumption index								
0–19	47.2	41.5	47.0	42.8	+1.4	+2.5	271	234
20–24	51.2	43.4	47.5	42.5	+1.9	+2.2	217	205

25–29	48.2	51.1	46.8	47.6	+1.2	+7.3	226	237
30–34	36.2	31.0	45.9	34.9	+.3	−5.4	174	203
35–39	56.1	45.0	49.2	32.4	+3.6	−7.9	114	131
40–49	43.3	40.0	42.2	38.4	−3.4	−1.9	120	120
50 and above	40.2	34.3	41.6	39.3	−4.0	−1.0	291	350
Ethnicity and occupation combined								
Professional and semiprofessional	56.8	56.4	57.0	56.1	+11.4	+15.8	213	156
Farmers	63.7	56.0	51.6	46.5	+6.0	+6.2	179	150
White collar and skilled (foreign-born)	32.7	35.5	36.3	33.6	−9.3	−6.7	98	169
White collar and skilled (native-born)	49.2	63.5	46.9	60.8	+1.3	+20.5	443	156
Semiskilled and unskilled (foreign-born)	25.0	27.0	29.2	29.1	−16.4	−11.2	164	407
Semiskilled and unskilled (native-born)	37.6	45.0	44.8	43.8	−.8	+3.5	109	200
Father absent, mother working	33.0	32.2	39.8	37.0	−5.8	−3.3	97	59
Father absent, mother not working	40.9	25.7	46.7	32.9	+1.1	−7.4	110	183
Age of parent								
0–34	75.0	43.8	58.8	35.2	+13.2	−5.1	32	32
35–39	60.0	47.0	46.3	35.8	+.7	−4.5	150	164
40–44	48.1	41.9	43.8	38.6	−1.8	−1.7	339	334
45–49	45.6	42.4	48.9	43.3	+3.3	+3.0	349	340
50–54	39.4	39.7	44.4	41.7	−1.2	+1.4	310	310
55–59	40.1	35.0	37.0	42.8	−8.6	+2.5	137	160
60 and above	32.3	30.7	50.4	38.1	+4.8	−2.2	96	140
Total	45.6	40.3					1413	1480

Conclusion

Our data illuminate the transitional processes of entering and leaving school. Although family and economic variables influenced somewhat the timing of those transitions, both decisions, and particularly school entry, were governed very strongly by the subject's age. The aggregate transition from 20% attending to 80% attending was accomplished in 3 years. School leaving was somewhat more spread out along the teenage portion of the life course and was thus more influenced by other considerations. Nonetheless, the transition from 80% attending to 20% attending was made in 4 years.[19]

This generalization should not be allowed to obscure different school experiences by different groups. There were surely substantial differences in the quality and quantity of education received by different groups in nineteenth-century Essex County, differences that are not reflected in our crude data on school entry and school leaving. Nor do we wish to minimize the differences that do appear in our data, particularly the group differences in the age of school leaving.

Our main conclusion is that not only was entry age virtually uniform, but that participation in the aged 9–12 group was virtually universal. Rudimentary schooling was an established, uniform feature of American childhood by 1860 and probably long before. It was based on the assumption that all had a right to be brought equally to the starting point at the public expense. By midcentury, school systems had been established in the North and West that implemented this faith. Beyond the age of 13, however, young people began experiencing choices, sometimes forced choices, between work and school. Even teenagers from native and comfortable backgrounds, although they had higher attendance rates than their immigrant and working class contemporaries, were not attending school nearly as long as they did 40 years later, when the high school had become a mass institution. Despite the lack of compulsory legislation, length of schooling was not as widely varied in late nineteenth-century Massachusetts as one might have predicted. But a small difference can mean a lot, not because education is so precious, but because the marginal choices were shaped by cultural differences and economic exigencies. Whatever was learned in school, school leaving taught Essex County youth something about how their world was ordered.

---

[19]For changes in the length of these transitions from 1880 to 1970, see Modell et al. (1976:7–33).

Appendix: The Use of
Multiple Classification Analysis

Since many of the readers of this essay may not be familiar with multiple classification analysis, we will try to provide a brief introduction to this technique in order to facilitate a better comprehension of our results. Multiple classification analysis (MCA) is a form of multiple regression analysis with dummy variables which express results in terms of adjusted deviations from the grand mean of the dependent variable associated with the various classes of the predictor variables.[20] For example, MCA answers the question: How much decrease in average school attendance is associated with being the child of an unskilled laborer, while controlling for such other variables as age of parents, ethnicity, and community. Similarly, it provides an approximate answer to the question: Ceteris paribus, what is the effect on youths' school attendance of the family's life-course stage as measured by the age of the parents? Multiple classification analysis "controls" for other variables by assuming while it looks at one class of a predictor variable that the distribution of all other predictor variables will be the same in that class as in the total population, thus "holding constant" their effects. Although traditional multiple regression programs also do this, MCA has three advantages: It does not require variables to be interval variables, it does not require or assume linearity and thus can capture discontinuities in the direction of association and, finally, it is useful descriptively because it presents the reader with the gross effects of a predictor class, that is, the actual mean of each class, as well as the mean after adjusting for the influence of other variables.

Although MCA does not assume linearity, it does, like other forms of regression analysis, assume that the effects of the various predictors are additive, that is, independent of one another. In fact, of course, for most variables this is not true. In our sample, for example, children's sex is not correlated with father's occupational status, but ethnicity and occupational status are correlated substantially. However, the problem of the interaction effects of variables can be ascertained both conceptually and empirically and then corrected, if necessary, by creating a new variable that combines those two variables.[21]

[20]For an excellent, well-written introduction to multiple classification analysis, see Andrews et al. (1973). Demographers and sociologists have long used MCA. For example, see Duncan (1964–1965:82–89) and Sweet (1973). Stepwise MCA may be used when a group of predictors is logically prior to others; see Schnaiberg (1971).

[21]For a detailed discussion of the interaction problem, see Sonquist (1970).

The statistics generated by MCA analysis provide information to answer a variety of different, but related issues. If one asks how "important" an independent variable (X) is in determining the variation in a dependent variable (Y), the question can mean several things. Most studies that have used MCA have dealt primarily or exclusively with the magnitude and direction of the adjusted means within the classes of a given predictor variable X; that is, they have emphasized the question: How much of the difference in Y is attributable to membership in a particular class of X? The statistics that are the most useful in analyzing this issue are the class mean, the adjusted mean, and the net deviation of the independent variables. The class mean (often called the gross mean) is simply the value of the dependent variable for that class or category of that independent variable. The adjusted mean indicates what the mean would have been for that class or category if that group had been exactly like the total population with respect to its distribution over all the other predictor classifications. The net deviation of a class category of a predictor variable is simply the adjusted mean minus the grand mean of the dependent variable.

Another question, however, is: "how important" is the whole predictor variable X_1 compared to predictor variable X_2 or X_n in explaining variation in dependent variable Y? Here we ask, not how much higher is the attendance rate for professionals' children as opposed to unskilled workers' children, when controlling for other variables, but rather, how much of the variation in attendance rates is explained by father's occupational status, in comparison with the amount of variation explained by a child's ethnicity. To attempt to answer this question we must turn to the predictor summary statistics which provide expressions of each predictor's unadjusted and adjusted contribution to explaining the variance in the dependent variable. A word of caution, however. These statistics are heavily dependent upon the particular distribution of the sample and are not simply comparable across samples. We present them as indicators of the relative importance of our variables in explaining school attendance in each year. The β^2 statistics are an unadjusted measure of variance explained, that is, they express the zero-order relationship between the predictor variable and the dependent variable. They are thus analogous to the square of Pearson correlation coefficients for interval variables. Our adjusted measure is β, the partial β coefficient. The rank order of these betas indicates the relative importance of each variable in explaining variance in the dependent variable while controlling for all other included variables. However, β^2 does not express percent of variance explained.

Finally, we may want to know how much of the total variance of the dependent variable can be accounted for by our series of predictor variables. To measure this we use R^2 adjusted which indicates the proportion of the variance of the dependent variable explained by all the predictor variables together after adjusting for the number of cases, categories, and predictors, that is, adjusting for the degrees of freedom, that have been used in the analysis.

In order to present the reader with adequate statistical information on our MCA analyses, we will present two tables for each of our major runs. The first table (Tables 5.13 and 5.15) will contain the β^2 and β coefficients for each of the predictor variables as well as the overall adjusted R^2. The second table (Tables 5.14 and 5.16) will present the class means, the adjusted means, the net deviations, and the number of cases for each class or category of each of the predictor variables as well as the grand mean and the total number of cases for that particular MCA.

Acknowledgments

This work was prepared for the Mathematics Social Science Board Conference on The Family Life Course in Historical Perspective. The authors gratefully acknowledge the financial support of the Mathematics Social Science Board of the National Science Foundation, as well as grants from the Rockefeller Foundation, under which the 1880 data were prepared, and from the National Institute of Education, under which the 1860 data were prepared and much of the supporting research conducted. The opinions expressed herein do not necessarily reflect the position of the National Institute of Education, and no official endorsement by the Institute should be inferred. We are indebted to Stephen Shedd for programming our condensed file of children and to Mary Vinovskis for programming our MCA runs.

References

Andrews, Frank, J. N. Morgan, John A. Sonquist, and Laura Klem
    1973   Multiple Classification Analysis (2nd edition). Ann Arbor: University of Michigan, Survey Research Center.
Blumin, Stuart
    1968   "The historical study of vertical mobility." Historical Methods Newsletter I (September): 1–13.
    1975   "Rip Van Winkle's grandchildren: family and household in the Hudson Valley, 1800–1860." Journal of Urban History I (May):293–315.
Bowles, Samuel, and Herbert Gintis
    1975   Schooling in Capitalist America: Educational Reform and the Contradictions of Economic Life. New York: Basic Books.
Calhoun, Daniel
    1974   "Letter to the editor." History of Education Quarterly (Winter): 545–546.

Denton, Frank, and Peter George
  1974a   "Socio-economic influences on school attendance: a study of a Canadian
           county in 1871." History of Education Quarterly XIV (Summer): 223–232.
  1974b   "Socio-economic influences on school attendance: a response to Professor
           Katz." History of Education Quarterly XIV (Fall):367–369.
Duncan, Otis Dudley
  1964   "Residential areas and differential fertility." Eugenics Quarterly XI 82–89.
Ensign, Forest C.
  1921   Compulsory School Attendance and Child Labor. Iowa City: Athens Press.
Fabricant, Solomon
  1949   "The changing industrial distribution of gainful workers: comments on the
           dicennial statistics, 1820–1940." Studies in Income and Wealth I:3–45.
Field, Alexander J.
  Unpub-   "Educational Reform and Manufacturing Development in Mid-Nineteenth
  lished   Century Massachusetts." Unpublished doctoral dissertation, University of
           California, Berkeley, 1974.
Fishlow, Albert
  1966   "The American common school revival: fact or fancy?" Pp. 40–67 in N.
           Rosovsky (ed.), Industrialization in Two Systems: Essays in Honor of Alex-
           ander Gerschenkron. New York: Wiley.
Griffen, Clyde
  1972   "Occupational mobility in noneteenth-century America: problems and
           possibilities." Journal of Social History V (Spring):310–330.
Hershberg, Theodore Michael Katz, Stuart Blumin, Laurence Glasco, and Clyde Griffen
  1974   "Occupation and ethnicity in five nineteenth-century cities: a collabora-
           tive inquiry." Historical Methods Newsletter VII (June): 174–216.
Kaestle, Carl, and Maris A. Vinovskis
  1974   "Quantification, urbanization, and the history of education: an analysis of
           the determinants of school attendance in New York State in 1845." Histori-
           cal Methods Newsletter VIII (December):1–9.
  Forth-   Education and Social Change in Nineteenth-Century Massachusetts. Cam-
  coming   bridge: Cambridge University Press.
Katz, Michael B.
  1968   The Irony of Early School Reform. Cambridge, Massachusetts: Harvard
           University Press.
  1972a   "Who went to school?" History of Education Quarterly XII (Fall):432–454.
  1972b   "Occupational classification in history." Journal of Interdisciplinary His-
           tory II (Summer): 63–88.
  1974   "Reply." History of Education Quarterly XIV (Summer):233–234.
Lawrence School Committee
  1880   Annual Report. Lawrence: A. & C. Morrison.
Lindert, Peter
  1978   Fertility and Scarcity in America. Princeton: Princeton University Press.
Lynn School Committee
  1880   Annual Report. Lynn: Lynn Record Press.
Massachusetts Board of Education
  1839–40 Annual Report.
  1849–50 Annual Report.
  1859–60 Annual Report.
  1879–80 Annual Report.

Massachusetts Bureau of Labor Statistics
1870   Annual Report. Senate Document #120. Boston: Massachusetts Depart-
        ment of Labor and Industries.
1883   Annual Report. Boston: Massachusetts Department of Labor and Indus-
        tries.
May, Dean, and Maris A. Vinovskis
1976   "A ray of millenial light: early education and social reform in the infant
        school movement in Massachusetts, 1826–1840." Pp. 62–99 in Tamara K.
        Hareven (ed.), Family and Kin in American Urban Communities, 1790–
        1930. New York: Franklin and Watts.
McNeill, George E.
1875   Factory Children: Report on the Schooling and Hours of Labor of Children
        Employed in the Manufacturing and Mechanized Establishments of Mas-
        sachusetts. Massachusetts State Senate Document #50. Boston.
Modell, John, Frank Furstenberg, and Theodore Hershberg
1976   "Social change and transitions to adulthood in historical perspective."
        Journal of Family History I (Autumn):7–33.
Morgan, James N.
1974   Five Thousand American Families: Patterns of Economic Progress. Vol-
        umes I and II. Ann Arbor: University of Michigan, Survey Research Center.
Oliver, Henry K.
1869   Report of Henry K. Oliver, Deputy State Constable, Especially Appointed
        to Enforce the Laws Regulating the Employment of Children. Boston.
Perrin, John W.
1876   The History of Compulsory Education in New England. Ph.D. Dissertation,
        University of Chicago. Published in Meadville, Pennsylvania.
Salem School Committee
1881   Annual Report, 1880. Salem: Salem Observer Book and Job Print.
Schnaiberg, Allan
1971   "The Modernizing Impact of Urbanization: A Casual Analysis." Economic
        Development and Cultural Change XX (October):80–104.
Sonquist, John A.
1970   Multivariate Model Building: The Validation of a Search Strategy. Ann
        Arbor: University of Michigan, Survey Research Center.
Sweet, James A.
1973   Women in the Labor Force. New York: Seminar Press.
Troen, Selwyn K.
1973   "Popular education in nineteenth-century St. Louis." History of Education
        Quarterly XIII (Spring):23–40.
Vinovskis, Maris A.
1972   "Trends in Massachusetts education, 1826–1860." History of Education
        Quarterly XII (Winter):201–229.
Wenham School Committee
1880   Annual Report. Salem: Press of the Essex County Mercury.
Whelpton, P. K.
1926   "Occupational groups in the United States, 1820–1920." Journal of Ameri-
        can Statistical Association XXI:335–343.
Wright, C. D., and W. C. Hunt
1900   History and Growth of the United States Census. Washington, D.C.: U.S.
        Government Printing Office.

6

Women's Work and the Life Course in Essex County, Massachusetts, 1880

KAREN OPPENHEIM MASON
MARIS A. VINOVSKIS
TAMARA K. HAREVEN

This chapter examines the determinants of women's employment in Essex County, Massachusetts, as of 1880. Although we are interested in a number of social and economic factors that influenced women's work, we will pay special attention to the life course and its major transitions. Our primary concern is at what time in their lives and under what conditions late nineteenth-century women were gainfully employed.

In this period of history, women engaged in several kinds of work: unpaid housework, extensions of housework that brought in money (for example, taking in boarders or laundry), and work performed outside of the home in the paid labor force. We focus on the last of these three, mainly because of the increasing importance of market work to the family economy in this period of history. By 1880 in eastern Massachusetts the transition from a predominantly rural and agricultural economy to an urban–industrial one was well advanced. To be sure, urban families continued to produce some of their own food and clothing and occasionally produced goods for sale at home, but the self-sufficient farm family was largely a phenomenon of the past: Most families could only survive if at least some of their members entered the labor force. The usual expectation at that time was that men would go to work and earn the family's income while women cared for the

187

TRANSITIONS
The Family and the Life Course in
Historical Perspective

home. Indeed, as early as the 1850s the family-advice literature had already defined and glorified full-time motherhood and domesticity as women's primary pursuits. Nonetheless, in 1880 a large number of women were to be found on the rolls of the employed, working at a variety of occupations. In this chapter, we explore the circumstances that drew women into the labor force in the eight Essex County communities.

Background

Although historians have only recently begun the systematic study of female labor-force participation, a consensus has already arisen that women's employment must be understood in terms of their position within the family, the family's position within the community and the community's economic structure. As Kleinberg has argued:

> Any analysis of women's work must take into account the types of job available in the community, the attitudes of racial, ethnic, and class groups toward women and women's work, the age and marital status of the women who worked and those who did not, the number and age of children in the family, and the opportunities open to men, that is, their working conditions, jobs, and wages [1977: 23].

In the latter half of the nineteenth century, a woman's position within the family and household defined her domestic responsibilities and thus was likely to influence her ability or willingness to work for pay. While unmarried daughters generally had relatively few chores and were free to work outside the home, married women, especially those with young children, had to assume numerous domestic responsibilities, as well as maintain their husbands' status as breadwinners; their opportunities for gainful employment were, therefore, more restricted than were those of their daughters. By the late 1800s, the ideal of the domestic wife was widely held (Smuts, 1959), though some groups appear to have maintained this ideal more strongly than others. Yans-McLaughlin (1974), for example, has argued that South Italians were especially opposed to women's employment outside the home. Pleck (1978), on the other hand, suggests that blacks probably were less opposed to female employment than most other groups, and Hareven (1975) found that French-Canadian women continued to work after their marriages, despite the official censorship of married women's work in their culture. Thus, both a woman's life-course position and her ethnicity may have influenced the likelihood that she worked outside of the home.

Also of obvious importance was her family's economic status. Women, like men, worked primarily for income. The woman's and her family's need for her earnings was thus significant in determining whether she sought employment. A family that did not need a wife's or daughter's earnings probably had more to gain by keeping the women at home than by having them work. A family whose male members were unable to provide an adequate income, however, had a strong incentive for sending daughters or wives into the labor force. Since economic needs fluctuated considerably with the age configurations in the family, economic status was itself a life course variable. Especially when one considers the type of work done by late nineteenth–century women, work that was generally dirtier and more arduous than the clerical and semiprofessional work done by most employed women today, it seems likely that most women worked only when they needed the money.

Occupational opportunities for women in the local community should also have influenced women's work. In the nineteenth century, as today, the range of occupations open to women was relatively narrow (Oppenheimer, 1970). In 1880, domestic service was the most common form of employment for women, with a smaller number working in textile and shoe factories, and as school teachers, nurses, and seamstresses. Whether the local community had industries employing large numbers of women and whether its population was large or affluent enough to provide a number of openings in school teaching, dressmaking, and domestic service should therefore have influenced the ease with which women could find work when they needed to.

Although most historians seem to agree that the above were significant variables in determining female labor-force participation, they do not agree on the relative importance of each variable. Kleinberg, for example, states unequivocably that "[t]he most important factor in determining whether or not a woman worked outside the home was the occupational structure of the area [1977:23–24]." Yans-McLaughlin (1977), on the other hand, argues that cultural definitions of the appropriate role for women were more important than economic factors: Certain women would never work outside the home, regardless of economic circumstances or community structure. Unfortunately, such claims remain largely untested. Although many studies have shown that these factors influenced women's employment, few have been able to examine all of them simultaneously. One aim of this chapter is to ascertain the relative importance of life course, family economics, and community structure variables by examining how these factors together affected women's work.

This chapter has two additional aims as well. First, although there is considerable evidence that daughters worked more often than did wives in the late nineteenth century (Long, 1958), there is little systematic evidence about the differential influence of family and community variables on the work of these two categories of women. Did family income influence daughters' and wives' employment equally? Did the same occupations or industries that drew daughters into the labor force also attract wives? Or did certain types of occupations attract married women while others were more attractive to unmarried women? Groneman's (1977) analysis of New York women suggests the latter may well have been the case: The ease with which a wife could combine a job with her domestic duties may have been more important in determining whether she worked than the sheer availability of work or the wages it paid (though the latter were important factors in whether daughters worked). In this chapter, we will search for possible differences in the determinants of daughters' and wives' work.

Second, although past studies (e.g., Pleck, 1978) have shown that women's employment was influenced by family economic status, they have not explored whether economic status interacted with the wages that women were capable of earning in determining their employment. Modern economic theories (Bowen and Finegan, 1969) argue that women from affluent families will be less likely to work than those from poorer ones unless the women from affluent families are capable of earning an especially high wage. A woman's employment is, in other words, dictated by her earnings relative to her family's remaining income rather than relative to what other women earn. This assumption is difficult to test for the late nineteenth century because of the lack of information on women's wage levels in studies that also contain information on family economic status. In this chapter we will approach this problem by using community of residence to index the wages available to women. Because the New England textile industry offered lower wages in 1880 than the shoe industry offered (Abbott, 1910), communities with a heavy concentration of textile mills presumably provided lower wages for women than did communities with a heavy concentration of shoe factories. If economic theory is correct, women from high-status families should have been more likely to seek jobs in shoe towns than in textile towns, while the reverse may have been the case among women from poor families. The analysis that follows will test all these hypotheses.

Data

The Essex County data were drawn from the manuscript census of 1880 and represent the noninstitutional households of the eight Massachusetts towns previously mentioned. The dependent variable for our analysis—whether women worked for pay or did not—is inferred from the census question on usual occupation or trade (asked for all persons in the household aged 10 or older). The women in our sample reported over two dozen occupations, a number of which would normally have been pursued entirely at home or without pay (these include housewife, student, family worker, and retired). We combine these unpaid occupations to form the not employed category, reserving the remaining occupations (such as textile mill operative, domestic servant, seamstress, shoe factory operative, washerwoman, school teacher) to form the employed category.[1] As other historians have noted (e.g., Yans-McLaughlin, 1977:104), the usual occupation or trade question used by the census tends to underestimate part-time and seasonal work, especially that done by women with other clearly identifiable positions such as housewife or student. For this reason, our analysis is probably best considered an exploration of women's primary economic roles rather than a study of their total participation in remunerative work.

The 1880 census allows us to study a number of variables potentially influencing women's work. The first is community of residence, an indicator of the number of jobs and wages locally available to women. Of the eight communities we consider, Lawrence was in 1880 the largest and most industrialized, its industry consisting largely of textile mills. Employment opportunities for women were consequently numerous in Lawrence—indeed, Lawrence was a net importer of female labor in this period of history[2]—but wage levels were relatively low. Lynn, the second largest community we examine, was, in contrast to Lawrence, primarily a center for the boot and shoe industries; for this reason, Lynn offered a relatively large number of jobs for women

---

[1]Although we are interested in distinguishing work done outside of the home from that done within the home, we have no assurance that our classification of women's usual occupations and trades achieves this end. The census manuscripts record occupational titles only and for many titles (such as laundress) it is impossible to tell whether this work involved leaving the home. Auxiliary information for the textile and shoe industries suggests that most work was being done in mills or factories by 1880 rather than in women's homes. Since a sizable portion of the employed women in our sample worked as domestics and in textiles and shoes, our classification probably distinguishes market work from work done at home in most cases.

[2]We used the Massachusetts State Census of 1875 and 1885 for a life-table analysis of 5-year female cohorts to estimate net migration to or from each Essex town. Lawrence appears to have had the highest net in-migration of younger women in this period and several of the rural communities experienced net out-migration of these women. We would guess that much of this movement was produced by differential job opportunities across communities.

(though fewer than Lawrence did) and unusually high wages as well. Salem, the third largest community, was more diversified occupationally than either Lawrence or Lynn and had a lower rate of female employment than did Lawrence. The five remaining communities, which we treat as a block in our analysis,[3] were rural and had the lowest rates of female employment. Because of these differences among communities, we would expect that women living in Lawrence were generally more likely to have jobs than those living in Lynn, Salem or the five rural towns. Women from relatively well-off families, however, may have obtained jobs more often in Lynn than in Lawrence, because of the relatively high wages offered there.

In addition to community of residence, the 1880 census also provides information on marital status, relationship to household head, age, literacy, and place of birth of the woman, her mother, and her father. We use the first two variables to form a typology of women's household–family positions, which together with age can be used to make inferences about the typical life-course pattern of work. The third variable, literacy, is the only information we have on women's educational attainment. Although the overwhelming majority of Essex women in 1880 could read and write, the few who could not may have been at some disadvantage in gaining access to higher-wage jobs (Vinovskis, 1970). Literacy thus may have interacted with family economic status in determining women's employment, much as did community of residence. For this reason, we include literacy status in our analysis.

The information on place of birth for women and their parents provides us with measures of ethnicity and generation. These in turn are potential indicators of three factors: family economic status (third-generation families were generally better off than were immigrant families); the means through which immigration occurred (in New England, French–Canadian women were often brought to the United States by employers, whereas women from Europe rarely were); and cultural values about women's roles espoused by the family. Unfortunately, Essex County in 1880 had neither a significant number of South Italians or blacks, two groups previously identified as having had distinct values about women's roles. Whether attitudes toward women's employment varied among the ethnic groups present in Essex County is unknown. We will, however, assume that a tendency for fewer first-

---

[3]We combine the data for Boxford, Hamilton, Lynnfield, Topsfield, and Wenham not only because of their economic and demographic similarities, but also because each community provides an insufficient number of cases for separate analysis.

generation women to have jobs than second-generation ones—where other determinants of employment have been statistically controlled—reflected an especially conservative outlook towards women's work in the first generation. Although our analysis cannot test specific claims about Italians and blacks, it can ask whether certain other ethnic groups appeared to have had distinctive attitudes towards women's employment in the late 1800s.

Because the 1880 census asked no questions about family economic status, this status can be inferred only by examining the characteristics of coresident individuals; for example, their occupations or whether there were servants in the home. This means that family economic status is unknown for all women who lived apart from their kin. Unfortunately for our study, almost one-fifth of the women in our sample did not live at home; these women, moreover, were especially likely to work. Many of them were domestic servants who lived in their employers' homes, and many others were mill workers who boarded out while they worked. Thus, when family economic status is used in the analysis, the sample contains disproportionately few working women. Although it is not entirely clear how this is likely to affect our results, we suspect we are more likely to underestimate socioeconomic differences in women's employment than to overestimate them[4].

For this reason, we perform two distinct analyses of our data. First, we analyze all working-age women,[5] regardless of whether they lived with their kin, to assess the impact on employment of community, household–family position, age, literacy, ethnicity, and generation. This analysis provides a view of life-course and community variations in employment that is unbiased by the exclusion of boarders and servants. It does not, however, permit us to assess the impact on women's employment of family economic status, nor easily to compare the work patterns of daughters and wives. To do the latter, we use the subsample of all male-headed households that contained both an ever-married,

---

[4]Whether socioeconomic (SES) differences in daughters' employment are over- or underestimated depends on the relationship between SES and moving from home to find work. If lower SES girls were not only more likely to work than were higher SES girls, but were also more likely to leave home to do so, then the difference in proportion employed between high- and low-status girls will be smaller when studying only those girls who remained at home (as we must) than when studying all girls. SES differences in female employment would be overestimated only if high SES girls were less likely to work but more likely to leave home to do so. This strikes us as unlikely.

[5]Working-age is 15–59, inclusive. Although the full age range is found in the original Essex County sample, our analysis is restricted to 15–59-year-olds because virtually no women below or above this age were reported to have a gainful occupation or trade.

working-age daughter and another adult woman (usually the head's wife).[6] Although households of this kind were a minority of all Essex households in 1880, the male-headed sample allows us both to measure family economic status and to contrast the work patterns of daughters and wives.[7]

We have created five specific measures of family economic status from the 1880 data. The first is the household head's occupation, which we have grouped into six categories, four of them rank-ordered in terms of socioeconomic status. These categories are (a) professionals, non-farm owners of businesses and other proprietors; (b) skilled craftsmen and white collar workers; (c) semiskilled workers, such as factory oper-atives; and (d) unskilled laborers; the remaining two categories com-prise farmers and men without known occupations. The second mea-sure is whether the household contained any servants: We assume that households with servants were generally more affluent than those without servants. The third measure is whether the household in-cluded boarders, tenants, or lodgers: We assume the presence of board-ers to mean that the family needed additional income, although we recognize that boarders usually brought in income as well. The fourth measure is a ratio indexing the adequacy of the family's male-derived income for its total consumption needs. The numerator of this ratio is the number of employed adult men in the family, while the de-nominator is a weighted sum of all related individuals in the family, with children weighted less heavily than adults on the ground that their consumption needs were more modest.[8]

---

[6]In creating this subsample, we counted as daughters any female descendants of the household head (such as granddaughter, niece). Most daughters, however, were in fact the head's natural, adopted or stepdaughter.

[7]The rationale for restricting the sample to male-headed households was largely statistical. When female-headed households were included we were unable to use several measures of family economic status without encountering problems of multicollinearity. The rationale for restricting the sample to households containing both daughters and wives was to be able to contrast the impact of family traits on wives' versus daughters' employment without having to worry about the effects of unmeasured variables.

[8]The weights used in the denominator were .55 for children aged 0–4, .65 for chil-dren aged 5–9, and .75 for children aged 10–14. Adults—those 15 and over—were weighted 1.0. We thank Peter Lindert for access to the manuscript of his book, *Fertility and Scarcity in America* (1978). In this book, Lindert assembles age-specific consumption data from a variety of late-nineteenth- and early-twentieth-century surveys, and converts these figures into consumption ratios (expenditures on a child age x as a proportion of expenditures on an adult). To obtain the above weights, we selected the samples that seemed most comparable to the 1880 Essex County population and took averages of the

The fifth and final measure of family economic status is the household head's age. We are interested in this variable because we suspect it was one of the few that may have influenced wives' employment more than daughters'. The traditional definition of a wife's role made employment in times of financial crisis far more acceptable than steady employment designed to compensate for a husband's generally low earnings; wives were expected to manage on what their men earned, unless there was a sudden change in economic status brought about by strikes, unemployment, or illness. In the late nineteenth century, as men moved into their fifties and sixties, a number undoubtedly suffered illness and disabilities that made it difficult for them to maintain their normal level of earnings. When this happened, the wife's employment outside the home may have become more socially acceptable, as well as more necessary financially. If this were the case, then we should see an increase in wives' employment as their husbands grew older.

One additional variable will be used in the analysis. This is whether the household contained children of the head under 5-years-old. Studies of women's employment in western Europe suggest that wives were especially unlikely to work when they had young children (Scott and Tilly, 1974). Whether this was also generally the case in North America has not yet been determined. Since the age of the youngest child in the household is today the strongest determinant of married women's employment (Sweet, 1973), it is of interest to see whether this same variable influenced women's employment a century ago.

Findings

In 1880, the great majority of coresident families in Essex County were nuclear units rather than extended ones, although many were augmented by servants and boarders. The two most common household–family positions held by working-age women were wife to a

---

consumption ratios found in these surveys. (Professor Lindert is in no way to blame for any misuse of his data this may have involved.) Although these weights provide only a crude estimate of age differences in consumption burdens, the numerator of our ratio also provides only a crude estimate of the family's male-derived income. It should be noted that a similar family–income adequacy ratio is used in Kaestle and Vinovskis's analysis of children's schooling in Chapter 5 of this volume.

male household head (42% of our sample) and never-married daughter
of this head (24%). Our typology of family positions distinguishes these
two groups from seven others:

1. Women who were themselves the household head because they
   were widowed;
2. Other female household heads (most of whom were designated
   head because their husbands were disabled or missing);
3. Never-married relatives of the head other than daughters (sisters, cousins, aunts, etc.);
4. All other female relatives of the head;
5. Women with the relationship of "servant" or "servant's relative" to the household head;
6. Women who were boarders, tenants or lodgers and who were
   also married; and
7. All other boarders, tenants, or lodgers (single or widowed).[9]

Our typology thus distinguishes among women according to their marital status, kin relationship to household head, and generational position within the coresident family. Although we are unable to speculate
about all the variations in economic status, cultural norms, and domestic responsibilities associated with these positions that might have influenced women's employment, we expect married women to have
worked in the market less often than the unmarried did, and those
living with kin to have worked less often than those living apart from
their kin.

The percentage gainfully employed in each household–family position is shown in Table 6.1, both for each community in our sample
and for all communities combined. These figures make clear that
enormous variations in women's employment were associated with
household and family position in 1880, even though married women
did not invariably work less often than the unmarried. The lowest
reported rate of gainful employment was, however, for wives of household heads. Less than 5% of these women worked, with, at most, 10%
doing so in Lawrence. In clear contrast were unmarried daughters:
Over half of these women were working in 1880, with this figure ex-
ceeding 75% in Lawrence. Other female relatives were less likely to
work than were unmarried daughters, but were far more likely to work

---

[9]Because of coding errors, there is also a residual category of women with "other"
relationships to the household head.

TABLE 6.1
*Percentage Gainfully Employed by Relationship to Household Head and Community:
Essex Women Ages 15–59, 1880*

Relationship to household head	Total sample	Lawrence	Lynn	Salem	Rural
Wives	4.3	9.9	4.5	2.0	.8
	(2196)[a]	(545)	(598)	(401)	(652)
Single daughters	54.5	75.9	59.8	54.1	28.3
	(1245)	(344)	(286)	(279)	(336)
Other single relatives	47.6	73.9	55.8	47.7	21.0
	(204)	(46)	(52)	(44)	(62)
Other relatives	30.6	46.8	43.7	20.5	15.3
	(242)	(47)	(71)	(39)	(85)
Widowed household heads	24.6	35.6	29.4	19.4	8.3
	(256)	(73)	(68)	(67)	(48)
Other household heads	38.8	56.7	38.9	30.0	17.6
	(103)	(30)	(36)	(20)	(17)
Married boarders, tenants, and lodgers	65.4	80.0	54.1	50.0	36.4
	(162)	(80)	(61)	(10)	(11)
Other boarders, tenants, and lodgers	89.1	95.6	79.6	88.9	48.3
	(469)	(320)	(93)	(27)	(29)
Servants and servants' relatives	89.2	97.9	97.1	98.9	67.4
	(344)	(48)	(105)	(93)	(98)
Other	43.6	22.2	—	76.5	10.0
	(39)	(9)	(3)	(17)	(10)
All women	36.0	54.0	36.6	34.2	16.2
	(5260)	(1542)	(1373)	(997)	(1348)

[a] Numbers shown in parentheses are the base Ns for the percentages above them and to the left.

than were wives. Household heads held a similar position between wives and unmarried daughters.[10]

In general, women who had no kin relationship to the household head worked more often than women living with kin, a fact that most likely reflected the influence that taking up certain forms of employment had on whether women resided at home rather than vice versa. Most domestic servants in 1880 were expected to live with their employer. To find work in textiles, moreover, many young women migrated to communities like Lowell and Lawrence where they lived in

[10]The reader will note that widowed household heads were somewhat less likely to work than were other household heads. Directly standardizing work rates for age does not remove this difference. It would appear that the widowed heads had greater financial resources than did the other female heads and did not have to work as often.

boarding houses or with other families.[11] It is thus not surprising that the servants and boarders in our sample were more often employed than were the women who lived with their kin. What is surprising is the high rate of employment among married boarders. Proportionately more of these women had gainful occupations in 1880 than did the unmarried daughters who were living at home. Marriage per se thus appears to have been less a deterrent to gainful employment than were the domestic responsibilities associated with being the mistress of a household. A married woman would work if she did not have a household of her own.

The figures in Table 6.1 not only suggest the importance of household and family position for women's employment, but also the importance of community of residence. In almost all household–family positions, a job was far more common if the woman resided in Lawrence than if she lived in Lynn, Salem, or one of the five rural towns. Indeed, the only exception to this occurred among servants, who, because their household position was synonymous with their employment, worked at uniformly high rates in all urban communities. The variations in employment associated with community were, however, far smaller than those associated with household–family position. This remains the case even when boarders and servants are ignored.

Table 6.1 thus suggests a typical life-sequence of roles in the late nineteenth century that involved relatively short-term attachment to the labor force for most women. If census data are to be believed, very few women were gainfully employed during childhood and early adolescence.[12] Upon leaving school, a majority of them worked for pay for some period of time, especially if they lived in a community offering numerous employment opportunities for women. Upon marrying, most women appear to have stopped working, or at least, no longer worked full-time or outside of the home; their chances of returning to the job market later in life also appear to have been low. Some widows

[11]In our sample, 72% of all women with unskilled or domestic service occupations had the relationship of "servant" to the household head. This figure suggests that entering service while living at home was uncommon in Essex County. A number of employed women in our sample also had the relationship of boarder or lodger to the household head; in Lawrence, this figure was 44%, while in Lynn and Salem it was 21 and 8%, respectively. Boarding out, while not an inevitable accompaniment of female employment, was fairly common.

[12]Contemporary reports on lax enforcement of child labor laws suggest that low employment rates among girls under 15 may have resulted from lies told to census takers rather than from a lack of participation in the labor force. We have no way of establishing the true rate of employment under age 15, but certainly suspect that employment was far less common at these ages than at later ones.

did work, as did some women whose husbands were disabled or missing, but most did not. There undoubtedly were class differences in this life-course pattern of employment. The high employment rate among married boarders suggests greater lifelong labor-force involvement among low-status women than among higher-status ones. Women from affluent families undoubtedly avoided working for pay altogether. Among women who were neither very poor nor very rich, however, the typical life sequence of roles appears to have been school followed by a combination of domestic activity and paid work, then marriage, and little or only irregular paid work outside of the home.[13]

Although this picture is quite consistent with what we know from other studies (e.g., Groneman, 1977), there is some need to insure that apparent life-course variations in employment are not a spurious reflection of other variables influencing women's work. For example, in our sample household–family position happens to be correlated with ethnicity. Thus, if ethnicity influenced women's work, then the effects of family–household position on work shown in Table 6.1 may be overstated. To insure that we are not seeing spurious effects of this kind, and so that we can assess the relative importance of community versus life-course variables, we turn to multivariate analysis using dummy-variable regressions. This regression technique, which produces estimated percentages employed among various categories of women, allows us to understand the impact on women's employment of each variable net of the effects of all other variables.[14] Because we wish to include servants and unmarried boarders in this analysis, we are unable to use our measures of family economic status. We thus ask how community of residence, household–family position, age, literacy, ethnicity, and generation influenced women's employment. Three regression equations intended to answer this question are shown in Table 6.2. The first two equations are similar except that each employs an

---

[13]Hareven's analysis (1975) of women's work careers derived from longitudinal data in a city dominated by the textile industry (Manchester, New Hampshire) suggests a partly variant pattern to the one derived from the census data. Immigrant women working in textiles continued to hold jobs after their marriages, some sporadically and others consistently. Many were in the reserve labor force, thereby relying on the mill as a source of employment even though they were not working continuously.

[14]In dummy-variable regression (which is often referred to as Multiple Classification Analysis or MCA; see Andrews et al., 1967) all variables are treated as classifications, rather than as numerical scales, each category of a classification being represented by a zero–one variable (the so-called dummy). Use of regression analysis with a dichotomous dependent variable violates the assumptions of the underlying statistical model, thus rendering all tests of statistical significance invalid. These tests are presented only as a rough guideline for interpreting the results.

alternative measure of ethnicity. The third equation is identical in form to the second one, but is estimated for only a subsample of the cases.

Table 6.2 makes clear that differences in women's employment according to household–family position in 1880 were by no means spurious; the estimated percentages in Table 6.2 are almost identical to the percentages seen earlier in Table 6.1. The multiple-partial R^2's (MPR^2's) shown above and to the right of each variable in the second equation also make clear that household–family position accounted for far more variance in female employment than did any other variable: 34% as against 2–4%. Although some of this ability to account for variance is the result of including the unmarried boarders and servants

TABLE 6.2

Estimated Net Percentages Gainfully Employed According to Relationship to Household Head, Age, Place Resided, Ethnicity and Literacy: Regression Analysis, Essex Women Ages 15–59

Independent variables	Total sample			Subsample[a]		Number of cases[b]
	(1)	(2)	MPR^2	(3)	MPR^2	
Relationship to household head			.34*		.20*	
Wife[c]	6.3	6.4		5.6		2235
Single daughter	55.0	54.6		54.3		1245
Single relative	49.0	49.1		48.4		204
Other relative	33.3	33.1		32.1		242
Head	30.8	31.2		30.6		359
Married boarder	58.9	58.6		58.1		162
Other boarder	80.6	80.7		—		469
Servant	88.2	88.5		—		344
Age			.02*		.02*	
15–19	29.3	28.6		17.2		772
20–24	43.0	42.5		34.1		955
25–29	38.7	38.6		28.9		773
30–39	37.9	38.1		28.9		1173
40–49	34.6	35.2		25.7		928
50–59	29.1	29.5		20.6		659
Place resided			.04*		.03*	
Lawrence	45.1	45.7		35.7		1542
Lynn	38.4	38.1		28.9		1373
Salem	34.3	34.0		23.6		997
Rural	24.4	24.2		16.7		1348

TABLE 6.2 (continued)

Independent variables	Total sample			Subsample[a]		Number of cases[b]
	(1)	(2)	MPR²	(3)	MPR²	
Ethnicity[d]						
French Canadian	47.9	—		—		295
Irish	41.9	—		—		1295
English	39.3	—		—		382
English Canadian	33.6	—		—		276
Other (non-U.S.A.)	40.7	—		—		147
U.S.A.	31.6	—		—		2825
Ethnicity/generation			.02*		.02*	
French Canadian/first	—	49.6		41.7		266
French Canadian/second	—	30.9		19.4		29
Irish/first	—	38.7		29.2		868
Irish/second	—	47.7		40.5		427
Other/first	—	37.7		28.8		554
Other/second	—	37.2		27.7		251
U.S.A.	—	31.7		21.7		2825
Literacy			.00		.00	
Can read and write	36.3	36.2		26.6		
Other	31.5	32.4		21.7		
Equation R²	.480	.481		.352		5220
Total percentage gainfully employed	36.0	36.0		26.3		5260

*The increment in the R² when this classification is added to the regression would be significant, .05 level, were the assumptions of the test met. All numbers in these columns are multiple-partial R²s. These measure the proportion of the variance in women's employment not explained by the other variables that each variable can explain. The MPR²s for a given regression equation do not normally sum to the equation R².

[a] This subsample excludes unmarried boarders and servants.

[b] The number of cases shown is for the total sample. The total N varies across variables because of missing data. The total sample has 5260 cases (5220 of which have data on ethnic group) while the subsample has 4447 cases (4418 of which have data on ethnic group). The smaller Ns are used in computing statistical tests.

[c] This category includes 39 women with a relationship to the household head other than those listed in the table.

[d] U.S.-born women are classified as second generation if either of their parents were born abroad. They are classified as third generation or higher only if they and both parents were born in the U.S. and its territories. Women are categorized as belonging to a particular ethnicity if they were born in the country of origin, if both of their parents were born there, or if one parent was born there and the other was born in the U.S. Women born in the U.S. whose parents were born in different non-U.S. countries are classified under "other (non-U.S.)" (e.g., one parent born in Ireland, the other in England). English stock includes England, Scotland and Wales.

in the analysis (women whose distinct family–household positions were largely determined by the fact that they were employed) the MPR^2 of .20 in the third equation, which excludes unmarried boarders and servants, shows that family–household position was still the most important determinant of employment.

In addition to household–family position, a woman's age had an independent influence on whether she worked, as the second set of percentages in Table 6.2 shows. Between ages 15–19 and 20–24, the percentage of women at work rose by more than 14 points; it then declined at later ages, especially after age 49. Although we do not show the figures here, this age profile of employment was more marked among unmarried women than among wives; explanations for it should therefore refer primarily to unmarried women.

Two obvious explanations for the age profile were decreasing school attendance between ages 15–19 and 20–24 and the increasing difficulty of obtaining employment between ages 40–49 and 50–59, either because of employers' prejudices against older workers (Oppenheimer, 1970) or because of the physical difficulties women in their fifties may have had doing certain kinds of paid work. While the latter factors may account for the dropoff in women's employment after age 49, school attendance cannot account for its rise between ages 15–19 and 20–24. We know that at least one-quarter of the 15–19-year-olds in our sample were neither in school nor at work in 1880; the decline in the proportion enrolled between 15–19 and 20–24 thus seems an unlikely explanation for the rise in employment. We would suggest that part of the explanation for this rise involved a shift with age in the family's utilization of daughters in their internal division of labor. It would appear that many daughters were first employed at home, helping with chores and looking after younger children, only later entering the labor force.

The precise circumstances bringing this about probably varied among families. Some parents may have considered work in service or a mill too dangerous or immoral to permit their daughters to do it until they were older. Others may have demanded that a daughter help pay her way by working only after she had been out of school for several years and clearly was not about to get married. In still other families, it may have been the daughters themselves who became tired of being at home full time and who sought employment as an escape from their domestic confines. In other families, it may simply have been that by the time the daughter was 20, her younger brothers and sisters were in school and her help in the home consequently no longer needed.[15] Whatever the specific reason for 15–19-year-olds being at home more than 20–24-year-olds, it would appear there were subtle life-course variations in women's employment beyond those associated with the major transitions in marital and family roles. For many unmarried women, the typical life-sequence of roles involved schooling followed by domestic employment, then market work.

Although the strongest effects on employment in Table 6.2 are associated with life-course variables, the community variables have important effects on women's work, too. Place of residence was strongly associated with women's employment. Lawrence women were most likely to have jobs, while rural women were least likely to have them. To some extent, these community differences in employment may have reflected the impact of local job opportunities on patterns of in- and out-migration among young women, rather than their impact on the employment decisions of resident women. The third equation in Table 6.2, however, suggests that job opportunities also influenced local women's work. This equation pertains only to women who were unlikely to have migrated to or from a community specifically to find employment; the community differences in employment are almost identical to those seen in earlier equations.

Women's ethnic backgrounds also appear to have influenced their likelihood of working, although in ways that were somewhat complex. In general, French-Canadian women had the highest rates of employment, while English-Canadians and native Americans had the lowest rates (women of English, Irish, and other European stock were intermediate). The higher rates among French-Canadians probably reflected their disproportionate chances of entering the United States with a job already guaranteed, while the low rates among English-Canadians and third-generation Americans probably reflected their higher-than-average economic status. Although these patterns make sense, the second equation in Table 6.2 makes clear that they varied considerably between first- and second-generation women. Among French-Canadians, for example, it was only the foreign-born who had high employment rates; second-generation French-Canadians had extremely low rates. Likewise, among the Irish it was only the foreign-born who worked at intermediate rates; second-generation Irish women worked almost as frequently as did women born in French Canada.

---

[15]Results from the analysis of male-headed households contradict this last idea. In that analysis, unmarried daughters were less likely to work outside of the home in families without young children than in those with infants or toddlers.

Since these estimates take into account underlying differences between ethnic groups in women's family positions, ages, and literacy levels, they must be explained in other terms. We are unable to understand the low employment rates among second-generation French-Canadians, although it makes sense that these women worked less frequently than did their mothers, many of whom came to the United States specifically to take up employment. The higher employment rates of second-generation Irish women compared with women born in Ireland may be one example of conservative attitudes about women's employment among the foreign-born. Women born in the United States of Irish parents may have been less reluctant to work outside of the home than were their foreign-born mothers because they were more assimilated to American values. If this was the case, however, then the hold of the family over Irish women would appear to have been considerably weaker than the hold of Italian families over their daughters.

The only variable in Table 6.2 with virtually no influence on women's employment was literacy. The few Essex women who in 1880 were unable to both read and write worked somewhat less often than other women did, but the differences were extremely small. Whether literacy had greater importance in interaction with family economic status remains to be seen.

This first analysis of the 1880 data thus suggests the paramount importance of life-course variables for Essex women's employment. While a majority of young, unmarried women were gainfully employed, only a tiny minority of wives were employed regularly enough to report themselves as having a gainful occupation or trade. Community of residence was also important for whether women worked, as was their ethnicity. Neither of these variables, however, was as important as life-course position.

While this first analysis suggests the overwhelming significance of the life course for women's employment, we have yet to assess the impact on work of family economic status. How community and familial characteristics differentially affected the employment of daughters and wives also remains unexplored. In order to take up these issues, we now turn to the data for male-headed households. In dealing with this sample, we treat the household itself as the unit of analysis and thus analyze two dependent variables: the percentage of daughters in a household who were gainfully employed, and the percentage of other adult women in the family who were gainfully employed.[16] (The two

---

[16]Because most households had only one other adult woman, the percentage of these women employed is usually either zero or 100; this variable is thus a dichotomy for all practical purposes.

are also combined to form a summary variable measuring the percentage of all adult women employed.) We now use regression analysis in which the predictors of gainful employment are treated both as categoric variables and as scaled variables.[17] The coefficients for the former are net deviations from the total percentage employed, while the coefficients for the latter are slopes stating the number of units of change in the dependent variable for each unit of change in the independent variable. Because of problems of multicollinearity, the age distribution of the daughters in the household is not included in the analysis.[18] Preliminary regressions indicated, however, that daughters' ages had the same impact on their gainful employment in the male-headed sample as they had in the total sample of all working-age women (the more daughters aged 20–24, rather than younger or older, the higher the proportion of daughters employed). The regression analysis of the male-headed households is shown in Table 6.3.

Although the variables in this analysis can account for only one-quarter of the variance in daughters' work and for almost none of the variance in wives' work, the regression results nonetheless make clear the importance of family economic status for women's employment, especially for daughters'. Among daughters, the five measures of economic status included in our regressions all have the expected relationship to employment. As the first set of coefficients in Table 6.3 shows, the higher the socioeconomic status of the father, the lower the proportion of daughters employed. (The especially low rate of employment among farm daughters may have reflected the economic self-sufficiency of farm families, rather than an unusually high level of affluence among these families.) Likewise, as the negative coefficient for the income adequacy ratio suggests, the more money that male family members brought into the household (relative to what the household needed to survive), the fewer the daughters who went out to work. In addition, households with servants had fewer daughters in the labor force than did households without servants, and those taking in boarders had somewhat more daughters at work than did other households. (The weakness of this latter relationship may reflect the fact that boarders brought income into the family and were thus partial substi-

[17]The categoric variables are head's occupation, the presence of servants and of boarders in the household, whether the household had an illiterate daughter, community of residence, and ethnicity. The scaled variables are the income–adequacy index and the head of household's age. To allow the latter variable to have a curvilinear relationship to women's work, we enter it into the regressions both in linear and in squared form.

[18]For the same reason, the measure of whether there were children under 5 cannot be included in the general regressions. We report on this variable later in this chapter.

TABLE 6.3

Multiple Regression Analysis of Daughters' versus Wives' Employment as a Function of Household Characteristics (Male-Headed Essex Households)[a]

Independent variables	Percentage of all women employed	MPR²	Percentage of never-married daughters employed	MPR²	Percentage of wives employed	MPR²
Head's occupation[b]		.02*		.02*		.01
Unskilled	6.5		9.3		−1.0	
Semiskilled	4.5		7.7		−.08	
WC, craft[b]	−2.5		−2.7		−2.0	
Professional, etc.[c]	−4.0		−8.4		3.3	
Farm	−5.0		−9.9		1.9	
Other, none	1.4		5.7		1.7	
		.01*		.00		.00
Income adequacy ratio[d]	−26.7		−18.9		−8.0	
		.01*		.01*		.00
Whether servants	−9.8		−14.0		−3.9	
		.01		.00		.00
Whether boarders	4.9		5.6		2.2	
Head's age		.02*		.01		.02*
Linear	.17		−.12		−1.43	
Squared	0		.01		.02	
[minimum]	[−]		[12]		[48]	
Place resided		.04		.04		.01
Lawrence	4.8		8.8		1.3	
Lynn	5.8		8.8		3.0	
Salem	−.8		−2.0		−1.3	
Rural	−8.4		−13.6		−2.7	

tutes for daughters' employment.[19]) The household head's age also influenced the probability that his daughters worked; the older the head, the more daughters worked. For example, when the head was 60-years-old, 11% more of his daughters held jobs than when he was 40-years-old. Although some of this increase may have been due to the

[19]Taking in boarders was, of course, a common way in which housewives contributed to family income without entering the outside labor force. For example, close to one-fifth of the male-headed households in Essex County had boarders or lodgers. Although we do not treat the presence of boarders as gainful employment for the wife in this analysis, it is clear that many wives helped to improve the family's finances through this practice.

TABLE 6.3 (*continued*)

Independent variables	Percentage of all women employed	MPR²	Percentage of never-married daughters employed	MPR²	Percentage of wives employed	MPR²
Generation[e]		.08*		.06*		.01
First generation	15.9		21.7		2.8	
Second, Irish	8.4		14.1		−2.6	
Second, other	.1		−2.7		1.5	
Third or higher	−6.7		−9.3		−.5	
		.00		.01		.00
Whether an illiterate daughter	−8.6		−17.2		−.9	
Intercept	11.7		31.6		39.3	
R²	283		.247		.050	
Total percentage employed	29.6		49.1		4.9	
N	662		662		662	

*Increment in R^2 when this variable is added to the regression would be significant, .05 level, were the assumptions of the test met.

[a] The coefficients shown in the table for head's occupation, place resided, and generation are estimated net deviations from the total percentage employed, shown at the bottom of the table. The coefficients for servants, boarders, and illiterate daughters are estimated net deviations from the opposite category (those households without servants, boarders, or an illiterate daughter). The remaining coefficients are the usual metric regression coefficients.

[b] Includes men with white collar and skilled craft occupations.

[c] Includes men with professional, managerial, and nonfarm proprietary occupations.

[d] The numerator of this ratio is the number of employed male relatives in the household. The denominator is the weighted sum of all related persons in the household, children 0–4 being weighted .55, those 5–9, .65 and those 10–14, .75 (all adults are weighted 1.0).

[e] The generation is that of the unmarried daughter(s). If any of these daughters was born abroad, then the household is classified as first generation. If none of the daughters was born abroad, but at least one parent was, then the household is classified as second generation. It is classified as third generation only if all daughters and all parents were born in the U.S.

daughters' coming of age, it seems likely that it was also due to the father's declining income.

Because so few wives worked, the variations in their employment associated with varying family economic statuses were necessarily small.[20] Even taking this into account, however, it would still appear that family economic status had a much greater impact on daughters'

[20] The extreme skew in the percentage of wives gainfully employed makes it likely that some of the results found in Table 6.3 would be statistically significant were a more appropriate estimation technique used. Unfortunately, time did not permit reestimation of the equations for wives' work using such a technique.

employment than on wives', something that suggests relatively uniform standards for a wife's role across socioeconomic strata. The one exception was the household head's age, which accounted for more variance in wives' work than in daughters'. The relationship between a man's age and his wife's likelihood of working was curvilinear. Up until age 48, his wife's chances of working declined somewhat each year, but after his forty-eighth birthday, her chances of working started to increase, almost doubling between ages 60 and 70. This pattern seems quite consistent with the idea that a wife's full-time employment was far more acceptable if her husband was sick or disabled than if he was young and healthy but unable to earn a good living. One way to test this interpretation is to see whether the age pattern of wive's employment was more pronounced in families that had low incomes to begin with than in families with greater economic resources. If declining income associated with husband's age produced the relationship with wife's work seen in Table 6.3, then the rise in her work during her husband's old age should have been more pronounced in poor families than in wealthier ones.

Although Table 6.3 suggests the importance of family economic status for female employment, especially for daughters' employment, it again shows the importance of community and ethnicity as well. The relationships observed for these variables in male-headed households, however, are somewhat different from those observed earlier among all working-age women. First, in the male-headed households, although both daughters and wives were less likely to work if they lived in a rural community than in an urban one, their chances of working were no higher if they lived in Lawrence than in Lynn—a clear difference from the earlier results, which showed higher work rates in Lawrence. This change in the relationship of community to employment may reflect the somewhat higher-than-average economic status of male-headed households. We may thus find the original rank-ordering between Lawrence and Lynn if we examine low-status families, and find higher work rates in Lynn than in Lawrence among the higher-status families.

Because there are fewer cases in the present analysis than in the first one and because these cases are disproportionately American and Irish, we are able to use only four ethnic categories in this analysis. These categories are (a) families in which at least one daughter was born abroad; (b) those from Ireland whose daughters were all born in the United States; (c) those from other foreign countries whose daughters were all United States-born; and (d) those in which both the parents and all daughters were American-born. This grouping is not directly comparable with the ones used earlier. Nevertheless, it is clear from Table 6.3 that the tendency for Irish-born women to work less frequently than their American-born descendants is no longer observed in these households. In the male-headed households, first-generation women were more likely to be employed than were second-generation women, both Irish and other, a pattern that is more consistent with an economic interpretation than with a cultural one. It is consequently questionable whether the ethnic groups found in Essex County in the late 1800s varied significantly in their outlook towards women's roles.

The final variable appearing in Table 6.3 is literacy. Although by no means having as strong an influence on daughters' employment as other variables, literacy status has a stronger relationship to women's work in this analysis than in the earlier one for all Essex women. This may reflect the higher-than-average status of the households involved in this analysis. If illiterate daughters earned less than literate ones, this variation in wages may have been especially important to relatively well-off parents. To ascertain whether this was the case requires that we analyze high- and low-status families separately.

The variable measuring whether there were young children at home does not appear in Table 6.3. However, a special set of regressions (not given) shows that young children's presence had little effect on wives' employment.[21] Mothers with young children were somewhat less likely to work outside the home than were mothers without young children, but the difference between the two groups in proportion employed was only 2 percentage points. The failure of young children's presence to influence the mother's employment may, of course, reflect the presence in all of these households of working-age daughters, girls whom the mother could send to work in place of herself even when no small children were in the home. However, the percentage of wives employed in the male-headed sample, 4.9%, is if anything slightly higher than the percentage employed among all Essex wives, 4.3%. The results for the presence of young children are thus unlikely to be unique to households containing both working-age daughters and mothers.

Although the analysis presented in Table 6.3 makes clear that women's employment was affected by family economic status, it does not make clear whether economic status was more or less important for

[21]The young children variable (like the daughters' age variable mentioned earlier) is highly correlated with the income–adequacy ratio and consequently the two cannot be included in the same regression. To analyze the impact of small children on their mother's employment, we excluded the income–adequacy ratio from the analysis, but retained all the other variables shown in Table 6.3.

women's participation in the labor force than was life-course position or the community's industrial and occupational structure. The measures of family economic status in Table 6.3 clearly account for less variance in women's work than do the measures of life-course position in Table 6.2. But to conclude that economic status had less impact on women's employment could be misleading for two reasons. First, as we noted earlier, the estimates of socioeconomic differences in female employment shown in Table 6.3 are likely to be too small, not only because of the exclusion of servants and boarders from the analysis, but also because by focusing on male-headed households we are probably excluding many of the poorest families from our consideration. Second, it is difficult to disentangle culturally based life-course effects on employment from economic effects. For example, the greater tendency for widows than wives to have worked, although associated with life-cycle position, was probably caused by differences in economic status rather than by social norms about women's roles in distinct phases of the life course. The most we can conclude is that life-course position and family economic status were both important determinants of women's employment in 1880.

We have raised several questions about differences in the determinants of women's work between high- and low-status families: Whether head's age affected wives' employment more in poor families than in wealthier ones; whether employment was more common in Lynn than in Lawrence among better-off families, while being more common in Lawrence among the less well-off ones; and whether illiterate daughters were especially unlikely to work in better-off households. To answer these questions, we have subdivided the households in our sample according to the head of household's occupation. Because the status of men with farm and unknown occupations is ambiguous, households headed by men with these occupations are excluded from the analysis. Regression equations examining the employment of daughters and wives within high- and low-status groups are shown in Table 6.4.

The results for household head's age are consistent with our earlier interpretation. In low-status families, daughters and especially wives were increasingly likely to work outside the home as the head grew older. In higher-status families, however, the age of the husband or father made little difference for female employment, at least when compared with the lower-status homes. A decline in men's incomes with increasing age, especially in low-status families, appears to have been an important factor in sending wives as well as daughters into the labor force.

The results for community of residence seen in Table 6.4 are also consistent with our earlier speculations. Daughters in high-status

tiple Regression Analysis of Daughters' and Wives' Employment as a Function of Household
racteristics, Separately by Head's Occupational Status (Male-Headed Essex Households)[a]

Independent variable	Percentage of daughters employed				Percentage of wives employed			
	High status	MPR²	Low status	MPR²	High status	MPR²	Low status	MPR²
d's occupation		.00		.00		.01		.00
nskilled	—		1.9		—		-.3	
emiskilled	—		-.9		—		.2	
VC, craft[b]	.1		—		-1.8		—	
rofessional, etc.[c]	-.2		—		3.0		—	
arm	—		—		—		—	
ther, none	—		—		—		—	
		.00		.02		.00		.01
ome adequacy ratio	-.8		-47.6		3.8		-18.5	
		.03*		.00		.00		.00
vants	-23.9		-16.3		-2.0		-5.0	
		.01		.01		.01		.00
rders	9.5		9.5		3.7		3.1	
d's age		.00		.03*		.01		.05*
inear	-1.30		.66		-1.17		-2.74	
quared	.01		0		.01		.03	
Maximum/minimum]	[54]		[—]		[49]		[49]	
ce resided		.02		.07*		.01		.03
awrence	1.8		10.0		-.7		1.4	
ynn	7.7		6.1		1.7		3.6	
alem	-3 3		-4.4		.3		-5.0	
ural	-8.9		-23.3		-2.1		-4.0	
eration		.07*		.04*		.00		.01
irst	22.4		11.6		-2.4		3.1	
econd	13.8		1.6		2.0		-1.5	
hird or higher	-9.4		-11.1		-.4		-1.1	
		.00		.02*		.01		.00
ether an illiterate aughter	.5		-26.9		16.7		-2.0	
rcept	83.0		27.7		28.4		67.4	
	.147		.228		.046		.112	
al percentage mployed	42.6		64.9		4.5		5.2	
	286		249		286		249	

*Increment in the R^2 when this variable is added to the regression would be significant, .05 level, were assumptions of the test met.

[a] The households designated high status are those in which the head had a professional, managerial, white ar, or skilled craft occupation. Those designated low status are those in which he had an unskilled or semi- ed occupation. Farm households and households headed by men with other or unknown occupations are uded from this analysis.

[b] Includes men with white collar and skilled craft occupations.

[c] Includes men with professional, managerial, and nonfarm proprietary occupations.

families were more likely to work if they lived in Lynn than in Lawrence, while among daughters from low-status homes the reverse was true. It thus appears that the availability of numerous but low-paying jobs in Lawrence was insufficient to attract many daughters from higher-status homes into the labor force. Only the relatively well-paying jobs available in Lynn made work attractive enough to these women to cause them to enter the work force in large numbers. The high wages offered to shoe workers in Lynn may also have accounted for the somewhat greater proportion of wives at work in Lynn than elsewhere. However, the greater availability of work that could be done in the home may have been equally important.[22] In any case, these results suggest strongly that it was more than the number of jobs that communities offered to women that influenced whether they worked. The wages attached to jobs were also important, especially when measured against the additional income that a woman's family needed.

The results for literacy in Table 6.4 are somewhat unexpected; it was in low-status homes, rather than in higher status ones, that literacy had the greatest impact on daughters' employment. This finding may reflect little more than the virtual absence of illiterate daughters from higher-status homes. The literacy variable is treacherously close to being a constant for those households, something that makes a weak correlation unsurprising. Also, the difference between what an illiterate and a literate daughter could earn may have been so small that it was important only to families with relatively low incomes. Thus, these findings, although contrary to expectations, may nonetheless be consistent with the notion that wage levels and family income interacted with each other in determining women's employment.

The impact of the remaining variables in Table 6.4 on women's work varied between the high- and low-status families. For example, the income–adequacy ratio was more important for women's work in low-status families than in high-status ones, while the presence of servants was more important in the high-status homes. While speculation might be offered for each of these differences, we are inclined to regard them as chance occurrences. The income–adequacy ratio, the servants and boarders measures, and even the measure of ethnicity can all be regarded as imperfect, alternative measures of socioeconomic status. That some happen to predict daughters' employment more strongly in high-

[22]Although the stitching of uppers had by 1880 become largely an operation done in factories, rather than in the home (Hazard, 1921), Lynn nevertheless had many more women working at home in 1875 than did either Lawrence or Salem (Census of Massachusetts, 1875). This may have helped to account for the somewhat greater employment of wives in Lynn than elsewhere (cf. Groneman, 1977).

status families than in low-status ones, while others operate in the reverse manner, does not therefore strike us as having had great significance. Taken together, the results for these variables suggest that within both the high- and the low-status strata, further distinctions in socioeconomic status were important for women's employment.

Conclusion

This chapter has suggested the importance of life-course, community, and family economic factors for women's employment in the late nineteenth century. The roles and responsibilities that married women normally assumed made steady or full-time labor force participation difficult; most wives who were mistresses of their own households consequently did not report having a gainful occupation or trade in 1880. On the other hand, young, unmarried women in the transitional state between schooling and marriage worked in large numbers, especially if they came from a low-status family and lived in a town offering large numbers of jobs to women. Ethnic group and generation also affected women's work patterns, but seemingly for reasons other than cultural values about women's roles. Essex County had only English, Canadian, and Irish immigrants in large numbers in 1880 and thus cannot be regarded as having been a complete microcosm of late nineteenth-century American ethnic groups. Nevertheless, the tendency for ethnic variations in female employment to follow along economic lines rather than along cultural ones in Essex County raises questions about the significance of cultural factors for variations in women's work in the United States as a whole. An understanding of this issue must await studies that compare a number of ethnic groups across a wide range of communities. In Essex County, however, it would appear that life-course stage, community, and family economic status were far more important for women's employment than were variations in cultural values associated with ethnicity.

Our analysis has also suggested that distinct considerations often entered into the employment decisions of daughters and wives. In general, wives' work was less responsive to family and community conditions than was daughters' work. Whether a daughter worked was strongly determined by her age, her family's economic status, and her community's occupational structure. A wife's work, however, was little influenced by her age and by most other factors as well, including whether she had small children at home. There appears to have been only one important exception to this rule: Wives were influenced more strongly by the husband's age than were daughters. This suggests that one condition that made wives' work both necessary and socially acceptable was when a husband's normal earning ability was temporarily impaired. In other circumstances, if wives contributed to family income, it was typically by taking in boarders or doing other work at home rather than by entering the labor force as their daughters did.

Finally, this chapter has also confirmed that women's work was influenced not only by family economic status and by wage levels, but by the interaction of these two factors as well. We at least saw that women from higher-status homes were more likely to work in the community offering high wages than in the community that offered the largest number of jobs, while the reverse was the case among lower-status daughters. The economic principles that governed decisions about women's work in the late 1800s thus appear to be quite similar to those governing such decisions today. What has changed is the women most likely to work. One hundred years ago, it was unmarried daughters who composed the majority of the female labor force while today it is mothers and wives.

While this chapter has provided a useful picture of women's participation in market work during the late 1800s, it has ignored a number of important issues. For one thing, the view we have provided is cross-sectional rather than longitudinal and thus leaves unclear the dynamics of historical change in women's work. To be sure, by understanding the determinants of female employment at one point in time, we may make it possible to understand why women's work changed over time. For example, the tendency for immigrant women to seek employment may help to explain the rise in female labor-force participation during the first decades of the twentieth century when the population was greatly swelled by immigration. Analyses that focus directly on the dynamics of change are needed, however. Also, as we noted at the start of this chapter, women labored at many kinds of work in the late nineteenth century, not just the work that was recorded on census forms as a gainful occupation or trade. If we are to understand the full nature of women's economic roles in this period of history, we need to explore their participation in all productive work, not just that done in the factory, shop, and school.

Acknowledgments

Funds for this research were provided by the Mathematical Social Sciences Board of the National Science Foundation and by the Population Studies Center, University of Michigan. The authors thank Deborah Freedman, Louise Tilly, the members of the Eco-

nomic Demography Seminar at the University of Michigan, and the participants in the
MSSB workshops on family history for their helpful comments on earlier drafts.

References

Abbott, Edith
    1910   Women in Industry. New York: Appleton.
Andrews, Frank, J. N. Morgan, John A. Sonquist, and Laura Klem
    1967   Multiple Classification Analysis. Ann Arbor: University of Michigan Survey Research Center.
Bowen, William G., and T. Aldrich Finegan
    1969   The Economics of Labor Force Participation. Princeton: Princeton University Press.
Census of Massachusetts
    1875   Manufactures and Occupations. Volume II. Boston: Massachusetts Bureau of Labor Statistics.
Groneman, Carol
    1977   "'She earns as a child; she pays as a man': women workers in a mid-nineteenth-century New York City community." Pp. 83–100 in Milton Cantor and Bruce Laurie (eds.), Class, Sex, and the Woman Worker. Westport, Connecticut: Greenwood Press.
Hareven, Tamara K.
    1975   "Family time and industrial time: family and work in a planned corporation town, 1900–1924." Journal of Urban History 1:365–389.
Hazard, Blanch
    1921   The Organization of the Boot and Shoe Industry in Massachusetts Before 1875. Cambridge, Massachusetts: Harvard University Press.
Kleinberg, Susan J.
    1977   "The systematic study of urban women." Pp. 20–42 in Milton Cantor and Bruce Laurie (eds.), Class, Sex and the Woman Worker. Westport, Connecticut: Greenwood Press.
Lindert, Peter H.
    1978   Fertility and Scarcity in America. Princeton: Princeton University Press.
Long, Clarence D.
    1958   The Labor Force Under Changing Income and Employment. Princeton: Princeton University Press.
Oppenheimer, Valerie K.
    1970   The Female Labor Force in the United States. Berkeley: University of California, Population Monograph Series, No. 5.
Pleck, Elizabeth H.
    1978   "A mother's wages: income earning among married Black and Italian women, 1896–1911." Pp. 490–510 in Michael Gordon (ed.), The American Family in Socio-Historical Perspective. Second edition. New York: St. Martin's Press.
Scott, Joan, and Louise Tilly
    Unpub-   "Daughters, wives, mothers, workers: peasants and working class women
    lished   in the transition to an industrial economy in France." Paper presented at The Second Berkshire Conference on the History of Women, October, 1974.

Smuts, Robert W.
    1959   Women and Work in America. New York: Columbia University Press.
Sweet, James A.
    1973   Women in the Labor Force. New York: Seminar Press.
Vinovskis, Maris A.
    1970   "Horace Mann on the economic productivity of education." New England
            Quarterly 43 (4, December): 550–571.
Yans-McLaughlin, Virginia
    1974   "A flexible tradition: South Italian immigrants confront a new work ex-
            perience." Journal of Social History 7 (Summer): 429–445.
    1977   "Italian women and work: experience and perception." Pp. 101–119 in
            Milton Cantor and Bruce Laurie (eds.), Class, Sex, and the Woman Worker.
            Westport, Connecticut: Greenwood Press.

7

Family Transitions into Old Age

HOWARD P. CHUDACOFF
TAMARA K. HAREVEN

Our investigation of the later years of life in the second half of the nineteenth century focuses on two questions: (*a*) What were the changes in household and family structure of the aged? and (*b*) What were the functions of old people in the family, and how did they contribute resources to the family over the life course? To pursue these questions, we will examine patterns of household structure of older people in Essex County along two major lines: the position of older people in the household and patterns of kin interaction.

The only historical studies to date that identify some of these patterns are those focusing on the colonial American family. Demos (1970), Greven (1970), and Smith (1973:419–420), have documented the power which parents exerted over their progeny in colonial America. By holding on to family estates, fathers were able to control the careers of their adult sons and to delay their marriages and establishment of independent families. This suggests power and control, but also reveals the insecurities and anxieties of old people for their future support. These anxieties were expressed in wills, in particular, where fathers imposed on their sons a series of provisions for parental support in old age in exchange for property promised in inheritance. In rural society, the distance between the families of orientation and procrea-

217

TRANSITIONS
The Family and the Life Course in
Historical Perspective

tion was smaller, allowing a continuity of interaction between parents and children which extended beyond the children's marriage.

None of the historical studies have explicitly examined the family arrangements of individuals in the later years of life and the extent of their relationships with kin. We propose to analyze some aspects of the family and household status of the aged, and their interaction with other family members in late nineteenth-century communities, by exploring the changing patterns of household structure of individuals older than 50 who headed their own households. By necessity, our analysis is also limited to household data, which is cross-sectional by its very nature. We are inferring, therefore, longitudinal patterns from cross-sectional information. We base our analysis on the following assumptions:

1. The nineteenth-century urban population which we are studying did not experience clear transitions between adult family-cycle stages; the empty-nest stage, for example, which is a characteristic feature of the life course in current society, rarely occurred in the period studied here. Even though sons and daughters were reaching adulthood as their parents entered the later years, the family and household did not dissolve. Urban families continue to maintain the antonomy of their households through the persistence of children in the home or through the addition of surrogate kin.

2. An increase in the numbers and proportions of old people who were living with others did not necessarily indicate a growing dependency among old people, if dependency is defined as being a burden or lacking in reciprocal abilities.[1] Rather, much of the pattern of household extension was characterized by mutual support and assistance between older and younger generations. This assumption forms the basis for our hypothesis that in 1860 and 1880 in Essex County large numbers of older people assumed important community and family functions by sharing the housing space that they controlled with younger family members or strangers.

3. Household composition depends not only upon the internal conditions of the family, but also upon influences and exigencies arising from societal and economic contexts in the commu-

---

[1]For elaboration of this definition, see Clark (1969); also Troll (1971:263–290). For a discussion of aging in American society, see Hareven (1976).

nity.[2] Thus, we hypothesize strong interrelationships between family patterns and community growth, the business cycle, and local housing markets.

One critical element in the historical analysis of kinship is the control and exchange of resources by and between kin. As modern studies have suggested, family resources, whether they be land, money, time, or some other asset, become crucial factors in times of crisis. Times of stress on an individual family, such as illness and death, and periods of societal crisis, such as war or economic depression, have tended to push family members into more interdependent relationships (Litwak, 1965; Sussman and Burchinal, 1959:333–340; Rosser and Harris, 1965; Adams, 1968; Hill, 1970; Sussman, 1977; Hareven, 1977). These relationships, which have received little historical attention, raise important questions about family adaptability. How, for example, did an imbalance in resources between generations affect family members at different points along the life-course continuum? Were steps taken to equalize resources by means of exchange between generations? Our research suggests that one important manifestation of exchange involving old people as "resource suppliers" occurred in the area of housing.

Data and Methods

This chapter employs the census data for eight select communities in Essex County used throughout this book, as well as supplementary materials relating directly to our particular approach and hypotheses. We have used the 1860 and 1880 Essex County census samples to identify various conditions of the aged in different communities and to compare the derived patterns with those of other age groups. For purposes of definition, we have adopted the convention of considering age 55 as old age in our analysis. This definition is admittedly arbitrary and differs from the twentieth-century boundary, which is usually 65. From the viewpoint of the nineteenth-century family, age 55 has some application, because family dissolution would have normally started at this age.

Our analysis of the census samples involved separate tables for Salem, Lawrence, and Lynn, and joint tables for Boxford, Hamilton, Lynnfield, Topsfield, and Wenham. This last category combines the

[2]For elaboration of this hypothesis, see Chudacoff (1977).

agricultural communities of Boxford and Hamilton with Lynnfield, which, at the time, had developed the characteristics of a suburb of Lynn. We see, however, some justification for aggregating these nonurban places. No rural community in Essex County was purely agricultural in character, and for our purposes the social and economic contrasts between the five smaller towns on the one hand and three urban, industrial places on the other were more salient than any similarities.

Whenever possible, we used published aggregate census data to reinforce and to extend the individual samples, particularly for analysis of comparative patterns between age groups and for identification of social and demographic trends within separate communities. Age and sex distributions from Massachusetts state censuses of 1865, 1875, and 1885, and from the 1860 federal census, were especially useful since the 1870 and 1880 federal censuses did not include age by sex breakdowns for individual communities. The aggregate censuses also provided generally uniform information on family size and the number of dwellings in each community.

Other documentary sources were less helpful for our purpose. However, of these, newspapers and deed records were the most useful. *The Essex County Mercury* and *The Salem Gazette* provided much of the information on local conditions, particularly for the onset and impact of the business depression in the 1870s. Most local news reports, however, consisted of announcements and gossip; the papers very rarely presented statistics or analysis of local conditions. Information on trends in local housing markets was even more scarce. Neither the Essex Institute nor the Essex County courthouse has collected data on residential real estate transactions, housing starts, vacancy rates, or other possible indicators; and newspapers did not yet publish advertisements that might have yielded some information about housing availability, prices, and rents. Faced with a lack of direct information, we tried to construct a rough gauge of local housing markets from annual numbers of deeds recorded for property in Salem and Lynn. These indexes were derived from tabulations of 10% samples taken from grantor index books.[3]

---

[3]There were no summaries of annual numbers of deeds recorded in any Essex County town under examination. The index books listed all deeds recorded in the country between 1853 and 1879. The entries were arranged alphabetically by name of grantor and included the location of the property and year of record. There are 29 index books for these years, each with several thousand entries. We randomly selected 3 of the books and tabulated for each year between 1860 and 1879 the total number of deeds recorded in Salem and Lynn. We assume that this selection yielded an approximate 10% sample of all deeds recorded in these towns during the years under examination, and thus our estimates of annual totals are reasonably accurate.

In order to set the eight sampled communities within the total context of all 35 Essex County towns in the period under examination, we have attempted to identify what town-level variables most closely related to incidences of old age. We began by running multiple regressions of several variables on the proportion of people in older age groups in each town. Using aggregate data from the 1875 Massachusetts census, we chose as dependent variables the proportion of each town's population that was aged 55 and above, that which was aged 60 and above, and that which was aged 75 and above. We then experimented with a number of independent variables, regressing them on our separate dependent variables.

These regressions have suggested that two primary variables and three secondary variables were the strongest "influencing factors" in determining the proportion of old people in any of the 35 Essex County towns. The two primary factors were the proportion of the population that was foreign-born and the proportion of the workforce that was engaged in agricultural occupations. The former had a negative influence; the latter, positive. The lower the proportion foreign-born, the higher the proportion aged; the higher the percentage in agricultural pursuits, the higher the proportion aged. The secondary factors included the proportion of families with four or more members (negative influence), the proportion of the workforce engaged in manufacturing occupations (negative influence), and the proportion of the population that was female (negative influence). The primary variables accounted for about half of the town-to-town variation in the proportion of the population aged 55 and over, slightly less than half of the variation in the proportion aged 60 and over, and the same for the proportion aged 75 and over. The five variables together explained 68.1% of the variation in the proportion 55 and over.[4] These findings seem intuitively logical. A community with large numbers of immigrants and industrial workers would have bulges in the young adult segments of its age pyramid and a consequent narrowing of the pyramid in older age groups. A community characterized by farming and out-migration of young people would tend to have larger than usual proportions of old people.

Comparisons among town-level variables that strongly influenced

---

[4]One of the secondary independent variables, the proportion of total families that consisted of four or more members, had higher beta weights than either of the primary variables, although it explained less of the variance in proportions that were aged. This was expected, since old people generally lived in smaller households than other age groups. Also, we should note that although we tried to choose independent variables so as to minimize multicollinearity, we were unable to remove all effects.

incidences of old age reveal that the 8 sampled towns represent the extremes of community types in Essex County. Among the 35 towns, Salem, Lawrence, and Lynn ranked among the highest in proportions of foreign-born, among the highest in proportions working in manufacturing occupations, and among the lowest in proportions engaged in agriculture. Clearly they were the most urbanized communities in the county. Boxford, Hamilton, Lynnfield, Topsfield, and Wenham were the most agrarian, ranking among the lowest in proportions foreign-born and in manufacturing occupations and among the highest in proportions in agricultural pursuits. Moreover, the three large cities had the lowest proportions of old people, and the five other places had among the highest proportions of aged in the county.

Although the eight sampled communities are not completely representative of all Essex County, they are important to the study of conditions of old people because they do represent distinct, rather than marginal, community types. We would expect that in cities, where social and economic conditions were changing dynamically, patterns and conditions of old age would differ from those in rural and semiurban areas. Where land was less of a common resource, issues of kinship and exchange between generations—and support of old people— would have different dimensions. These problems could best be analyzed in communities of contrasting natures rather than in those more closely approaching the average for the entire county. Because of limitations in source availability, we have had to focus chiefly on the cities; yet we can note some specific urban–nonurban comparisons, and a number of others are implicit throughout the following pages.

General Pattern

As in other settled eastern regions during the second half of the nineteenth century, the population of Essex County was beginning to age. Between 1860 and 1865, proportions of older people in nearly every community in the county increased, in some instances quite remarkably. As Table 7.1 reveals, the three cities and the combined nonurban places all experienced steady increases in that segment of the population 50 years of age and older.[5] In absolute numbers, the in-

---

[5]In this table, the age of 50, rather than 55, was used because the 1860 and 1865 censuses divided age cohorts into 10-year, rather than 5-year, divisions. The 1870 federal census did not include age by sex distributions and our 1880 figures were derived from the sample file.

TABLE 7.1
Proportions and Numbers of Population Aged 50 and Above by Sex, Essex County, Massachusetts, 1860–1885

	1860		1865		1875		1880		1885	
	Male	Female	Male	Female	Male	Female	Male	Female	Male	Female
Salem										
Percentage	13.1	15.8	15.8	17.7	16.1	18.1	16.9[a]	17.6[a]	16.8	20.6
N	1288	1891	1462	2112	1881	2564			2152	3157
Lawrence										
Percentage	7.4	6.9	9.7	7.9	10.6	10.7	13.1[a]	12.5[a]	13.1	14.3
N	599	656	904	1014	1673	2050			2329	3010
Lynn										
Percentage	10.8	11.9	12.3	13.1	12.3	13.7	12.4[a]	14.7[a]	13.4	14.9
N	978	1165	1201	1436	1887	2464			2918	3610
Nonurban										
Percentage	17.6	19.6	21.9	21.6	24.6	24.0	24.8	25.4	26.2	26.0
N	453	489	481	499	550	551	538	591	577	591

[a] Sample.
Source: U.S. Bureau of the Census (1860); Massachusetts Censuses (1865, 1875, 1885); manuscript census samples (1880).

crease in the number of old people is even more dramatic, especially in the cities. In Salem, the total number of people over 50 rose from 3179 in 1860 to 5309 in 1885; in Lawrence the number swelled from 1255 to 5339; and in Lynn, it climbed from 2143 to 6528. These increases outran total population growth rates in each city by a considerable margin. Clearly, the aged were becoming significant parts of the population. By the 1880s, proportions of people 55 years and older (returning to the convention mentioned earlier in this chapter) had exceeded 1 in 10 in the three cities and approached 1 in 5 in the smaller towns.

Typically, women, as they have longer life expectancies than men, constituted a large majority of old people in the cities. In the period under examination, Salem, Lawrence, and Lynn had about 75 to 80 men for every 100 women in the cohort aged 60–69, and only between 35 and 40 men for every 100 women aged 70 and above. In addition to conforming to general demographic patterns, these sex ratios also reflect unusually high surpluses of women at younger ages in the three cities. Salem, Lawrence, and Lynn all employed large numbers of young women in industry and domestic service; in every age cohort in the cities, except that of children under 15, the sex ratio was very low. In the five smaller towns, there was near parity between the sexes, even at older ages. Only among the very oldest groups, those over 80, did the sex ratios show heavy surpluses of women. The more even sex ratios in these towns probably resulted from smaller differentials in migration rates between men and women. The generally high female in-migration and high male out-migration characteristics of these cities contrasts with the nearly equal persistence rates of both sexes in the nonurban areas.

Differences in marital status clearly separated the experiences of men from those of women. In 1880, the only census year for which marital status is available, nearly 80% of men over 55 in each Essex community were married. Only about 15% were widowed. On the other hand, about 47% of the aged women in the three urban places were widows, and only about 42% were married. Widows constituted a slightly smaller proportion in the nonurban communities because percentages of single women were higher—about 15% in the nonurban areas compared with 10% in the cities. Women were more likely to be susceptible to isolation than men because they tended never to have married or to have lost their spouses through death more often than men. Yet, these women were not isolated; in the 1880 Essex County communities, 60% of widows over 55 lived in extended households, and only 20% of widowed heads lived completely alone.

Contemporary analysts express concern about the growing dependency of the aged who, because of failing health or reduced incomes, are forced to move in with their children or to enter old age in nursing homes.[6] Conditions in nineteenth-century Essex County do not convey the impression that old people were displaced. Tables 7.2 and 7.3 indicate that in 1860 and 1880, between 80% and 90% of all men over age 55 were heads of households, and generally over 60% of older women were heads or wives of heads. Only among those aged 75 and up did incidences of headship decline. There was a small increase in the proportions of males who were in the "parent" category, that is, living in a household headed by one of their children. Still, these incidences were quite infrequent, generally remaining below 10%, suggesting that few older men were dependent on their children or other kin for housing.[7]

An analysis of the household status of older women in Table 7.3 poses a greater problem than that of men because of the relatively large proportions of women in the "other" category in 1860. As noted earlier, because the 1860 census did not specify relation to head, coders had to deduce this variable. Any person whose relationship was not obvious was assigned to the "other" category. The "other" group consists mainly of three subgroups: boarders not related to the primary nuclear family in the household; resident servants employed by the family; and kin who could not be identified as such because they had different surnames than that of the head. The relatively large number of older women in the "other" category in 1860 could have included homeless spinsters and widows forced to lodge with strangers, aged servants working in the household, or widowed mothers and other older relatives of the head's wife. Probably, most were members of the last subgroup because the decline in the "other" division in 1880, when the census did specify relation to head, was balanced by increases in the "parent" and "other kin" categories. In both 1860 and 1880, between 30% and 40% of all aged women did not live in their own households, and these proportions rose considerably in the oldest age cohorts. Thus, the household status of older women seems to have been more varied than that of older men. These women outnumbered their male

---

[6]See, for example, "New Outlook for the Aged," *Time*, June 2, 1975.

[7]These observations depend upon assumptions that the first person whom census enumerators listed in each household in 1860, where no relation to the head was specified, was legitimately the head of household and that those persons designated as head by the 1880 enumerators were indeed of that status. No one to our knowledge has rigorously tested nineteenth-century enumerators' accuracy in classifying people's household status, but our experiences suggest that our assumptions are reasonably acceptable.

TABLE 7.2
Relation to Head of Household by Age, Males 55 and Over, Essex County, Massachusetts, 1860 and 1880

	Head		Parent		Other kin		Other		N	
	1860	1880	1860	1880	1860	1880	1860	1880	1860	1880
Salem										
55–64	89.4	90.8	14.1	2.6	1.4	2.6	5.5	3.9	73	76
65–74	87.9	76.1	9.1	13.0	0	2.2	3.0	8.7	33	46
75+	78.6	61.3	0	16.1	0	0	21.4	22.6	14	31
Total	87.5	80.4	5.0	18.5	.8	2.0	6.7	9.2	120	153
Lawrence										
55–64	97.2	90.9	0	0	0	1.0	2.8	8.1	36	99
65–74	66.7	90.3	11.1	3.2	0	0	22.2	6.5	9	31
75+	100.0	72.7	0	9.1	0	0	0	18.2	2	11
Total	91.5	89.4	2.1	1.4	0	.7	6.4	8.5	47	141
Lynn										
55–64	85.3	83.1	1.3	2.4	2.7	2.4	10.7	12.0	75	83
65–74	90.9	84.9	4.5	11.3	0	1.9	4.5	1.9	22	53
75+	88.9	71.4	0	9.5	0	4.8	11.1	14.3	9	21
Total	86.8	82.2	1.9	6.4	1.9	2.5	9.4	8.9	106	157
Nonurban										
55–64	83.6	87.0	2.2	0	2.7	6.0	10.9	7.1	183	194
65–74	86.0	82.4	2.2	3.8	1.1	3.8	11.8	10.9	105	156
75+	69.2	72.2	5.8	12.7	1.9	3.8	23.0	11.4	52	80
Total	81.4	82.1	2.7	3.8	3.0	4.8	13.1	9.3	340	430

counterparts, and they encountered greater difficulty, particularly as widows, in sustaining themselves in their own households.

Starting in the middle of the nineteenth century, families gradually saw their protective functions assumed by welfare institutions. Our data suggests, however, that late nineteenth-century society was still strongly familistic. Even when older people became dependents, they were not likely to be put in institutions. A survey of the alms houses, prisons, poor farms, and hotels of Lawrence and Lynn reveals that less than 1% of both men and women in the age group 55 and above, in either city, were inmates in these institutions, although the fear of having to end up in the poor farm or the old ladies' home may still have haunted the minds of older people.

Socioeconomic status constitutes another important index of the conditions of old people in Essex County. Given the scarcity and un-

TABLE 7.3

Relation to Head of Household by Age, Females 55 and Over, Essex County, Massachusetts, 1860 and 1880

	Head or spouse		Parent		Other kin		Other		N	
	1860	1880	1860	1880	1860	1880	1860	1880	1860	1880
Salem										
55–64	57.1	84.7	17.8	3.5	2.8	8.2	22.4	3.5	107	85
65–74	46.4	56.7	20.3	16.4	1.4	19.4	31.9	7.5	69	67
75+	34.7	64.7	20.4	17.6	2.0	11.8	42.9	5.9	49	34
Total	48.9	71.0	19.1	10.8	2.2	12.9	29.8	5.4	225	186
Lawrence										
55–64	68.4	76.5	7.9	7.8	5.3	2.0	18.4	13.7	38	102
65–74	45.0	62.2	10.0	24.4	0	4.4	45.0	8.9	20	45
75+	41.7	21.1	8.3	68.4	0	0	50.0	11.1	12	19
Total	57.1	66.3	7.9	19.3	3.2	2.4	31.7	12.0	60	166
Lynn										
55–64	69.0	70.7	7.1	10.9	3.6	6.5	20.2	12.0	84	92
65–74	70.0	61.1	12.2	27.8	4.9	2.8	22.2	8.3	41	72
75+	60.0	31.4	6.7	34.3	0	17.1	33.3	17.1	15	35
Total	65.7	60.3	8.6	21.1	3.6	7.0	22.1	11.6	140	199
Nonurban										
55–64	75.7	77.2	5.3	7.3	5.3	9.2	13.6	6.3	169	206
65–74	63.4	61.2	11.6	17.1	.9	11.8	23.2	6.5	112	166
75+	49.3	58.7	17.9	17.4	0	13.8	32.8	10.9	67	91
Total	67.8	67.7	9.8	12.8	2.9	10.9	19.5	7.3	348	463

even quality of pertinent historical data, historians have not been able to devise rigorous, comprehensive methods for the identification of class or status. For purposes of expediency and estimation, we have adopted a scheme of occupational classification.[8] We fully recognize the drawbacks of occupational categories as determinants of socioeconomic status, but we believe that for our purposes occupational variables are important because they yield information about an individual's dependency.

We have aggregated occupations into the following categories:

[8]Our categories basically integrate those used in the Comparative Cities Project, Brown University, and the Five Cities Project involving Blumin, Glasco, Griffen, Hershberg, and Katz. See Hershberg et al. (1974) and Shorter (1971:145).

1. Nonmanual—combines professional, managerial, proprietary, and clerical subgroups (because sample numbers in any one subgroup alone would have been too small for analysis)
2. Skilled—includes blue-collar artisans and tradesmen
3. Semiskilled—consists primarily of factory workers
4. Unskilled—encompasses general laborers and lowest-level service workers
5. Dependent and other—contains those without occupations, mainly those who presumably depended on others for support

In addition, because of the way in which occupations were originally coded from the 1860 and 1880 census, farmers, that is, farm proprietors, were included in the nonmanual category.

Given the present situation, where one-half of American employers have instituted forced retirement at age 65 and where social analysts express concern over discrimination against older job seekers, data from a century ago offer a significant contrast. Very few aged males in late nineteenth-century Essex County did not work. According to the totals in Table 7.4, only about 1 in 10 aged men had no means of support; 90% or more appear to have been employed.[9] Dependency increased with age, but relatively high incidences of male nonemployment occurred only beyond the age of 75. There seem to have been a few changes in occupational patterns of aged men between 1860 and 1880: slightly higher dependency in Salem and Lawrence, and a shift from skilled to semiskilled in Lynn. These trends pose analytical difficulties because the sample sizes are fairly small. Thus, for us, the consistently high levels of gainful employment among older age cohorts remain the most remarkable pattern.[10]

The types of employment held by older men did differ from the jobs of younger workers. In 1880, in Salem, Lawrence, and Lynn, about 60% of employed males younger than 50 worked in manufacturing occupations, while only about 35% of nondependent men aged 50–75 held manufacturing jobs. In other sectors, such as building, retailing, service, and general labor, proportions of older men were generally one-third higher than those of men below age 50. At first glance, these contrasts seem to suggest that as men began to approach old age, they left or were forced out of industrial jobs and either used accumulated

---

[9]We assume that the occupation the census listed for each individual meant gainful, not former, means of employment.

[10]As would be expected, 90% of all employed aged males were heads of households. Among those with no occupations, half to two-thirds were heads, which is still a relatively high proportion.

TABLE 7.4
Age by Occupational Status, Males 55 and Over, Essex County, Massachusetts, 1860 and 1880

	Nonmanual		Skilled		Semiskilled		Unskilled		Dependent and other		N	
	1860	1880	1860	1880	1860	1880	1860	1880	1860	1880	1860	1880
Salem												
55–59	35.5	29.0	48.4	41.9	9.7	12.9	6.5	12.9	0	3.2	31	31
60–64	27.0	34.2	29.7	34.2	5.4	2.6	32.4	23.7	5.4	5.2	37	38
65–74	23.1	38.5	46.2	28.2	26.9	12.8	3.8	7.7	0	12.8	26	39
75+	30.0	43.5	30.0	8.7	10.0	21.7	0	8.7	30.0	17.4	10	23
Total	28.8	35.9	39.4	29.8	12.5	11.5	14.4	13.7	4.8	9.2	104	131
Lawrence												
55–59	36.4	17.0	31.8	23.4	4.5	25.5	27.3	25.5	0	8.5	22	47
60–64	16.7	19.6	25.0	19.6	0	32.6	58.3	19.6	0	8.7	12	46
65–74	11.1	17.2	22.2	24.1	11.1	17.2	45.5	24.1	0	17.2	9	29
75+	0	0	0	33.3	0	0	100.0	11.1	0	55.6	2	9
Total	24.4	16.8	26.7	22.9	4.4	24.4	44.4	22.1	0	13.7	45	131
Lynn												
55–59	33.3	28.6	46.7	33.3	3.3	21.4	10.0	9.5	6.7	7.2	30	42
60–64	12.8	13.5	48.7	24.3	17.9	35.1	10.3	21.6	10.3	5.4	39	37
65–74	10.0	18.8	60.0	35.4	10.0	25.0	10.0	10.4	10.0	10.4	20	48
75+	33.3	17.6	33.3	35.3	0	11.8	0	5.9	33.3	29.4	6	17
Total	20.0	20.1	49.5	31.9	10.5	25.0	9.5	12.5	10.5	10.4	95	144
Nonurban												
55–59	61.7[a]	51.1[a]	30.9	14.4	1.1	5.6	6.4	21.1	0	7.7	94	90
60–64	48.1[a]	56.7[a]	40.5	21.1	0	8.9	11.4	7.8	0	5.5	79	90
65–74	66.7[a]	56.3[a]	23.0	14.5	2.4	5.9	12.2	19.7	0	3.3	84	151
75+	59.5[a]	63.6[a]	23.3	11.7	0	1.3	4.7	14.3	7.0	10.0	44	77
Total	58.5[a]	56.6[a]	29.9	15.4	1.0	5.6	9.0	16.4	1.0	5.9	301	408

[a]Includes farm proprietors.

229

capital to start their own businesses (contracting or retailing, for example) or sought whatever menial work was available to sustain themselves. Considerably more research is needed to determine whether the contrasts are real or whether they result from cohort effects. The low proportions of older men in manufacturing could be explained by the fact that many of these men entered the labor force before factory jobs were widely available, and therefore, they had fewer opportunities to acquire industrial employment as young men. By 1880, they were not leaving manufacturing. Rather, they were not holding jobs in the areas where they had no experience. Both explanations are plausible and deserve further attention.

Nearly 90% or more of aged women in 1860 and 1880 had no recorded occupation (see Table 7.5). The only exception occurred in Lawrence in 1860 where almost one-third of the 60 sampled women 55 years and older held unskilled jobs, most of them probably working as domestics and washerwomen. There were slight declines in the "dependent" category of Salem and Lynn between 1860 and 1880, from 92 to 87% in Salem and from 98 to 91% in Lynn. Nevertheless, the generally high rates of nonemployment among older women, even among those between 55 and 65, suggest that very few women in Essex County were entering or reentering the job market after childbearing responsibilities had ended. The figures, however, do not measure the extent of unpaid women's work, mainly taking in boarders, which seems to have been quite common, especially among widows. This issue is important because employment figures reveal that even among those aged women who were heads of households, 9 out of 10 had no recorded occupation and thus were supported by others in their households.

In general, the aged in the Essex County communities grew rapidly in numbers and proportions between 1860 and 1880, frequently retained at least titular control of their own households, and the men continued gainful employment while the women remained outside the labor market. In effect, we have established that old people did not differ considerably from other adult groups in their efforts to retain economic independence by heading their own households and, for men, by continuing their working careers. However, the extent to which old people were able to maintain this independence varied according to changing social and economic conditions in the community.

Changing Economic Conditions

The interactions among the aged, their families, and the community offer revealing insights into the ways that people adjusted during a

TABLE 7.5
Age by Occupational Status, Females 55 and Over, Essex County, Massachusetts, 1860 and 1880

	Nonmanual		Skilled		Semiskilled		Unskilled		Dependent and other		N	
	1860	1880	1860	1880	1860	1880	1860	1880	1860	1880	1860	1880
Salem												
55–59	1.9	8.4	9.3	2.1	0	0	1.9	4.2	87.0	85.4	54	48
60–64	1.9	3.7	3.8	7.4	0	0	5.7	0	88.7	88.9	53	27
65–74	1.4	0	2.9	7.8	0	0	1.4	7.8	94.2	84.3	69	51
75+	0	0	4.1	0	0	0	0	0	95.9	100.0	49	21
Total	1.3	3.4	4.9	4.8	0	0	2.2	4.1	91.6	87.2	225	147
Lawrence												
55–59	0	3.7	0	0	4.0	7.4	28.0	9.3	68.0	79.6	25	54
60–64	0	2.3	0	2.3	0	0	23.1	0	76.9	95.4	13	44
65–74	0	0	5.0	2.4	0	0	45.0	4.9	50.0	92.7	20	41
75+	0	0	50.0	0	0	6.7	0	0	50.0	91.7	2	12
Total	0	2.0	3.3	1.3	1.7	3.3	31.7	4.6	63.3	89.7	60	151
Lynn												
55–59	0	0	0	0	0	4.9	0	2.4	100.0	92.7	40	41
60–64	2.3	4.7	2.3	2.3	0	0	0	4.7	95.4	88.4	44	43
65–74	0	1.5	0	1.5	0	0	0	4.4	100.0	92.6	41	68
75+	0	0	0	0	0	11.1	0	0	100.0	88.9	15	27
Total	.7	1.7	.7	1.1	0	2.8	0	3.4	98.6	91.1	140	179
Nonurban												
55–59	1.1	0	1.1	1.1	1.1	0	2.3	3.3	94.3	97.6	88	91
60–64	1.2	.9	2.5	1.9	8.6	0	2.5	2.8	85.2	95.5	81	108
65–74	1.8	0	3.6	2.6	.9	0	6.3	2.6	87.5	94.7	68	76
75+	1.5	0	5.9	1.3	1.5	0	0.	1.3	91.2	97.4	68	76
Total	1.4	.2	3.2	1.9	2.9	0	3.2	2.6	89.4	95.3	305	351

period of social and economic change. Between 1860 and 1880 in Essex County, two converging forces—one demographic and the other economic—profoundly influenced family patterns. On the one hand, the region's cities experienced extraordinary population growth. In two decades, the populations of Lawrence and Lynn each more than doubled, and that of Salem increased by one-fourth. Such rapid expansion necessarily strained existing resources and created problems of absorbing newcomers into housing and job markets. During the same period, the regional and national economies completed a full business cycle, rising broadly and rapidly through the 1860s and early 1870s, then falling precipitously during the depression that followed the crash of 1873 (Easterlin, 1968; Long, 1960).

Trends traced in Figure 7.1 yield important clues about changes in interdependency and family formation (a form of independence) over time. The Ch curves represent proportions of particular age cohorts who were children of the head living at home, and the H/S curves represent proportions who were either heads of households or spouses of heads. The graph shows two significant patterns. First, the location of the 1880 Ch curves is consistently to the right of the 1860 Ch curves, suggesting that by 1880 it had become more difficult for young people

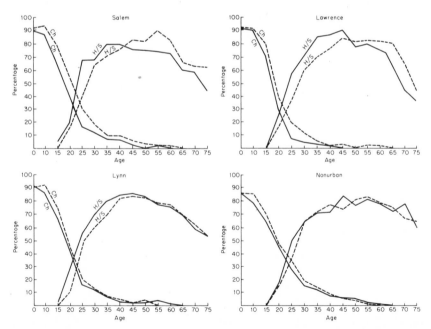

FIGURE 7.1. *Proportion, by age, of total population who were children of head of household (Ch) or who were either the head of household or the spouse of the head (H/S).*

to achieve independence. That is, increasing numbers of sons and daughters, particularly between the ages 15–35, were remaining in their parents' households for a longer period of time. Some of the adult children may have been married and were living as secondary family units; others could have been unmarried young adults unprepared or unable to strike out on their own.

Second, aging adults in 1880 were retaining the status of head of household, or wife of head, in somewhat larger proportions than old people in 1860 had, at least in the three cities. In Salem, Lawrence, and Lynn, the 1880 H/S curves are consistently higher than 1860 H/S curves for people in their fifties, sixties, and seventies. Moreover, for the ages 20–40, the 1880 curves are to the right of the 1860 curves, supporting the observation that it became more difficult for young adults to establish their own households. The high incidences of headship among old people with delayed headship among younger adults suggest the existence of conditions that encouraged generational interdependence.

Although direct evidence is difficult to find, these patterns seem to be linked to the economic conditions of the period. Salem, Lawrence, and Lynn all underwent impressive economic growth during the 1860s. The textile and shoe mills of Lawrence and Lynn expanded, and Salem shippers offset losses in foreign commerce with increased coastal trade (Robotti, 1948:69, 75, 78). Property valuations in Salem and Lawrence more than doubled between 1858 and 1872, and real estate markets experienced higher levels of activity. Basically, in Essex County cities, it appears that job and housing opportunities were relatively abundant in the 1860s.

The aftermath of the 1873 Panic saw a reverse in economic trends in Essex County, as declines in employment, real wages, and general business swept the region. Reduced demand and fiscal uncertainty slowed down production in the factories of Salem, Lawrence, and Lynn; and Salem's overseas shipping, once its most prominent livelihood, halted completely.[11] *The Essex County Mercury* cautiously observed in 1876 that:

[11]Salem city directories, 1858–1872; Dorgan (1924:174). Evidence on economic conditions in Boxford, Hamilton, Lynnfield, Topsfield, and Wenham is even more obscure. State census information suggests that some of these communities, notably Lynnfield, were tightening economic bonds with nearby cities and were losing traditional agrarian characteristics in favor of more manufacturing. The problem of interpretation, however, is further complicated by the impact of the Civil War, which seems to have depleted, at least temporarily, the population of young men in these communities. Census records show a decline of 35.3% in the number of males between the ages of 15 and 29 in these five communities, a decline that accounts for half the population loss in these places in the years 1860–1865. No local indexes have been discovered, but for regional data, see Long (1960:Chapter 5).

It is really quite impossible for anyone to foretell with certainty, the day when
we may expect a revival of business, but it seems safe enough to say that almost
any change is likely to be for the better. . . . Here and there people may be found
who think the times will be worse before they grow better; but for the most part,
there seems to be an impression that there is to be a general revival of business
in the near future. Although few look for a great revival, the feeling is general
that there is to be a steady improvement for the better. That the people generally are examining their affairs, and giving their earnest attention to learn how
to do business as well as live within their means, and to avoid drawing ahead
on "luck" in the future, as too many have done in the past, is considered as one
of the best signs of the times [February 16, 1876].

Certainly these conditions could have inhibited young adults from
separating themselves from their parents. Conceivably, these proportions could have been even higher in the middle and late 1870s when
effects of the depression were more severe, although in many places
recovery was barely under way in 1880. And if more young adults were
being forced to live at home longer, then older parents were assuming
additional responsibilities, or at least functions, by providing household space.

Besides general economic conditions, trends in local housing markets also seem to have created conditions that would have increased
and prolonged situations in which older and younger generations
shared housing in the residences of the older generation. Unfortunately, data on nineteenth-century housing markets are very scarce.
Economists have collected information on building trends and real
estate transactions for only a very few cities, so that full assessment of
local and regional cycles must rely on incomplete records. Nevertheless, studies based on existing data all indicate a sharp rise in building
and real estate exchange before 1873 and a dramatic slump afterward,
lasting until 1879 or 1880 (Maverick, 1932:192–199, 1933:52–56;
Newman, 1935; Colean, 1944:186; Gottlieb, 1964:65; Long, 1940).

The curves in Figures 7.2 and 7.3 confirm the general trend for two
communities in Essex County. Since no direct information on new
housing starts and availability of existing housing could be practically
assembled, we have attempted to estimate conditions of the Salem and
Lynn housing markets by tabulating annual numbers of deeds recorded. The two figures show, albeit indirectly, that real estate activity
generally expanded from 1860 until 1869 or 1870 and then dropped
drastically until the late 1870s. The cycle was somewhat less abrupt,
peaked earlier, and recovered earlier in Salem than in Lynn; nevertheless, the paths of the curves were the same. These trends suggest that by
the middle and late 1870s, ostensibly as an effect of the depression, the
Salem and Lynn housing markets had shrunk dramatically and that this
contraction may well have prompted coresidency among people who

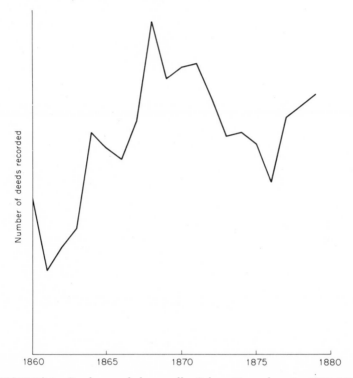

FIGURE 7.2.   *Deeds recorded annually, Salem, Massachusetts, 1860–1879.*

ordinarily would have lived apart. Moreover, the pressures of this assumed housing shortage would have been intensified by continuing
population growth in these cities as well as by economic hard times.
Between 1875 and 1880, the population of Lynn increased by 18%
while the number of available dwellings grew by only 11%; in Salem,
the population grew by 6% during these years, while the number of
dwellings increased by 4%.[12] There is even some more direct indication of a housing slump. *The Salem Gazette* noted early in 1875 that:

[12]Ratios of estimated deeds recorded to total population provide further evidence of
real estate contraction relative to population growth:

Deeds recorded per capita

	Salem	Lynn
1860	.018	.061
1865	.025	.071
1870	.031	.094
1875	.021	.077
1879/1880	.025	.037

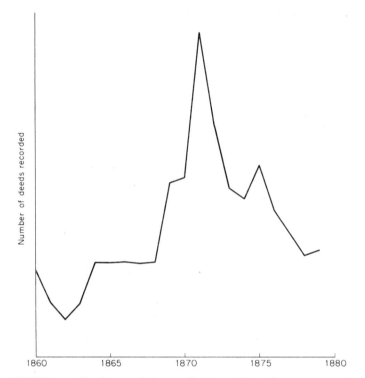

FIGURE 7.3. *Deeds recorded annually, Lynn, Massachusetts, 1860–1879.*

"Here, as elsewhere, building has been falling off the past few years, pending the return of better times. In 1872, there were 73 notices [i.e., intentions to build]; in 1873, 50 notices, and in 1874, 44 notices, in all [February 5, 1875]."

Thus, the evidence seems to indicate that there were constraints in Essex County housing markets by the mid-1870s. Deed records, of course, pertain only to owned property and shed little light on rental markets—an important sector since probably half or more of the urban families lived in rented quarters. Still, the data previously noted on the timing of the establishment of one's own household, owned or rented, by sons and daughters, confirm the tightening conditions of the 1870s. Direct references to housing shortages in Essex County have been difficult to uncover, although such shortages did exist in nearby Worcester County, which experienced similar economic and housing problems during the same period (Chudacoff, 1977). Nevertheless, the circumstances strongly suggest that housing scarcity did develop and that this condition combined with employment and business adversities to modify family compositions so that adult generations coresided more frequently than they did when economic and housing opportunities were more elastic.

Data on the type of household in which each person lived in 1880 reveal remarkably high frequencies of cases where old people coresided with others. Table 7.6 shows that less than half of the males aged 55 and up in 1880 Essex County communities, and less than one-third of females in the same age group, lived in nuclear households consisting only of husband, wife, and unmarried children with no other kin or strangers. These proportions are very low when viewed in a total context of about 70% of all people in these communities living in isolated nuclear households. About 20 to 30% of aged males and 30 to 40% of aged females lived with kin in extended households (lines 3 and 4 in Table 7.6). This represents at least twice the proportion of the total population living with extended kin. About one-third of both aged males and females lived in households with nonkin, or lived as boarders and lodgers in other peoples' households (lines 2, 4, and 6 in Table 7.6). Only very small percentages of old people lived alone (line 5 in Table 7.6).

In 1880, then, nearly half of the aged men and three-fifths of aged women lived with others besides their spouses and/or married children. Studies of the nearby cities of Worcester and Providence have confirmed increased household extension and augmentation in 1880 for these communities and we have every reason to assume similar trends in Essex County (Chudacoff, 1975; Rosenthal, 1975). In addition, because most aged men and a majority of aged women were either

TABLE 7.6

Household Types Inhabited by People Age 55 and Older, Essex County, Massachusetts, 1880

	Salem		Lawrence		Lynn		Nonurban	
	Male	Female	Male	Female	Male	Female	Male	Female
Nuclear, isolated	47.1	33.2	52.9	34.9	48.4	29.9	39.0	31.2
Nuclear, augmented	22.2	9.8	25.7	23.5	19.7	14.7	21.9	15.7
Extended	16.3	21.7	10.7	24.1	19.1	25.9	21.0	25.3
Extended, augmented	9.8	12.0	7.9	12.0	8.9	15.2	10.8	14.8
Single member	2.0	10.3	2.1	1.8	1.9	6.1	2.4	6.5
Single member, augmented	2.0	3.3	0	1.2	.6	1.5	2.2	2.0
Other	.7	9.8	.7	2.4	1.3	6.6	2.7	4.6
N	153	184	140	166	157	197	415	459

household heads or wives of heads (see Tables 7.2 and 8.3), it appears that the extra kin and nonkin were being attached to households headed by old people.[13]

All of these circumstances lead us to conclude that the demographic and economic conditions of the cities in 1880 created conditions which prompted old people to enter into interdependent relationships with others. Such arrangements enabled many of the aged to remain integral and functional family members instead of becoming burdens. Since by 1880 residential space was at a premium, many old people, as occupants of this space, held an advantageous position. As household heads, they had acquired residences and raised their families in the 1850s and 1860s when local economies were booming and, at least in the later decade, housing markets were relatively open. When hard times spread over communities in the 1870s and closed off employment and housing possibilities, younger people increasingly looked to their elders for continued provision of housing. We note that whether older people owned their quarters is not central to our interpretation. Rather, occupancy was the chief asset, for sharing space constituted the issue of concern, not ownership. In this regard, there may well have been considerable opportunities for instrumentality, as conceptualized by Michael Anderson, to have operated. That is, mutually advantageous situations could have arisen, where, in a tightening economy, aging household heads exchanged household space with younger people, either adult offspring or boarders, in return for remuneration or other forms of compensation such as running errands, doing household chores, and providing company (Anderson, 1971).

Of course, not all old people in Essex County, particularly not all women, were household heads or wives of heads. Some lived as tenants in other people's housing space. Yet even in these situations, they may not have been completely dependent. About 75% of male boarders, parents, and other kin (that is, those aged men who were not household heads) had an occupation and could have contributed to the household income. Although most women in similar categories (that is, not heads or wives of heads) did not hold jobs, they could have exchanged ser-

[13]This information also is in the process of being created. We hope to extend the individual files for Essex County by adding to each record the summary information about the household in which each individual lived. That summary information will include the head's age and thus enable us to construct distributions of extended kin, including married children, and nonkin according to the age of the head of household in which such groups were living. If our hypotheses are correct, we would expect disproportionate numbers of extended kin and nonkin to be residing with older household heads and frequencies of these cases to have increased between 1860 and 1880.

vices such as housecleaning, washing, and babysitting for their lodging.

Although economic conditions in Essex County in 1873–1880 put pressure on individuals and families, we hypothesize that as a result people tightened intergenerational bonds, and situations of reciprocal assistance rather than dependency emerged. Under such circumstances, the aged and aging were not being pushed into isolation and segregation; rather, they were participating in and contributing to family sustenance. If we carry our interpretation further, it is possible that some families recreated new variants of the early American experience discussed previously. In hard times, some could have substituted the valuable resource of housing for land. By allowing grown children to remain at home even after they married, nineteenth-century aged parents might have been able to use their housing resource as an exchange commodity for assistance, just as their ancestors had used land more than a century earlier.

The process of urbanization, with its uncertainty and different requisites for housing and employment, may well have fostered a new type of intergenerational exchange, at least in Essex County. At a time when theorists began to lament the anomie and atomization resulting from urban growth, household data suggest considerable interdependence among family members, whether voluntary or forced. In Salem, Lawrence, and Lynn combined, 64% of men aged 55 and over in 1880 lived in the same household with one or more offspring who were aged 16 or older; 60.7% of aged women lived with late adolescent or adult children. By contrast, in nonurban areas, percentages for men and women in these categories were only 46.5 and 35.5%, respectively, which were statistically significant differences. Moreover, in the cities, older people retained at least titular control of their families. Of all aged men living with adult offspring, over 90% were heads of households, and over 70% of older women in this category were either heads or spouses of heads. Conditions of late nineteenth-century urbanization moved aging parents closer to their progeny rather than isolating them.

Our limited evidence at this stage suggests that the incidence of the empty nest was less pervasive in the late nineteenth century than in modern society. A number of sociologists have challenged the assumption that the later years of life are marked by isolation and dependence, on the basis of the modified extended family model. Litwak (1965), Shanas et al. (1968), and Sussman (1963), for example, have emphasized patterns of kin interaction outside the household between older parents and adult children in modern society. Our study suggests that these patterns occurred in the past as well. The household contracted and expanded at different points along the family cycle. While the household was predominantly nuclear during the childbearing and launching years, it extended itself to include other kin and strangers in later years.

Life-course transitions are determined by demographic and socioeconomic characteristics, as well as by cultural norms. Several demographic trends, some of which are involuntary, determine the timing of family events along the life course. At the same time, cultural norms of family behavior and economic needs affect the timing of transitions along the life course, as well as the boundaries of each stage. The relative role of cultural and economic factors affecting different stages of family life has not been developed yet historically. This chapter documents a familial response to economic needs in later years of life. It shows the degree to which exchanges along the life course were built into family relations. Instrumental relationships integrated older people into viable family roles. Our data suggest that a familial ideology played an important role in the position of older people. How cultural factors interacted specifically with economic needs still remains open to investigation.

This chapter has attempted to probe possible kin functions and relationships among old people in nineteenth-century communities. Our evidence, admittedly circumstantial, but strongly so, leads to conclusions that older people, particularly old household heads, assumed important familial and quasifamilial functions during times of social stress. In this respect, issues of dependence and independence appear less important than relationships of mutual assistance or reciprocity. Historical evidence implies that during emergencies resulting from personal adversities such as death or illness and societal crises such as natural disasters or economic depressions the family remained the most ready agency of assistance, particularly in eras predating institutions of public aid and welfare. Historical situations, with support from more recent data, also suggest that the aged seem to have been most comfortable when they were in mutually dependent relationships where they could offer something to others (in the form of services such as babysitting or housekeeping, or in the form of resources such as housing, financial assistance, or gifts) in return for aid and/or companionship (Anderson, 1971; Townsend, 1957; Hill, 1970; Adams, 1968:78–79). This does not mean that such exchange relationships were formal or that old people did not strive for independence, but rather that these exchanges flowed naturally from kinship norms.

In this discussion, we have focused primarily on housing as an example of resource sharing. There are other types of resources, such as food, clothing, and time, that are important factors in family exchanges but which cannot be measured by data currently available to us. To some extent, housing space can act for these other resources; however, it provides only the most tangible factor out of a large number of possible resources.

The foregoing is admittedly highly speculative. There are large gaps in the historical evidence, and our examination has overlooked some prominent variables such as ethnicity, class, and sex differentials. Our hypotheses demand more quantitative and qualitative support. Still, we believe that our particular approach to interrelationships among the aged, the family, and the community points toward a more functional view of old people and toward a dynamic interplay between community and family patterns.

This chapter suggests several directions of further research. It is important to know at what points in the life course resource exchanges among kin were most intensive and to differentiate between exchanges that were responses to temporary crises and those that were structured into the life-course continuum, such as the investment of parents in raising their children with the expectation of reciprocal support in old age. In the populations discussed here, demographic and economic factors combined to encourage more intensive interaction among kin, minimizing the isolation of distinct age groups.

References

Adams, Bert
    1968   Kinship in an Urban Setting. Chicago: Markham.
Anderson, Michael
    1971   Family Structure in Nineteenth Century Lancashire. Cambridge, England: Cambridge University Press.
Chudacoff, Howard I.
    1977   "A new branch on the tree: family formation and family extension in Worcester, Massachusetts, 1860–1880." Proceedings of the American Antiquarian Society XXXVI:303–320.
Clark, Margaret
    1969   "Cultural values and dependency in later life." In Richard Kalish (ed.), The Dependencies of Old People. Ann Arbor: Institute for Gerontology.
Colean, Miles
    1944   American Housing: Problems and Prospects. New York: Twentieth Century Fund.
Demos, John
    1970   A Little Commonwealth: Family Life in Plymouth Colony. New York: Oxford University Press.

Dorgan, Maurice B.
   1924   History of Lawrence, Massachusetts with War Records. Lawrence, Mas-
          sachusetts: Author.
Glick, Paul
   1957   American Families. New York: Wiley.
Gottlieb, Manuel
   1964   "Estimates of residential building: United States, 1875–1939." Technical
          Paper 17, National Bureau of Economic Research.
Greven, Philip
   1970   Four Generations: Population, Land, and Family in Colonial Andover,
          Massachusetts. Ithaca, New York: Cornell University Press.
Hareven, Tamara K.
   1976   "The last stage: historical adulthood and old age." Daedalus 105
          (Fall):13–28.
   1977   "Family time and historical time." Daedalus 106 (Spring):57–70.
Hershberg, Theodore, Michael Katz, Stuart Blumin, Lawrence Glasco, and Clyde Griffen
   1974   "Occupation and ethnicity in five nineteenth-century cities: a collabora-
          tive inquiry." Historical Methods Newsletter VII (June):174–216.
Hill, Reuben
   1970   Family Development in Three Generations. Cambridge, Massachusetts:
          Schenkman.
Litwak, Eugene
   1965   "Extended kin relations in an industrial democratic society." In Ethel
          Shanas and Gordon F. Streib (eds.), Social Structure and the Family: Gen-
          erational Relations. Englewood Cliffs, New Jersey: Prentice-Hall.
Long, Clarence D. Jr.
   1940   Building Cycles and the Theory of Investment. Princeton, New Jersey:
          Princeton University Press.
   1960   Wages and Earnings in the United States, 1860–90. National Bureau of
          Economic Research, Number 67, General Series. Princeton, New Jersey:
          Princeton University Press.
Massachusetts Census
   1865   Boston: Bureau of Labor Statistics.
   1875   Boston: Bureau of Labor Statistics.
   1885   Boston: Bureau of Labor Statistics.
Maverick, Lewis A.
   1932   "Cycles in real estate activity." Journal of Land and Public Utility Econom-
          ics VII (May):192–199.
   1933   "Cycles in real estate activity, Los Angeles County." Journal of Land and
          Public Utility Economics IX (February):52–56.
Newman, Willian
   1935   The Building Industry and Business Cycles. Privately printed part of a
          dissertation distributed by the University of Chicago Press.
Robotti, Frances Diane
   1948   Chronicles of Old Salem. Salem: Newcomb and Gauss.
Rosenthal, Regina
   Unpub-   "The changing status of the aged in Providence, Rhode Island, 1850–
   lished   1880." Providence, Rhode Island: Brown University. Seminar paper, 1975.
Rosser, Colin and Christopher Harris
   1965   The Family and Social Change. London: Routledge and Kegan Paul.

Shanas, Ethel, P. Townsend, D. Wedderburn, H. Friis, P. Milhøj, and J. Stehoywer
    1968   Old People in Three Industrial Societies. New York: Atherton.
Shorter, Edward
    1971   The Historian and the Computer. Englewood Cliffs, New Jersey: Prentice-Hall.
Smith, Daniel Scott
    1973   "Parental power and marriage partners: an analysis of historical trends in Hingham, Massachusetts." Journal of Marriage and the Family 35 (August): 419–429.
Sussman, Marvin B.
    1963   "Parental aid to married children: implications for family functioning." Marriage and Family Living 24:320–332.
    1977   "The family life of old people." Pp. 218–243 in Robert H. Binstock and Ethel Shanas (eds.), Handbook of Aging and the Social Sciences. New York: Van Nostrand.
Sussman, Marvin B. and Lee Burchinal
    1959   "The isolated nuclear family: fact or fiction?" Social Problems VI:333–340.

Time
    1975   "New outlook for the aged." June 2:44–46.
Townsend, Peter
    1957   Family Life of Old People. London: Routledge and Kegan Paul.
Troll, Lillian E.
    1971   "The family of later life: a decade review." Journal of Marriage and the Family 33 (May):263–290.
U.S. Bureau of the Census
    1860   United States Census: 1860. Washington, D.C.: U.S. Government Printing Office.

8

Transitions:
Patterns of Timing

JOHN MODELL
TAMARA K. HAREVEN

This chapter attempts to synthesize the individual chapters about Essex County in this volume insofar as they discuss patterns of timing of different transitions along the life course and their determinants. Despite variety in substantive focus and methodological approaches, the chapters point to a common set of concerns, which Elder characterizes as the life-course perspective. Specifically, we seek the determinants of "social timetables" in patterned sequences of individual events, of the interaction between the history of the family and that of individual members, and between the course of events in the family and other institutional sectors (Elder, Chapter 1 of this volume).

Factors Affecting Transitions

The individual life course is punctuated at several points by transitions, in the timing of which individual preference plays a large although not wholly determinate part. A variety of constraints limits the freedom of such choices as when to begin or end school, to marry, to set up an independent household, to have a child or another child, and to retire. Individuals or couples take these actions, by and large recognizing both that they are consequential, and that they will, to a degree, be

TRANSITIONS
The Family and the Life Course in
Historical Perspective

held responsible for the decisions they make. That is to say, the timing of certain events is socially recognized, socially monitored, socially sanctioned. For example, "married" is a status carrying obligations and privileges distinct from those accruing to "single." "Schoolboys" are treated as such; "retirees" in their own way.

Sanctioned social norms may be among the considerations affecting an individual's timing of a particular transition. Some transitions are more strongly or precisely sanctioned in their timing than others. The degree of their sanctioning may also change over time. The appearance of the pejorative word "dropout" in the past few decades is evidence for the development of age norms regarding school departure, just as the fact of dropouts reminds us that the existence of a norm does not prevent its transgression. One reason why norms are inconsistently followed in practice is that a complex society such as the United States is composed of different groups that, while they obviously share enough to understand and predict one another's behavior, act somewhat differently from one another. Different ethnic cultures and different socioeconomic groups in the nineteenth century may have had their own values about the appropriate timing of events. Under certain conditions, a group may not be able to live by the norms of the culture, even if it accepts them, because it lacks the resources to do so.

Even age norms specific to ethnic and socioeconomic groups would not be likely to prescribe the exact moment in the life course for a particular transition, but rather to suggest appropriate ranges. As Uhlenberg demonstrates in Chapter 2, nonnormative considerations such as cohort size and composition may likewise affect the timing, as well as the possibility of role transitions. Social, demographic, and economic circumstances may also affect an imbalance between roles and their potential occupants. For example, even though all women in a certain cohort might be expected to marry at a certain age, some women might not be able to do so because of a shortage of eligible men. The uncertainties of the circumstances, the lack of institutional responses, and dependence on family mechanisms produced wide variations among members of a population in the timing of a given transition.

Ankarloo's chapter on marriage provides a suggestive instance of how dependence upon familial mechanisms in the mid-nineteenth century fed back into a larger and interrelated set of family decisions, extending over time. Premarital pregnancy, for instance, often led to marriage sooner than the couple could afford it. This failure of timing was dealt with by temporary coresidence with the parents of the bride or groom. Couples who had a choice became to a marked degree matrilocal. Yet, Ankarloo suggests, this was a calculated decision, as the couple strove to repair the consequences of earlier passionate miscalculation: The parents chosen most often were the set best able to afford to take in the young couple until they gained the wherewithal to establish an independent residence. These decisions, to coreside and to do so matrilocally, probably had further consequences for family relationships in nonmaterial realms, consequences that historians would be unable to reconstruct.

In addition to economic factors, institutional conditions were also important in affecting the timing of life-course transitions. In a society and time period when most educational, economic, and welfare functions were concentrated within the family, the timing of transitions was more family-centered than in societies where social institutions outside the family contribute to determining the pace or the nature of certain transitions. Two types of institutions in the context of which family life-course decisions were made are featured in this book: old-age institutions and schools. In Chapter 7, Chudacoff and Hareven develop the theme of family and kin self-sufficiency in the absence of institutions performing support functions for the aged. Social insurance hardly existed and private and medical insurance contributorships barely touched most of the American population. Only a minute fraction of the elderly resorted to old age homes or homes of refuge. Kaestle and Vinovskis, in Chapter 5, discuss the relationship of school-age legislation and school attendance. In the latter half of the nineteenth century, schools were provided universally, but offered schooling that while well-geared to the enlargement of "human capital," nevertheless was taken advantage of by only a portion of the population of the eligible age.

Individual calculations of utility also affect the way transitions are timed. Individuals weigh the benefits of acting now rather than later by considering the nature of the present state as against the quality of the future state, discounted for the uncertainties of attaining the desired state in the future. An additional year of school will be undertaken when either the school itself or its consequences are desirable; or when leaving school immediately would not lead one into a new job, a new family status, or some other utility. Leaving school will not be deferred, however beneficial further schooling might be, if waiting involves a serious chance of losing the job, or the intended spouse. Thus the timing of present transitions depends upon the intended timing of subsequent (or simultaneous) ones and upon the certainty with which one can predict subsequent conditions.

The social framework within which transitions are made may also make a difference. Rules govern the exchange of utilities. As Uhlenberg's cohort analysis shows, certain utilities may be in high demand at particular moments. (Obviously, our language here is drawn from market theory, and indeed one talks of "marriage markets" and "job markets.") The authors often refer to this framework in explaining timing differentials in marriage, labor-force behavior, or coresidence, referring more frequently to supply-and-demand considerations than to the rules of exchange. The kind of cross-sectional quantitative evidence we use here does not tell much about the rules, but we do know how many men per women there were in a given locality, how many jobs per family, and how many occupied dwellings per household.

Individuals come to transition decisions controlling differing amounts of resources. Those best endowed have more latitude in their choice, being better able to afford to remain in school or to leave it, to marry or to remain single. The census documents analyzed here do not reflect very many of these resources. Beauty, intelligence, strength, health, wealth, and skill go unmeasured, leaving us with somewhat bare pickings in discussing this theoretically important element of timing. The test, by Mason, Vinovskis, and Hareven in Chapter 6 of the efficacy of one such resource, literacy, on female labor-force participation is judged ambiguous by the authors.

It would be consistent with the arguments of Chudacoff and Hareven to hypothesize that older men who were employed (and thus evidently employable) would be more able to forestall the transition to dependency status within the household. Work in progress on a study of marriage in late nineteenth-century Philadelphia based on a 10-year census trace indicates that unmarried men at any given age who held, or gained wealth during the decade, were twice as likely to marry than were those wholly and consistently lacking wealth.

In contemplating transitions of the sort we are discussing here, individuals did not enter the market wholly as free agents, considering only their own utilities. They operated, instead, within a system in which family responses played a large role. The collective familistic character of decisions affecting transitions in the past was an essential feature of timing and may distinguish many categories of "historical" decisions from contemporary ones. The chapters here can only hint at mechanisms (such as power) for reconciling conflicts of interest among different family members. Most of the ongoing research in the history of the family has focused primarily on behavioral variables. The paucity of qualitative sources on this subject offers little insight into internal processes of family decision making. The examination of timing can, at least, provide insight into priorities in the collective strategies of the family. For, as we shall show further in our discussion, the timing of transitions into different roles was closely related to family responses to economic conditions.

The Pace and Sequence of Transitions

In this section, we will examine two interrelated aspects of transitions: (a) the pace at which a population group accomplishes a transition; (b) the ways in which one transition affected others for individuals and their families.

In examining the timing of different life-course transitions we can observe the incidence of status changes by age, an indication of the pace at which a population group would make a transition in and out of a status. (We do this assuming no dramatic cohort or period change in the incidence of the transition and that migration and death are unrelated to the transition in question.) Since each status is, in fact, strongly related to age, we can represent the approximate pace at which a population passes through a transition as a function of the proportion who ultimately undergo it, and the number of years between the first in a cohort to change their status and the last to change. Operationally, we are estimating what proportion of all the population makes the transition in an average year during the transition ages. In nineteenth-century Essex County it seems to be the case that transitions are paced more rapidly earlier in the life course than later.

School entry in mid-nineteenth century Essex County increased an additional 19% or so with every year of age after the transition was begun. The percentage that left school per year of age after peak attendance approached 13–14%. This figure is considerably higher than that for entry into the labor force for women, and, not unlikely, for men. From the midteens to the early twenties, the slope seems to be in the neighborhood of 10% per year of new labor-force entrants for males, and around 8% for females. For women, departure from the labor force was less speedy than entrance, but was in keeping with the pace of marriage—about 5% more married annually. The transition to household headship included a clear lag between marriage and headship status for the population as a whole and seems to have been a percentage point or so slower than the rate of marriage.

The concerns of the Essex chapters pass over the middle years, and pick up again at old age. Here, two transitions are within our purview: retirement from the labor force and residential dependency, both characterized by Chudacoff and Hareven as surprisingly infrequent in

Essex County. Both transitions were quite leisurely in their pace. Only about 1% of men a year ceased being heads of households, about the same rate as the male decrement of labor-force participation during these years. Females moved somewhat more rapidly into dependent household statuses (with the deaths of their husbands, no doubt), but even so the pace of transitions into "old-age" statuses, if inexorable, was slow.

These estimates offer an abstracted summary of nineteenth-century age-grading, arrayed over the life course of individuals for the period 1860–1885 in Essex County. The more general findings is suggestive: In this series of age-graded events, a year of age made the most difference in the earliest part of life; each successive transition was more leisurely. As we shall suggest later on, the last transitions were also the most contingent, the most subject to both market and familial mechanisms discussed above.

What was the meaning of these different transitions within a family context? Ankarloo's construct of the "reproductive cycle," helps identify some of the interrelationships: Ankarloo points out that for native Americans the combination of age at marriage and age at first birth made for a relatively short period between the birth of a person and that of his first grandchild, but that for Irish immigrants a typical reproductive cycle was many years longer. Ankarloo (Chapter 4 of this volume) has found that these interrelated sequences had several familial consequences: age at marriage can thus to some extent be used as a predictor for the structural characteristics of the parental household. Those marrying late will more often have obligations to support a widowed mother or a retired father. On the other hand, those who marry early will also be more likely to live in quasi-dependence, after marriage, in their parents' household. The interrelationships of timing among several individuals to a degree "create" the household configurations typical of the group in question. The "reproductive cycle" concept and its correlates to which Ankarloo alludes suggest in less fully developed form Elder's prescription of studying integrated life course behavior by construction of complex time-tables linking ages at marriage, first birth, and last birth. As Ankarloo's argument suggests, problems of synchronization and coordination in family management arise from the sequencing and synchronization of life-course events in realms internal and external to the family.

To what extent are such patterns of timing related to the family's allocation of its members' efforts over the life course? The family cycle provides a useful way of summarizing how a family acquires and dispenses its resources over time. Our contributors have in several ways provided us with indications of how aspects of the family cycle (as indicated by the head's age) may have affected the timing of life-course transitions of its constituent members. The class means in Kaestle and Vinovskis's (Chapter 5 of this volume) Tables 5.1 and 5.2 suggest that both school entry and departure may, crudely measured, bear a relationship to parents' age, a critical factor in most family-cycle indicators. But almost all of the patterns disappear when other variables are controlled (whether age of parent was related to school attendance by way of child's age or in some other way is not discernible here). The only remaining relationship is an interesting one, however; very young families in three out of the four cases sent smaller than usual proportions of their children to school. Are we perhaps tapping some dimension of a lack of prudence leading both to young marriage and to keeping children out of school? Could we couple the finding (remembering how very unusual it was for any variable apart from child's age to affect school entry) with Ankarloo's discussion of premarital pregnancy to project an out-of-phase family cycle, with effects continuing long after the first elements of disorder?

On the other hand, the impact of the household heads' ages on the work of their daughters was inconsistent and weak, despite the fact that Table 6.4 shows that other women in these households, typically wives of the heads, dropped out of the work-force in older families. Young women most typically entered the labor force in their parents' middle years, and left it as their parents entered old age. Since most indexes of well-being followed a curvilinear course with the family cycle, indicating different constraints at different parental ages, the treatment of parents' age as a linear variable may have confused two contrary effects.

Ankarloo's analysis, on the other hand, points to a continuing significance to the timing of marriage of the "child's position in the parental family cycle," both birth order and parent's age at the birth of the individual in question. Ankarloo shows that this positioning affects the amount of pressure parents are able to place upon their children regarding marriage (though the linkages by which the pressure is applied are not specified), and that earlier-born children marry more often at average ages (Table 4.9). "As long as the family is intact (all members present, including younger siblings) the familial sanctions against deviation will be imposed by parents in their midcareer and motivated as a precaution against an uncontrolled transition to the empty-nest stage [Ankarloo, Chapter 4 of this volume:113]."

Table 7.3 shows that for females, age does not much affect the extent to which older women live outside familial settings, although through widowhood it does greatly affect the proportion who are living as dependent kin. "Control," or at any rate obligation, seems to affect most cases. Very old men (Table 7.2) seem to show a greater tendency to live outside of kin settings, although they are able to retain headship more often. Perhaps this speaks to a sex differential in the strength of networks of obligation, perhaps to the absence of comfortable roles within the family for older men, whereas older women could perhaps assist with child care and housekeeping. Whatever the cause, the overall figures presented in Chapter 7 point to a well-functioning system of continuing familial obligation, owing, perhaps, to the care with which children's marital careers were integrated into the parental family cycle (following Ankarloo's argument). It seems as though, in this regard, coresidence and marriage had an order of importance different from schooling and work. They are, we should remind the reader, later transitions, and their pace less rapid. Perhaps it was the end of the life course that was most problematic, and critical; and it is the end of one generation that affects the middle of the generation following.

The Impact of Ethnicity and Class

Ankarloo displays a particular concern for the ethnic context upon the timing of marriage and related life-course events. He finds that Irish immigrants and their American-born children were marrying later than native or Canadian-born. Ankarloo claims that class considerations of marriage timing, far from reinforcing these tendencies, countered some of them, so that if class were statistically controlled the medians would be even more disparate. The pace of marriage seems to have been essentially the same from group to group, although its beginning, middle, and end differed. This pattern suggests that age norms among different groups may have been each modified by similar mechanisms.

Ethnic differences were also evident in the interrelation of timing decisions in the context of the family. Hareven and Vinovskis (forthcoming) found that Essex County marital fertility patterns in 1880 offered some substantiation of this. Looking at recent fertility data for married women they discovered an age-specific fertility pattern for native women which was appreciably flatter than that of Irish or Canadians. The natives began their childbearing (it would seem) as they began their marriage—relatively early. By their mid-twenties, the foreign-born women had caught up. Already the recent fertility of the native group was declining, while the Canadians peaked in their late twenties and the Irish in their early thirties. Thus, natives were already segregating family-building activities to the beginning of their married lives. For the Irish, the whole enterprise was delayed, with childbearing spread over a longer period. As Ankarloo shows, this delay may have facilitated the establishment of an independent household after marriage among most Irish.

By the 1880s Irish immigrant families were reducing their tendency to have many children, to withdraw them from school relatively young, and to send them to work. This pattern can also be seen in Modell's (forthcoming) analysis of working families' budgets in 1889, which show a tendency in that direction. Higher fathers' incomes were beginning to allow the Irish to adapt their entire family income and expenditure strategies to the American models they had partially adopted in anticipation. Chapters 5 and 6 allow us to test this argument, and to measure the relative importance of ethnicity in schooling and labor-force transitions. Our strongest tests are to compare the experience of second-generation Irish-American children with third or subsequent generations of American natives.

Chapter 5 calculates a moderate difference in unadjusted means between the children of the immigrants and the children of native Americans in school attendance in 1860 (Table 5.1), less than the difference attributable to a single additional year of age. Although with controls much of this difference is eliminated, the difference is in the anticipated direction: In 1860, the Irish seem to have timed school entry a little later for their children than did natives. By 1880, the difference was reduced, though still present.

Not unexpectedly, the timing of leaving school was more dependent upon ethnic cultural context than that of entering, the most strictly age-structured transition. American-born children of Irish immigrants showed a decreasing propensity to early departure from school (Table 5.2). This propensity, according to the figures in Chapter 5, amounts to a typical departure for Irish of about one year earlier than native children. We note that this, while significant, is less substantial than the 3–4 year difference in marriage age Ankarloo found. Chapter 6 shows that American-born Irish girls living with their parents were considerably more likely to have been in the labor force than were non-Irish girls. Controlling for class and situation, we can conclude that the ethnic culture in which families developed affected the way they managed their children's transitions. As Modell's family budget study indicates, these timing patterns were part of the way families arranged their lives, particularly in relation to the family economy, present and anticipated, and to fertility, present and past (Modell, (forthcoming).

It stands to reason that couples integrated conscious images of both the boundaries and the content of the "reproductive cycles" that are characteristic of their cultures. We can speculate that the late marrying of the Irish, along with protracted fertility patterns, would encourage considerable coresidence of widows with their children. Irish immigrants were rarely well paid, and were often involved in seasonal labor that was unsuitable for the aged. Coresidence probably often involved dependence of parents upon their children, and in accepting this obligation, a protracted bachelorhood or spinsterhood on the part of one or more children. These family mechanisms did not differ from those employed by native Americans except in their frequency. But the parts of the "reproductive cycle" creating these patterns were very likely under pressure as contact with native values emphasized their costs. The pressure, one imagines, affected all elements of the cycle.

Class considerations affecting timing were deeply intertwined with ethnic ones. Unfortunately, they are far harder to measure because they are empirically entangled with momentary economic considerations which are conceptually different. Since their methodology offers the best approach to this problem, the chapters on school attendance and women's labor-force participation (using multiple classification analysis) are the logical starting points in a consideration of the effects of class on the timing of life-course decisions. In Chapter 5, our best indicator of class per se on schooling is parental occupation, excluding from consideration father-absent families. Departure from school often represented a simultaneous or nearly simultaneous decision to enter the labor force. Children aged 8 or younger, at the school-entry ages, earned virtually no income. We can thus compare the effects of parental occupational class on school entrance and departure in order to contrast the class-based value for schooling with the financially based tradeoff between continued schooling and immediate income. (An alternative view, indicated in Chapter 5, is that rather than a single attitude toward schooling, two distinct attitudes, one toward early and one toward late schooling, may have existed.) If we consider the difference between the professional and semiprofessional occupational class and the semi- and unskilled occupational class, findings, for the purposes we have outlined, are fairly strong.

Class culture, thus measured, has no effect to speak of on the timing of school entry. In 1860 and 1880, no percentage difference, gross or net, amounted to as much as 5%. But things are quite different for the timing of departure from school. The gross percentage difference is about 25% (equivalent to perhaps 2 years age difference). This is reduced by controls by about half, but the remaining net difference of 10 or 15%—about the same effect as ethnic culture had had—is still significant, and amounts to about a year's earlier departure from school by children from lower-class families. We are not surprised to find a similar order of effect of parent's occupational class in predicting labor-force participation of young women in Chapter 6. The effect of class culture upon the educational transitions seems to have operated not through any distinct attitude about schooling and childrearing. Instead (and we could assert this with substantial confidence if our controls for the differential resources held by the families of the different classes were perfect) working-class and white-collar cultures made different tradeoffs between immediate income and its deferral in behalf of continued schooling. In view of what we know of the precarious nature of many domestic economies in the industrial nineteenth century we need hardly explain the different tradeoffs by different class tastes.

If class-based decision patterns propelled lower-class persons out of school and into the labor force, we may then reasonably ask whether working-class children's earlier contribution to their parents' family gave them a bargaining lever with which to achieve earlier marriage. Alternatively, we might find that the presumed scarcity of family resources that accompanied lower-class membership instead delayed marriage. Ankarloo (Table 4.10) pushes strongly toward the former interpretation. The proportion of children of upper-class parental origin marrying late was almost twice the proportion for children from lower-class fathers. Ankarloo's (Chapter 4 of this volume:113) explanation is in terms of "full or sufficient access to the productive system . . . as in unskilled, industrial occupations," although this explanation might better apply directly to variation in occupations of the marrying persons themselves. The finding is also consistent with the bargaining-position argument advanced here, in view of the contribution already given by lower-class children to their families of origin by the time of their marriage. The interpretation, however, is clouded by Ankarloo's very suggestive finding that members of the lower-class who married (presumably despite their relative youth) were more likely (Table 4.3) than those of more favored origin to have lived independently of their parents before their marriage; when they did not live independently before marriage, they were not so prone as others to move to independent quarters with their new spouses (Tables 4.4 and 4.5).

The timing of marriage in the lower class seems to have been considerably less contingent upon the establishment of residential independence either before or after marriage. If, and this is indeed speculative in view of the lack of statistical controls, there are those kinds of class-based differences in the degrees of intergenerational continuity and interrelation in family (and kin group) economies, we can readily hypothesize that retirement and dependency, the old-age transitions, were more common among lower classes because they fit in more smoothly with the less uniform patterns of transitions characteristic of the poor.

Family Economy and the Timing of Transitions

The key to this and many earlier arguments in this chapter is the idea that the nineteenth-century family economy was of necessity flexible because individual resources were precarious and institutional buttressing was slim. For the Irish, for lower-class families, limited and uncertain resources may well have called forth traditional adaptations, or perhaps innovative ones. Several of the contributors to this volume endeavor to measure the relationship of family resources to family needs, as apart from class. The conceptual distinction is an important one, for norm-based preferences in organizing the life course, or in timing any single transition, are modified in particular cases by a variety of exigencies stemming from previous demographic events, earlier transition patterns, chance happenings, and the effects of social change beyond individual control.

The chapters examining school attendance and women's labor force participation have devised a "dependency ratio." The ratio includes an income proxy as its numerator: the number of adult-male-equivalent jobs listed for family members. Its denominator is the number of adult-equivalent family members, representing consumption demands. Ankarloo uses a slightly different set of weights for his measure of percentage "dependent members of a household." Chapter 6 treats the presence of boarders in the household as a special instance of increased family resources. Chapter 7 examines the taking in of boarders as family "augmentation," which could contribute to the household economy (Table 7.6). Ankarloo's findings in Chapter 4 are the most unequivocal for our purposes. Considering the particular question of postmarital residence (which, as we have seen, was a complex function of class and marital age), Ankarloo concludes that there was a threshold of the dependency percentage that, if exceeded, would deter newlywed coresidence with either parental couple. He further maintains that the choice between matrilocality and patrilocality can be understood by this type of calculation. Unfortunately, it is impossible to measure the extent to which such calculations affected the timing of marriage, although we can see in it one mechanism by which family resources may have permitted earlier marriage (often to achieve legitimation of unintended pregnancies, to be sure). The direction of this particular result is contrary to the class–culture emphasis we have examined earlier. Considered together with a model of intrafamilial resource allocation, the consumption index offers highly suggestive insights into the timing of marriage, and a way of thinking about the intriguing difference between lower-class and other children in proportions marrying directly out of their parent's households.

Chapter 6 employs a dependency index that excludes all female occupations from the numerator (since that is what is to be explained), and discovers a "somewhat ambiguous" relationship of resources to labor-force participation. Lower dependency ratios, it seems, simultaneously indicated needy families and families in which the head's occupation could support the entire family, and was thus probably remunerative and prestigious. Thus lower dependency ratios were associated with late entry or early departure from the labor force for daughters. This interpretation is reinforced by a strong negative relationship between the presence of servants and work of daughters, and by a generally positive relationship between taking in boarders and sending daughters to work. This, perhaps, strains a bit too hard for consistency, suggesting that we have no clear indicator in this data set for resources available to families. The puzzling finding in Chapter 5 reinforces this conclusion. The consumption index bears little relationship to the school entry of the very young, but older children of both sexes were more likely to be in school where the dependency index was low. This finding, too, holds even though it is weakened when controlling for the level of head's occupation.

The theoretical expectation is clearly that immediate resources will make markedly easier transitions to states that are themselves relatively expensive, or that imply earnings foregone. The implication so far as we can see from these data is that "class" is powerful indeed in its likely effect on the transitions under discussion, and that the family-resource-based explanation may be weaker than we would expect.[1]

Another measure of family economic advantage is in the control over housing space. Chapter 7 explains surprisingly high rates of headship by older people in terms of their control of the housing resource, especially during periods of housing shortage. It is striking in this

---

[1]Further consideration of these questions, perhaps using the wealth measures in the 1860 census (not available for 1880) as an unambiguous resource indicator, is needed.

context that higher proportions of the population live in households containing boarders (Table 7.6) than either themselves live as boarders (Table 7.2, 7.3) or head households containing boarders. This peculiar translation of the housing resource, then, does not seem a substitution for familial use, but rather a mechanism, employed by heads, and not only by the elderly, to support complex households including old people. In this sense, the response mitigates the fragmenting effects of transitions. Chapter 7 even suggests that extended households including old people are more likely to be augmented by a boarder than are nuclear households with old members (Table 7.6). The data are far from conclusive on this point, and the indicator of boarders is subject to the ambiguity that has been suggested.

Just as resources affect timing, so individual attributes or capabilities may facilitate particular timing decisions and encourage a particular life course. Overall, the evidence for the relevance of individually controlled capabilities to the timing of transitions seems strong, but in none of the chapters of this book is the subject treated in the kind of detail that would permit any conclusive statement beyond this, or the tentative suggestion that capabilities and resources increased in their variance over the life course. No doubt the ability to work remuneratively explains some of the difference between the older men and older women in their ability to maintain nuclear households, which was presumably the preferred arrangement. Chapter 7 (Table 7.6) shows that 60 to 70% of older men but only 40 to 60% of older women lived in nuclear settings. Tables 7.2 and 7.3 strongly suggest that this difference is not the result of differences in age structure.

Old-age dependency was the less expensive condition, because it economized on space, sick care, etc.; so, too, did delayed marriage. Yet Ankarloo's Table 4.12 would seem to imply that not only were people who marry young more likely not to have achieved the high occupational status of their fathers, but that the upwardly mobile people from lower-class origins married older. The attributes being considered here are occupational skills and wherewithal. Acquiring the background skills for high-paying occupations may have been hindered by early marriage. This, again, is at best suggestive, but does point to the likelihood that in marriage, even of people whose parents were still living, individual skills and class origins are indeed two conceptually distinct, if empirically related, dimensions. If so, we need to delineate the interactive relationship between the accumulation of occupational skills, economic resources and other capabilities, and the decision to marry at a given age.

Dropping out of school may indeed have followed in substantial measure (age effects only excepted) from individual capacities. There is no way of telling this from the census schedules. Similarly, we can not measure individual attributes such as beauty or efficiency which may have affected the work careers of Essex women. We do know a number of things, however, about the individual resources of Essex women, relevant to their labor-force behavior. Chapter 6 presents these in Table 6.2. Two are of substantial, and about equal, import: marital status and household relationship. A woman at this time could call upon the resources of a household to which she was related, and upon the resources of a husband, each greatly reducing the necessity of working for remuneration, and thus precipitating departure from the labor force. The labor-force behavior of women would indicate that almost two-thirds of the 50-year-old women would have remained in the labor force if they were still unmarried and living as unrelated persons, and about a third would have been working at that age if unmarried but a family member. At no age would this many married women with a spouse or other relations present have remained at work. Much of the gross age effect, indeed, was a function of simultaneous transitions with age into more advantageous marital and household statuses.

Communities and Local Markets

The ways individuals were able to accomplish transitions may have varied by location even when they and their families had similar resources and preferences. First, the operation of the local marriage market, as Chapter 4 points out, was measurably significant in allocating aspirants to immediate marriage or to delay, and Chapter 7 develops evidence for a tight housing market and its effect on the position of the younger generation vis a vis coresidence with the older.

Chapter 4 shows that the age–sex specificity of migration patterns leads to sex ratios that differ sharply from place to place for unmarried people of marriageable age. Ankarloo identifies one pattern of female competition and male opportunities and another of male competition and female opportunities, and shows that the proportion of apparent long-term residents who marry by given ages is a function of these patterns (Table 4.2).

Markets need not have inflexible operating rules. Eligibility for marriage will probably vary. Ankarloo is not able to examine this question either as regards nativity, class, or age differences of spouses, except in noting the fact of and the interrelationships among patterns of ethnic and class homogamy. The flexibility of the rules of the marriage market is itself an interesting question.

Chudacoff and Hareven, in their study of the local housing market, point (Figures 7.2 and 7.3) to the short-term tightness of housing in this period, thereby adding a suggestive dynamic element to the static picture derived from the census, and predict that coresidence would be high at the end of such a period of tightness in 1880. Moreover, they maintain that in such circumstances, "extra kin and nonkin," new to the search for housing, "were being attached to households headed by old people." Accordingly, the period 1875–1880 showed for all the Essex cities a sharp upward thrust in the average number of persons per household which receded again in the succeeding 5 years. Even more tenuously, the data suggest that in Lawrence only, these "excess" persons were accomodated by expanding the number of coresiding families, while in Salem and Lynn the number of conjugal units increased less rapidly. Conceivably, this is reflected in the preeminent "headship" solution in Lawrence for the residence of older men (Table 7.2). The linkages are very unclear, although the relationship of the housing market and coresidential patterns—and thereby family interactions, if only temporarily—is obviously important. Chudacoff and Hareven have provided an initial examination of this question.

Putting the several contributions side by side with attention to locale is strong evidence that place-to-place variation is, at any rate for mid-nineteenth century Essex, slight enough that the dominant patterns show through everywhere. It is impossible to construct any convincing view that life was organized in different ways in Salem and Lynn. Such differences as were present probably can be resolved to a combination of lower-order concerns: the patterns of net and gross migration and their consequence in age and sex structure, and job and housing-market differences. A consideration of local variation will help point us to further directions of investigation.

School entrance and departure show no consistent city-to-city pattern, and differences are small at best (except urban–rural, where at both ends of the school period rural places had more children at school). Local variations in female labor-force participation are consistent in direction as between offspring and other female household members, but the latter shows only very small variation. Consistent in direction, too, is the effect of locality on the labor-force participation of all women including those outside of the closely defined household sample. But the local effect is far greater on this less selective sample, suggesting that local differences in demand for female labor affects the supply of female labor in three ways that are conceptually different. Least responsive to demand was the supply of labor by "other" women in the households, that is, spouses primarily; next least responsive was the labor of coresident unmarried daughters; but most responsive was the rest of the female labor force, especially that part composed of immigrants and domestic migrants living outside of their families of origin. Migration, of course, is an event which has a determinate part in the life course of individuals and in the life of families. Unfortunately, its elucidation would seem to require longitudinal or retrospective data on individuals not at hand, although it is available in at least one state census.

Labor-force participation varied from town-to-town inversely as did school attendance for the older children, leading us to suspect that local variation in school departure was a function of local labor markets. Generally, children left school and girls entered the labor force earlier in Lynn and Lawrence, as compared with Salem and the rural places, although this generalization is perhaps reading undue clarity into a complicated situation. Ankarloo's refined female marriage rate seems to follow this same division, too, suggesting perhaps a younger "adulthood" overall for those in the more industrial places. Marital fertility was lower in these seats of industry, at least when nativity is controlled. Data not presented in the Essex chapters but derived from the same sample shows that husband–wife families in Salem were, at given ages, considerably more likely than those in Lawrence or Lynn (the rural patterns are confused, probably owing to small numbers) to have had at least one child living with them. A "modern" pattern of early marriage combined with controlled fertility may perhaps have been emerging most rapidly in the most industrial places, with implications for the organization of the life course and the family. The effects of the industrial context, too, may perhaps be seen in the higher-than-expected intermarriage rates for both foreign-born and native-born women in these cities, suggesting a homogenization of "inherited patterns." Clearly such an interpretation pushes the data hard. Additional observations and controls are needed if the consistencies cited are to be shown to be anything more than a chance set. Further, they will have to be reconciled with the lack of pattern in old-age residence and dependency patterns. Just an inkling of greater occupational dependency and nonfamilial dwelling can be seen in the two more industrial cities, but on the basis of what Chapter 7 figures show, one would rather conclude that what we think of as "modern" old-age patterns had about equal lack of currency everywhere in Essex in 1880.

We can make headway in the analysis of this table by recalling that

Salem, as distinct from Lawrence and Lynn, functioned as a central place for the surrounding rural community, was considerably older, had a lower growth rate, and was less narrowly industrial in its occupational structure. In its labor-market characteristics (as indicated by Table 8.1) Salem more nearly resembled the rural places than did Lawrence or Lynn. The number of jobs per family was low in Salem, lower in fact than in the rural places. Susceptibility to unemployment was less severe in Salem and the rural towns than in Lawrence and Lynn, especially for women's occupations. And while the contributions of family-age women were larger than in the rural places, and that of older men and women (who were rarer, of course) lower, in neither

TABLE 8.1
Ratios of Jobs to Families, by Age and Sex, Essex Places, 1885

		Jobs/family	Percentage of all jobs	Percentage unemployed 3 months or more
Rural places				
0–19	male	.181	9.1	26.2
	female	.128	6.4	8.7
20–59	male	1.039	52.1	16.5
	female	.318	15.9	12.9
60+	male	.278	13.9	18.7
	female	.050	2.5	0
Salem				
0–19	male	.168	9.0	20.4
	female	.126	6.8	14.8
20–59	male	1.004	54.0	23.7
	female	.404	21.8	10.7
60+	male	.124	6.7	22.7
	female	.033	1.8	7.9
Lawrence				
0–19	male	.211	9.4	34.7
	female	.156	7.0	53.1
20–59	male	1.136	50.5	23.2
	female	.634	28.2	23.3
60+	male	.090	4.0	33.6
	female	.021	.9	15.4
Lynn				
0–19	male	.160	7.5	35.8
	female	.114	5.3	37.4
20–59	male	1.240	58.3	38.1
	female	.511	24.0	27.8
60+	male	.096	4.5	34.4
	female	.006	.3	21.7

case were these divergences so great as in the two more fully industrialized cities. Insofar as we can consider this range of employment opportunities to have been given by the local economy, we can predict that the contribution to the several Salem age–sex groups to the local family economies rather resembled that in rural places. To the degree that such contributions determine the relationship of members of the several age–sex groups to their families, we can predict that the characteristics of Salem transitions will resemble those in the rural towns.

The Lawrence and Lynn economies—the former especially—offered notably more jobs per family. In both, the male central-age adults make a per-family contribution above that in Salem or in the rural towns. In both, very little occupational support per family was available from older men or women; the seasonality of the predominant industries produced a relatively high level of unemployment; and occupational structures allowed high per-family contributions by central-age women. In Lawrence especially, the census counted almost two-thirds of a job per family from this portion of the population, and with a far lower incidence of unemployment than among the young, who also made relatively large contributions. In Lynn, where female employment was about half a job per family, unemployment for this group was higher than in Lawrence. At the same time, it was lower than for the males there, who were especially subject to unemployment.

There were also significant differences in household patterns among these communities. Even though nonfamilial living was rare, different localities had different modes of attaching individuals to private families: notably, boarding and lodging varied from place to place. Once again, however, migration complicates patterns. The analysis of age structures helps us but does not entirely solve this problem. It suggests that the structures of labor forces were significantly variable and an important aspect of local context. In the rural towns and in Salem, we would anticipate youthful marriage for females, since competing working roles were relatively rare, and by the same token we would expect relatively high fertility within marriage. The low unemployment rate would lead us to anticipate relatively few complex residential adaptations to family economies hit by depletion through unemployment. In Salem, and in the rural places particularly, important economic contributions were made by older people, whose dependency would be correspondingly low.

The position of the old must have been weak in Lawrence and Lynn, at least insofar as it depended upon occupational contribution. The position of young adult women, by contrast, must have been quite strong. We anticipate this to be indexed by relatively late marriage and

low fertility, and thus either long coresidence with parents or as a
boarder or servant. Whether the difference between the two cities in
youth employment (and thereby the cost-offsetting benefits of each
child) would be reflected in fertility patterns (we would expect Lynn to
have the lowest fertility on this basis) is a function of how strong this
connection was, and how long it had existed. Both the high jobs-per-
family ratio and the high unemployment rates in the two industrial
cities would make for a more varied set of family economies at any
moment, and presumably a more varied set of coresidence patterns.

Historical Implications

The question now arises as to what these chapters teach us about
the timing of life-course transitions, family and household behavior,
and on a larger scale, about ethnicity, class, and social change. Without
attempting to generalize from the transitions examined here to the entire life course, or from the experience of Essex County, Massachusetts,
to the entire society, it is still possible to draw some broad and suggestive conclusions that transcend the immediate circumstances of the
studies.

First, it is clear that there was a significant difference between the
pacing of early and later life-course transitions. The early transitions
for children into schooling, and for women, into and out of the labor
force, were more strictly related to age than the later life-course transitions out of the labor force and out of parental roles. Transitions into
adult roles were more rapidly timed. On the other hand, later life-
course transitions, such as exit from parental roles, were much more
gradual and slow, and in many instances, did not occur until the end of
life. In the early phases of the life course, individuals moved rapidly
into new roles. Once they assumed these roles, they stayed within them
through major portions of their adult lives. While entry into these roles
was considered the normatively established sequence, and therefore,
an accomplishment, exit from them was associated with decline and
dependency. (Couples are congratulated when they marry and when
they become parents. They are not congratulated when their children
leave home, or when they have to break up their household.)

Essential to our understanding of nineteenth-century life-course
transitions is their integration around the family. Most transitions, except for schooling and labor-force participation, were family transitions.
The family was the arena within which and out of which most of these
moves by individuals or couples took place. Transitions entailed mov-

ing from one status to another within the family, or from one family to the next: from one's family of orientation to one's family of procreation, and on rare occasions, after marriage back to one's family of orientation. Even seemingly nonfamilial transitions, such as entry into and exit from school or the labor force, were closely related to family considerations.

The question arises then: How did individuals and families cope with conflicting goals and allegiances to their families of orientation and their families of procreation? How did they make their transitions from one to the other, without jeopardizing the independence and self-sufficiency of one at the expense of the other? Most of the findings in these chapters seem to revolve around this dilemma, a dilemma intensified by two conflicting tendencies in American culture. One was the frequently proscribed expectation that the integrity of the family be preserved. The other was the expectation that young adults achieve autonomy as soon as possible. Under a regime of limited resources, frequent migration, high risk, and overall insecurity, mutual assistance among kin was considered the very base of family continuity. In view of this heavy reliance on kin, how were individuals able to fulfill both of the roles prescribed in the culture? How could they become independent adults who headed their own households and cared for their own children and at the same time also assure support to their family of orientation, especially to their aging parents?

The dilemma was further intensified by yet another apparent commitment in American culture to the nuclearity of the household. As in our time, throughout the nineteenth century residence in nuclear households seems to have been the norm. By contrast to our time, the line was drawn excluding extended kin, but admitting strangers. Households more often included boarders and lodgers than cousins, aunts, adult siblings, or aging parents. Despite the overall commitment in the culture to the nuclearity of the household, extension did appear, when aged parents needed the continuing support of their children at home, or when adult children depended on shared household space with their parents in order to be able to marry. In many instances, when children were not available or willing to fulfill such functions surrogate kin (boarders and lodgers) engaged in reciprocal relations with older heads of household. Children's continued stay in their parents' household, bringing their newlywed spouses into the parental home, or conversely, for parents, readmitting into the household children who had left home after their marriage, were exceptions coming as concessions to economic pressures and to familial needs. Even in such cases, the commonly followed pattern was that of children staying in or moving into the parental home, rather than that of parents moving in with their children. Wherever aging couples were able to, they continued to hold onto the headship of their own households. Even aging widows tended to follow this pattern as much as possible. Autonomy of the household was clearly of supreme importance.

Viewed from the perspective of the collective needs of the family unit, it becomes clear that the needs of households and of families changed along the life course in relation to changing economic and social conditions. It thus appears that collective family needs and strategies were major proximate determinants of the timing of life-course transitions.

Having identified the extent to which individual life-course transitions may have been affected by overall familial considerations, especially under the impact of economic insecurity one would wish to know to what extent these patterns of timing are manifestations of class rather than culture or vice versa. Our answer to this is unsatisfactory, because of the imprecise measures for both class and culture in our data. For example, Irish timing may have been different from native American timing, because Irish families had higher fertility. Because of their large numbers of children, Irish families would have produced different age configurations at each stage of the life course than families with small numbers of children. In this instance, timing in Irish families would be affected by net fertility, which is the result of an ethnic preference. In assessing the relative impact of class and ethnicity on timing, it is also necessary to differentiate immediate decisions on timing from long range ones. Sending a child to work, leaving home, or taking in a boarder, are immediate decisions with limited consequences, while the decisions affecting the timing of marriage and number and spacing of children involve more lasting and consequential moves. Such decisions require careful planning that might be influenced by cultural background as well as socioeconomic status. In the population groups studied here, where economic insecurity was a pervasive pattern, economic needs often took priority over normatively established time schedules. But the ways in which different groups in the population went about meeting these needs may have been dictated by cultural differences emanating from ethnic traditions. Ethnicity may have affected timing in several ways: indirectly, through its impact on earlier behavior that affects subsequent timing (fertility), and directly, in making immediate choices pertaining to schooling, women's labor-force participation, or leaving home. Modell's (forthcoming) study of family budgets suggests that as Irish families adopted American tastes and standards of living, they gradually adjusted their timing and family-labor strategies accordingly. It is possible the people in 1880 Essex were in transition, both, in terms of their station along the life course and as part of the process of historical change.

The question arises, therefore: To what extent can the late nineteenth-century patterns examined here be placed in a long-range historical perspective on social change? Ideally, it would be necessary to compare different cohorts over time to find a satisfactory answer to this question. The answers offered here fall more within the realm of speculation and hypothesis.

First, as Uhlenberg suggests, over the past century American society has experienced a growing uniformity in the timing of life-course transitions. Survival of larger proportions of each cohort to adulthood and their increasing tendency to fulfill adult familial scripts of marriage, parenthood, and launching of children from the home, have contributed to this growing uniformity. The decline in mortality since the late nineteenth century has considerably increased the chances for intact survival of the family unit over the lifetime of its members. Thus, an increasing proportion of the population has entered prescribed family roles, and except for disruption by divorce, has lived out its life in family units. (The trend in solitary residence suggests a change in this pattern since the 1950s [Kobrin, 1976].)

The same demographic factors responsible for these continuities have also generated important discontinuities that have tended to enforce age segregation in American society. These increasing life-course discontinuities over the past century were expressed in the timing of transitions into and out of family roles, and are closely related to the gradual segmentation of the life course into socially acknowledged stages (childhood, youth, adolescence, adulthood, middle age, and old age). These discontinuities have affected the timing of transitions to adulthood in such areas as family formation and parenthood, entry into the post-parental or empty-nest period, and entry into old age. As Modell et al. (1976) have shown, transitions in the earlier part of the life course (out of the parental home to marriage, to household headship, and to parenthood) occurred more gradually and with less rigid timing in the nineteenth century. Among the differences: The time range necessary for a cohort to accomplish such transitions was wider; different transitions (leaving home, marriage, etc.) were not always timed in the same sequence; and there was no consistent congruity among various transitions. Over the past century, transitions to adulthood have become less uniform for the entire population but more rapidly timed. The factors determining such historical variation in timing also may have changed: "Timely action to nineteenth-century families consisted of helpful response in times of trouble; in the twentieth century, timeliness connotes adherence to a schedule [Modell et al., 1976:30]."

One can only begin to speculate what factors affected historical changes in timing (other than the demographic factors of declining mortality, declining fertility, and earlier marriage). First, institutional change was certainly important. The emergence of legislation affecting school attendance and regulating child labor set rigid age limits to leaving schooling and entering the labor force. Increasing efforts of enforcement of this legislation, combined with parents' increasing tendency to keep their children longer in school, have resulted in a more uniform observance of such schedules. On the other end of the life course, retirement and social security have imposed externally defined boundaries in the later years of life, resulting in greater independence of aging parents and adult children from each other. The separation between the family of procreation and the family of orientation has become more definite, thus enabling adult children to time their transitions into their new families more independently of their parents. The gradual transfer of responsibilities for the support and assistance from the family to that of the welfare state has relieved some of the traditional burdens carried by kin. Consequently, the family has ceased to be the exclusive central resource of support and survival. Related to the growing bureaucratization of some of the functions earlier held by kin is the erosion of instrumental relationships within the family. The growing privatization of the family, and a growing concentration on the family as a consumption unit and as a source of nurture, rather than as a productive economic unit, have clearly affected the timing of life-course transitions. The shrinking of intergenerational obligations, especially in later years of life, has resulted in a more distinct separation between the family of orientation and the family of procreation, and therefore, more clearly defined time schedules.

Third, the gradual adoption of American norms by immigrants, especially in the second and third generation, and the continuing adaptation of working-class families to middle-class family standards have further increased uniformity in timing and in related family organization. In accepting this generalization, one must keep in mind that this process has not been fully accomplished, and that traditional patterns of timing have persisted to different degrees among various ethnic groups.

References

Hareven, Tamara K., and Maris Vinovskis
    Forth-   "Patterns of childbearing in late nineteenth-century America: The deter-
    coming   minants of marital fertility in five Massachusetts towns in 1880." In Tam-
             ara K. Hareven and Maris Vinovskis (eds.), Family and Population in
             Nineteenth-Century America. Princeton: Princeton University Press.

Kobrin, Frances E.
    1976   "The fall of household size and the rise of the primary individual." De-
             mography 127–138.

Modell, John
    Forth-   "Patterns of consumption, acculturation, and family income strategy in
    coming   late nineteenth-century America." In Tamara K. Hareven and Maris
             Vinovskis (eds.), Family and Population in Nineteenth-Century America.
             Princeton: Princeton University Press.

Modell, John, Frank F. Furstenberg, Jr., and Theodore Hershberg
    1976   "Social change and transitions to adulthood in historical perspective."
             Journal of Family History 1:7–32.

9

Economic Perspectives on the Life Course

STANLEY ENGERMAN

The preceding chapters, presenting empirical studies of key decisions in the life course and a theoretical discussion of the conceptual framework in which such decisions can be studied, provide an important contribution to the social and economic history of the United States. Essex County, Massachusetts in the late nineteenth century has been used as a historical case study to analyze how individual decisions were affected by family life, and how these decisions varied with differences in social class and ethnic background. The empirical threads of these case studies are drawn together in Chapter 8 and there is no need to attempt a similar synthesis here. Instead, I would like to make some general remarks about the economic approach to historical problems and its significance to the study of these life-course problems.

The limited application of economic analysis has been a characteristic of the "new social history." Despite frequent calls to interdisciplinary studies, however, the different approaches of various disciplines often make communication difficult. In some cases this has resulted in historians being "more economic than the economists," without really benefiting from the analytical tools of the economist. In large part, this difficulty reflects the failure of historians and other social scientists to distinguish adequately between the application of

271

TRANSITIONS
The Family and the Life Course in
Historical Perspective

economic constructs and the conceptual applicability of an attributed "economic motive." There has been frequent confusion in contrasting an "economic motive" with other determinants of human behavior. Yet, properly understood, there is no conflict between economic analysis and the cultural or social explanations so often favored by historians. Since an economic motive can be, and has been, attributed without any real economic analysis, and because economic analysis permits the outcome of other motives, even those historians of an economic bent often have overlooked the value of the economic approach.

The economic approach represents an attempt to explain certain behavior, based on individual tastes, however formed, in response to external conditions. Yet these tastes and the external conditions generating responses are not necessarily economic as that term is often used (or misused). The basic tastes of individuals often are considered to be outside the realm of economic analysis, and are obviously molded by interactions in various social and cultural contexts. Indeed, a proper use of economic analysis can be of great importance in attempting to isolate the impact of "noneconomic" cultural and social variables. For example, several studies examine the varying adjustments made by members of different ethnic and immigrant groups to similar external stimuli. These behavioral differences permit us to describe better the nature of the differences in "tastes" (here, culturally derived attitudes) among these groups. Analyzing the economic variables involved permits us to depict the effect of a specified set of constraints on behavior. The concept of the budget constraint—an overall limit upon the expenditures that can be made—is meant to indicate that only so much command over the acquisition of goods and services, broadly defined, can be obtained by a family, given its numbers, skills, and training, and that this limit (independent of tastes which affect choice within these limits) affects what the family and its members can and will do. This is not to imply that decisions are made on purely economic grounds, but rather it provides the setting in which choices molded by preferences and other forces are made.

Certainly without a consideration of individual and family tastes it is impossible to explain or to understand the range of responses to variations in the economic environment. To use an analogy drawn from the market for an individual commodity, the fact that individuals face the same price for a commodity does not mean that each individual will purchase an identical quantity of that good. Some of the differences in quantities purchased can be explained by economic conditions, such as differences in income levels, but others can be attributed to what on an individual level could only be regarded as "tastes," and on the level of ethnic or class groups, would be called "norms" or the impact of "culture." By examining how people in similar conditions respond to similar stimuli, we can examine the "norms" that affect behavior in a manner that an improper description of economic influences would miss. Rather than being a source of contrasting explanations, a proper use of "economic" explanations can provide an important guide for the study of cultural norms.

Economic Variables and the Life Course

Several chapters in this book deal with various steps in the life course of individuals, and their relation to and interaction with family decisions. They discuss the nature and timing of specific key decisions made by individuals within a family context—the timing of marriage, the labor-force participation of females, the school attendance of children, the residential decisions of older individuals. As Elder's more theoretical chapter indicates, these are only a small subset of the crucial decisions made. Moreover, when analyzing these decisions, the empirical chapters can deal only with a limited number of independent variables (without full consideration of all the interactions among the choices at a moment in time as well as over future time). To note these limitations is not to differentiate these chapters from the studies of economists, but to point out that both in approach and subject these chapters are similar to empirical economic research. Each decision also has been studied by economists in terms of the influence of economic variables upon decision makers—individuals and families. While economists and historians have long been concerned with these key decisions, there has been, until recently, a failure to use such concepts as the life course. Even recent work has not explicitly drawn the very broad implications of the life course for the individual and the family as could theoretically be done. Yet even the present studies, informed as they are by the notion of a life course and the generally interrelated nature of various decisions, can deal best with only one decision at a time and, generally, in a format that does not permit fully the analysis of the sequence of interrelated decisions in response to changes in exogenous variables.

There is a substantial body of economic theory and empirical measurement which bears upon matters relating to the life course that would be of considerable importance to historians studying past patterns of behavior.[1] This body deals with only a limited number of decisions, made in presumed independence of each other, and thus loses much of the complexity of the actual decision-making process. There is no appreciable difference in this regard with this book's empirical studies. In attempting to handle the implications of one decision, which has broader implications for subsequent decisions of many kinds, all studies seem somewhat empirically intractable due to the large number of variables to be measured, even when, generally, we feel a basic model can be described. It is one thing to include, say, the presence of a child aged 5–9 as an independent variable in an equation explaining female labor-force participation, and then to include the women's presence or absence in the labor force as an independent variable in an equation accounting for school attendance of a child aged 5–9; it is quite another to try to analyze the forces explaining a decision which "simultaneously" determines both. At some time, the childbearing, schooling, and labor-force participation decisions are interrelated, and the answers are really determined at the same time. Thus, the next methodological step will be to pay more attention to methods of simultaneous estimation, but the limited success so far of such procedures applied to these specific problems is perhaps suggestive of the inherent difficulties in this seemingly obvious extension.

In discussing the individual life course, there are several aspects of the interrelations of decisions and their variations over time that make analysis complex. Some complications confront any attempt to explain economic or other behavior over time. The problem of trying to account for one decision when the individual is presumably weighing many influences and choosing from among more than two easily differentiated choices is a familiar one. Nevertheless, empirical studies confront a basic tradeoff between empirical understanding and full historical complexity. Similarly, the need to consider an entire sequence of decisions over a finite (or if there is a family and lineage concern, an infinite) horizon, where the considered choice at one particular moment of time affects the entire range of future options poses,

---

[1]There is no intention here to provide a detailed bibliography of economic work of interest. Such a list would be too long, and would include too many subjects to be useful. Rather I wish to note only a few general surveys that provide detailed bibliographies. Noteworthy are several published in the *Journal of Economic Literature*, particularly Hilda Kahne (1975). Also of importance as an indication of approach, as well as for bibliography, are Schultz (1974) and Terleckyj (1976). An ongoing longitudinal study of 5000 families, undertaken by the Institute for Social Research of the University of Michigan, deals with a large set of issues concerning patterns of family behavior and has led to several published volumes so far.

for the economist, a familiar problem.[2] Also important, for the interests expressed in this book, are the additional complications posed by the fact that the family, not an individual, is in essence the specific decision-making unit, and that family decisions affect more than one individual in ways not usually considered in economic analysis.[3] Family decision making has peculiar aspects of jointness, since it affects, and is meant to affect, the entire family group. Moreover, the existence of the group, its formation and its fission, is a subject of calculation, economic and otherwise. The family is, in essence, a group of individuals of varying ages with rather unequal decision-making power, and with a bond of "love" or "altruism" not generally thought to be found in other groups in our society. The family unit operates as a primary income redistribution unit, pooling the income (those funds actually received being only a part of its potential income since some of the potential is foregone for current or future family good) of one or more of its members, and allocating it among its members whether or not they earned it. Moreover, the "altruism" felt for offspring, and their futures, by parents requires considering the intergenerational impact of certain key decisions. This involves determining the magnitude of intergenerational transfers and their specific form, such as the choice between physical assets and educational expenditures that increase the value of human capital. These various complexities lead, no doubt, to the present piecemeal and tentative approach to life-course issues and the absence of any grand theories of family behavior. The range of possible choices and the factors involved in these decisions can be taxonomically described and theoretically analyzed, but the determination of which one of these choices was actually taken and for what reasons remains the subject of rather complex empirical study.

Theoretical and empirical studies of factors influencing major family decisions and on the impact of age and household status upon individual behavior have a long history among economists. There has been some resurgence of interest in these issues with the development of the so-called new home economics, and its concern with the economics of marriage, fertility, and education.[4] There have been important studies of the effects of age and marital status on consumption and savings decisions, using a life-course approach that suggests early fam-

---

[2]For a theoretical analysis of such problems within a life-cycle context, see Ghez and Becker (1975).

[3]For some comments on the implications of this, see the discussion in Part V of Schultz (1974).

[4]While much of this work has been at the University of Chicago, there are a number of other scholars who have made important contributions.

ily savings to provide a source of expenditures at older ages.[5] This has implications consistent with the relationship between age and wealth detailed in a number of studies for the nineteenth and twentieth centuries (Soltow, 1975). The literature on forming human capital, by formal education and by on-the-job training, points to a specific relationship between age and earned income, with investment costs of training and education lowering earned income at younger ages but providing for higher income at older ages (Mincer, 1970; Rosen, 1977). Systematic differences in labor-force participation by age, sex, and marital status, with their rather striking changes, particularly the increased participation by females in the twentieth century, have frequently been examined.[6] The relationship of age and migration has been studied, with migration being considered by economists as another form of investment in human capital. Social historians have also been concerned with geographic and occupational mobility in the process of United States development.[7] And age and marital status are key variables used in the explanation of decisions such as hours of work, the quantity and quality of children, and the duration of children's educations. These brief notes on economic studies bearing upon the life-course issues are meant to suggest the large body of theory and measurement that social historians can draw upon for both specific results and useful insights. To date much of this analysis has dealt with the most recent past, but given the availability of data for earlier periods in the manuscript censuses of the federal and state governments, it is expected that there will be more work by economists and economic historians on the nineteenth and early twentieth centuries.[8]

Budget Constraints

The concept of the budget constraint, widely used in microeconomic theory, can be, with some extension and modification, a very useful tool for the historical study of the family decision-making process. It would be necessary to employ a broad definition of potential

---

[5]For a survey, see Ferber (1973). For a detailed theoretical analysis, see Tobin (1968).

[6]See Long (1958). For other studies, see Bowen and Finegan (1969) and Cain (1966).

[7]For a survey of the economic literature, see Greenwood (1975). For a discussion of work, mainly by social historians dealing with the nineteenth and twentieth centuries, see Thernstrom (1973).

[8]For studies dealing with earlier periods, see Haines (forthcoming); Williamson (1967); Easterlin (1976); Modell (forthcoming); and Tilly (1978). For a detailed listing of the many budget studies in the U.S. and elsewhere which might be used to study these problems, see Williams and Zimmerman (1935).

income—the maximum that could be earned if all individuals in the family worked a maximum number of hours at jobs that yielded them maximum hourly incomes.[9] Such a maximum is, of course, hard to define but serves to remind us that people typically do not work at those jobs yielding the largest financial payoff, nor do they work as many hours as would be physically possible. Furthermore, many of the behavior patterns that are accepted by contemporaries and historians as "normal" without further question—such as the age at which children start work—are really the outcome of deliberate choices that impose costs upon society as well as upon the family. Individual families often are restricted in their earning opportunities by legislation or strong social consensus. The study of various life-course decisions needs to consider the effects of such socially imposed restrictions and to try to understand the social forces leading to them.

A consideration of maximum potential income is also conceptually important when trying to define subsistence income and when determining whether households were at, below, or above the subsistence level. As is clear from many studies, the socially defined subsistence is never the same as the physiological substance minimum.[10] This is not to deny that (a) there may be problems in achieving an acceptable level of living for many families; (b) a feeling of relative deprivation may exist. But it is useful to remember that this income level is generally not at a physiologically defined minimum, and reflects a certain number of decisions that result in lowered labor-force participation and a possible sacrifice of income for favorable working conditions on the part of individuals. In this sense the role of tastes in defining the "minimum acceptable" income level and its changes over time becomes a major subject for historical study. For example, the slave economy of the antebellum South made more "effective" use of its adult and child labor than did free societies because of a higher labor-force participation for children and females and because of the forced gang labor in large-scale units that free workers would not have voluntarily chosen at "reasonable" wage rates.[11] Free-labor societies apparently are willing to sacrifice some of their potential income, but while this is desirable

---

[9]Similar problems of adjustment for "non-pecuniary" items have long been discussed in the context of the measurement of national income, and over the past four decades Kuznets has examined the implications of various concepts of national income. For some estimates of the impact of various such adjustments, see Kuznets (1952, 1966) as well as National Bureau of Economic Research (1972), and Kendrick (1976).

[10]See Lebergott (1976). This book also includes much data of interest to historians, as well as a useful guide to sources on various aspects of living standards.

[11]For discussions and empirical estimates relating to this, see Fogel and Engerman (1974) and Ransom and Sutch (1977).

from a welfare standpoint, it must be considered when evaluating income levels and living standards.

The broad definition of potential income means that we must reconsider the treatment of some items not generally considered to be expenditures of income—such as leisure time, more pleasant working conditions, and the ability to forego labor-force participation. These appropriately should be regarded as forms by which individuals and families dispose of their potential income. The various attempts to expand the measurement of national income, to include the value of housewives' and students' time, and to measure the market value of increased leisure, can provide a more useful basis for historical studies than do the more familiar measures of personal and national income restricted to market production. Of course, before attempting to compare levels of family well-being and their changes over time, it is important to remember that not all of the foregoing of potential income can be regarded as consumption. A housewife's decision as to whether to enter the labor force will be influenced by the relative return from working and the possible need for and the alternative costs of providing for the performance of certain services in the home. Some loss of potential market income does not increase consumption, but serves as a form of family expenditure upon home services, child care, etc.[12] Similarly, while some nonlabor-force participation of children, such as school attendance, might be regarded as consumption uses of this "free" time they perhaps are better regarded as investment. Reallocating expenditures for schooling, on-the-job training, migration, and childrearing from consumption to investment reflects awareness of their intertemporal impact, distinguishing current satisfaction from deferral for higher levels of well-being in the future.[13] A detailed accounting scheme could show exactly how the maximum potential earnings were distributed among individuals and across expenditure categories and the implementation of such a scheme could provide a useful basis for understanding the nature of the interrelated decision processes of

[12]There are, of course, other costs which might enter into these decisions. Among the costs of working might be the contempt of neighbors if the commonly accepted norms of the community are violated. Here again it would be possible to place a price on the sanctions imposed by society.

[13]There are many conceptual problems in studying these decisions, and treatment may vary depending upon the specific perspective adopted. Thus, for example, while we may regard, following Kendrick, the raising of children as an investment from the point of view of society that has an interest in its future, for the parents children might be regarded as consumer goods (or at least consumer durables). Similar problems of classification exist for education and other forms of personal expenditures.

family members. Such a scheme would be of interest not only for the study of family decisions, but would add to our understanding of economic growth and social change.

It is too often assumed, for ease in handling certain problems, that maximum household income is a fixed sum, and that the household adjusts its needs and expenditures to some specified level of financial income. Carefully examining the implications of the possibilities for taking out potential income in many forms—including more leisure, more children, and better working conditions—can provide useful insights into the family decision-making process. In recent historical work, for example, the Malthusian presupposition that all individuals were working at a maximum to achieve subsistence has been modified by the view that not only were the marriage age and the number of children variables, but variations in amount and nature of work permitted alternative means of adjusting to changing economic conditions (Mendels, 1972). The suggestive work on the Russian peasantry by Chayanov, which analyzes systematic variations in family labor-force-participation rates with changes in the age structure and the number of dependents, indicates another form of adjusting work effort to needs within a culturally defined set of tastes (Millar, 1970).

These works can be expanded to provide a useful framework for studying economic aspects of the life course, increasing our awareness both of the complexity of the decision process and the interrelated nature of decisions within a family context. Thus, the use, in several of the chapters, of the ratio of dependents to earners within the household as a means of explaining female and child labor-force participation points to the importance of family and household conditions in influencing members' decisions. It suggests that whatever may be the success of analysis using the aggregate data published by the census bureau and other sources, a more complete understanding is possible only when we can examine the behavior of individual household units. Different behavior patterns result from regarding the family as a decision-making unit than from an assumption of individual decision making.

Alternative Responses to Economic Change

In this section a taxonomy of various possible changes in response to changing economic conditions will be presented. While listing these possible adjustments is a somewhat artificial approach to the issues posed in the study of the life course, the discussion can serve as a guide to understanding the possible systematic variations in choices made at specific times in the life course. It is, of course, impossible to be exhaustive and some variants or combinations may be selected that do not easily fit in a list. The choices themselves may be in response to social or cultural changes, not just economic ones. These points need not pose any difficulty here since the list is only meant to be suggestive.

Let us assume that the potential income of the principal wage-earner (a male) in a family increases because his hourly wage rate rises. Assume also that the wage-earner is already married so that we can abstract from that crucial decision with its implications for income-sharing and the reallocation of expenditures. Similarly, by omitting some important options in the responses of individuals and families, we assume that this wage change will not lead to a decision to dissolve the household and end family arrangements. Among the choices that might be made directly affecting the principal wage-earner, but also having implications for other family members, would be a Malthusian-type response of more children, with the additional resources used to provide an adequate subsistence level for the children to survive. A more refined discussion of responses, particularly applicable to modern times, would further consider the important choices to be made between the quantity and the quality of children. The financial ability to "pay for" more children (in quantity or quality units) requires that the wage-earner maintain sufficient labor input so that his financial income rises. Given an increased income due to maintained number of hours worked, a choice may be made to increase the number of children or to increase the consumption expenditures of the existing family. These increased expenditures could be usefully broken down into such categories as luxuries versus necessities, or nondurables (food, etc.) versus durables (housing, etc.). Increased income also might be used to change the net wealth of the household by repaying debt outstanding or by adding to assets held for future expenditures (or held indefinitely to provide self-insurance and security), or by providing legacies to offspring. Alternatively, the level of family consumption might be kept relatively constant while the leisure time of the household head is increased by some combination of working fewer hours per day, fewer days per week, or fewer weeks per year. Or, while keeping the income level constant, the hourly wage received might be lowered either because of a shift to employment with more pleasant working conditions (a form of consumption) or because of an investment in on-the-job training to enhance future earnings.

Each response by the family head may lead to some direct readjustments of the behavior of other family members. Thus, the increased potential income might permit his wife to reduce her labor-force participation, which would enable her to provide more home and household services or to enjoy the consumption of more leisure. It might permit one or more of the children to lower their labor-force participation and to increase their school attendance. If, as was more prevalent in the nineteenth century, there had been boarders within the household to provide an income supplement, their number could be reduced to offer more living space to family members. There are also possible adjustments to be made in the numbers of relatives or other individuals in the household, regardless of whether they were there to provide aid in family care and services or to be cared for by the family. Of course, if the increased income permitted migration to be financed more easily and if opportunities seemed better elsewhere, the entire family might change residence, either within a small area or interregionally, as well as employment. All of these decisions will affect how children are raised and how they are socialized. The responses are of more general interest because they are part of the process by which family ideology can influence social change.

This is a partial list of a rather complex set of possible reactions. While responses to an exogenous change in potential income are being discussed, there are other possible forces sparking change in individual and family behavior, and various combinations of responses that might be developed. For example, a decision to increase female labor-force participation might stem from the desire to raise funds for specific future expenses, such as the schooling of a child. The movement of older members of the kinship group into the house might be to provide for childcare to permit the female to work.

What factors might make certain decisions more probable at different points in the life course? Some influences, of course, are biological. Fertility is limited to part of the female life span and, therefore, tends to be concentrated early in family life. There are apparent relationships between age and physical capability in production and, perhaps, between sex and productive abilities in different types of work that have differing physical requirements. While some differences in type of work by age and by sex may have only a limited physiological basis, there have certainly been socially accepted norms that have restricted individual choices. Some bars to decisions clearly are socially imposed, such as restrictions on child and female labor, and legislated requirements for education.

Other important determinants reflect biologically influenced taste patterns of individual family members. The distinction between consumption and investment used by economists contrasts decisions that provide present satisfaction with those that involve the deferral of some current consumption in the interest of providing increased future consumption. Since human life is finite (although family lineage might not be so regarded), we would anticipate that as individuals age they would tend to invest less in human capital formation. This is consistent with observations relating age to occupational income, savings, migration, and the acquisition of consumer durables. The generally observed rise of income with age, particularly in jobs requiring skills and training, shows the importance of on-the-job training, while the observed decline in occupational and geographic mobility with age suggests a reduction in human capital investment with increasing age. The normal relationship of age and nonhuman wealth, with accumulated wealth rising with age to some peak late in life and then declining, is consistent with a life-cycle pattern of savings and consumer durable acquisition when younger. Accumulated assets are used to provide for consumption at older ages, when, due to lowered labor-force participation and the effect of age on earnings, incomes are generally lower.

The family's choices also are influenced by the number and ages of dependents, which, in turn, are related to the ages of the wage-earners. An increase in potential income of the principal wage-earner would be expected to have a different effect in a household with dependents too young to work whose consumption must be provided by parents than in a household in which all the children are earning incomes and there are no youthful dependents for which to provide.

We also anticipate some systematic patterns of differences at any moment in time. In addition to the effects of differential income and ethnicity, certain responses would vary with geographic region. The usual urban–rural distinction has been used widely as the basis for predicting different fertility, education, and labor force participation patterns.[14]

Concluding Remarks

To say that this book does not deal with the full complexity of life-course decisions is not to deny its usefulness in indicating some determinants of key life-course decisions, and in increasing our understanding of historical developments in the late nineteenth century.

[14]This explains the attention paid to this distinction in the chapters. Since the chapters cover a relatively urban area over a span of only 20 years, there is, however, limited insight possible into the importance of this set of problems.

There are certain problems in drawing implications from behavior patterns observed in cross-sectional samples, and the comparison of patterns across cross-sections.[15] Problems can arise because of changes in economic and other circumstances. Some response patterns might change as legal restrictions limit the family's choice of alternatives. (This is seen in the Chapter 5 discussion on education and child labor where pertinent legislation was passed in the years studied.) It is also necessary to consider the effects of seemingly exogenous factors. Changes in infant mortality rates would influence fertility decisions, and changes in occupational and industrial job structures and in the education system would affect decisions about investments in on-the-job training and children's education. Also, as Elder demonstrates, the level of economic activity and unemployment at the time of key decisions not only influences the choices, but leaves a residual impact upon subsequent responses.[16] Again, these chapters, limited in time-span, cannot explore such problems in detail.

Those chapters dealing with specific decisions highlight several issues for further examination. The determinants of women's labor participation are discussed in Chapter 6. Women's behavior within the family has become one of the most studied of all family economic problems and recent work has emphasized how the value of women's time is affected by education and changing wages. The present chapter emphasizes the crucial role of marriage in removing women from the labor force, an event that had more impact than the presence of children. What seems striking and worth more study is the extent to which older female children prior to marriage seem to maintain household residence without recorded employment or school attendance. This is in a region where female employment was relatively high; however, the functions, household and otherwise, performed by these young women remain somewhat unclear. Perhaps this reflects some problems of census recording, but the frequency of this pattern suggests that it did exist and merits further study. On the other hand, the apparent lower female labor-force participation of married women and mothers in urban areas is expected for several reasons. In rural areas, particularly on farms, productive employment at home was pos-

[15]In using studies drawn from cross-sections for specific years, there are important problems of interpretation and extrapolation. Any year's observation might represent a deviation from permanent levels, particularly so for economic variables. In addition, there is the general problem of using the distribution of observations in a cross-section to infer behavior over time, when the entire economic and social structure might be altered.

[16]For a similar observation relating the economic conditions at the same time of initial employment to the rate of occupational mobility, see Thernstrom (1973).

sible without limiting childcare and other household services. Indeed, one aspect of the change in female labor-force participation worth more attention is the effect on women of a shortened workday that would allow time for employment and household chores. Changes in female hours could also influence the school-enrollment rate of children. Also suggested by these chapters are strategies of substituting older children in household work for those prime-aged females who do enter the labor force, although this apparently occurred only to a limited extent, as well as the use of income from those older children in the labor force to permit younger children to attend school.

The chapters on marriage patterns and the location decisions of the elderly emphasize other types of problems, particularly those relating to coresidential choice. The income and wealth of the newly married, which affects their choice between a separate residence and coresidence with a parental family, and the role of these factors in determining the living arrangements of the elderly and their offspring seem of greatest importance. Ankarloo's finding concerning the relatively earlier marriage age of the unskilled, consistent with an age–income profile in which they approach their expected peak income earlier than do the more skilled, with a smaller investment of potential income to acquire training, is highly suggestive. Other implications of these chapters were drawn in the preceding synthesis, but even this summary indicates the wide range of questions suggested by the empirical analysis, questions of interest to economic, as well as social, historians.

Acknowledgments

I am most grateful to John Modell for detailed comments on several earlier drafts of this paper, as well as to Glen Elder for discussions and comment.

References

Bowen, William G., and T. Aldrich Finegan
    1969   The Economics of Labor Force Participation. Princeton: Princeton University Press.
Cain, Glen C.
    1966   Married Women in the Labor Force: An Economic Analysis. Chicago: University of Chicago Press.
Duncan, Greg J., and James N. Morgan (eds.)
    1975   Five Thousand American Families—Patterns of Economic Progress. Volume III. Ann Arbor: University of Michigan Institute for Social Research.

Easterlin, Richard A.
    1976   "Population change and farm settlement in the northern United States."
            Journal of Economic History XXXVI (March):45–75.
Ferber, Robert
    1973   "Consumer economics, a survey." Journal of Economic Literature XI
            (December):1303–1342.
Fogel, Robert W., and Stanley L. Engerman
    1974   Time on the Cross. Volumes 1 and 2. Boston: Little, Brown.
Ghez, Gilbert R., and Gary S. Becker
    1975   The Allocation of Time and Goods Over the Life Cycle. New York: Colum-
            bia University Press.
Greenwood, Michael J.
    1975   "Research on internal migration in the United States: a survey." Journal of
            Economic Literature XIII (June):397–433.
Haines, Michael R.
    Forth-   "Industrial work and the family cycle, 1889–1890." In Paul Uselding
    coming (ed.), Research in Economic History. Volume 4. Greenwich, Connecticut:
            JAI Press.
Kahne, Hilda
    1975   "Economic perspectives on the roles of women in the American economy."
            Journal of Economic Literature XIII (December):1249–1292.
Kendrick, John W.
    1976   The Formation and Stocks of Total Capital. New York: Columbia Univer-
            sity Press.
Kuznets, Simon
    1952   "Long-term changes in the national income of the United States of America
            since 1870." In Simon Kuznets (ed.), Income and Wealth of the United
            States: Trends and Structure, Income and Wealth. Series II. Cambridge,
            Massachusetts: Bowes & Bowes.
    1966   Modern Economic Growth: Rate, Structure, and Spread. New Haven and
            London: Yale University Press.
Lebergott, Stanley
    1976   The American Economy: Income, Wealth, and Want. Princeton: Princeton
            University Press.
Long, Clarence
    1958   The Labor Force Under Changing Income and Employment. Princeton:
            Princeton University Press.
Mendels, Franklin F.
    1972   "Proto-industrialization: the first phase of the industrialization process."
            Journal of Economic History XXXII (March):241–261.
Millar, James R.
    1970   "A reformulation of A. V. Chayanov's theory of the peasant economy." Eco-
            nomic Development and Cultural Change 18 (January):219–229.
Mincer, Jacob
    1970   "The distribution of labor incomes: a survey with special reference to the
            human capital approach." Journal of Economic Literature VIII (March):1–
            26.
Modell, John
    Forth-   "Patterns of consumption, acculturation, and family income strategy in
    coming late nineteenth-century America." In Tamara K. Hareven and Maris

Vinovskis (eds.), Family and Population in Nineteenth-Century America. Princeton: Princeton University Press.

National Bureau of Economic Research
1972   Economic Growth, Fiftieth Anniversary Colloquium V. New York: Columbia University Press.

Ransom, Roger, and Richard Sutch
1977   One Kind of Freedom: The Economic Consequences of Emancipation. Cambridge, England: Cambridge University Press.

Rosen, Sherwin
1977   "Human capital: a survey of empirical research." Pp. 3–39 in Ronald G. Ehrenberg (ed.), Research in Labor Economics. Volume 1. Greenwich, Connecticut: JAI Press.

Schultz, Theodore W. (ed.)
1974   Economics of the Family: Marriage, Children, and Human Capital. Chicago: University of Chicago Press.

Soltow, Lee
1975   Men and Wealth in the United States, 1850–1870. New Haven and London: Yale University Press.

Terleckyj, Nestor E. (ed.)
1976   Household Production and Consumption. Studies in Income and Wealth. Volume 40. New York: Columbia University Press.

Thernstrom, Stephan
1973   The Other Bostonians: Poverty and Progress in the American Metropolis, 1880–1970. Cambridge, Massachusetts: Harvard University Press.

Tilly, Charles (ed.)
1978   Historical Studies of Changing Fertility. Princeton: Princeton University Press.

Tobin, James
1968   "Life cycle saving and balanced growth." Pp. 231–256 in William Fellner et al., (eds.), Ten Economic Studies in the Tradition of Irving Fisher. New York: Wiley.

Williams, Faith M., and Carle C. Zimmerman
1935   Studies of Family Living in the United States and Other Countries: An Analysis of Material and Method. U.S. Department of Agriculture, Miscellaneous Publication No. 223. Washington, D.C.: U.S. Government Printing Office.

Williamson, Jeffrey G.
1967   "Consumer behavior in the nineteenth century; Carroll D. Wright's Massachusetts workers in 1875." Explorations in Entrepreneurial History, Second Series, 4 (Winter):98–135.

10
Comparative Notes on the Life Course

ROBERT A. LEVINE

As social scientists develop more generally applicable concepts and methods for investigating the life course, comparison of diverse cultures as well as historical periods becomes more feasible and instructive. The present volume, having presented a framework in which to describe the events of life course and family cycle in one historical context, exemplifies the common goal that historians share with social anthropologists: to develop a unified comparative perspective on the human life course, in which it is possible to describe universals and variations in a common language and to explain patterns of variation, stability, and change.

The development of this comparative perspective does not permit fixed assumptions about explanatory factors and directional processes, or other attempts to narrow the search for regularities, before a great deal more evidence is available. It requires broad historical and cross-cultural explorations of the connections between demographic constraints, economic pressures, and cultural norms and their impact on the structure of the family cycle and experience in the life course, over time. The theoretical and empirical studies of the present volume illustrate this disciplined eclecticism in a form that invites comparison with the societies studied by social anthropologists.

The society offered for comparison here is that of the Gusii, a rural

TRANSITIONS
The Family and the Life Course in
Historical Perspective

people of Western Kenya whose family patterns are strongly patrilineal, patrilocal, and polygynous (LeVine, 1964). In spite of this
characterization, the Gusii life course shows some remarkable
similarities to that of Essex County, Massachusetts in the late
nineteenth century. In both populations, for example, young adults
could look forward to a relatively advantageous old age, one in which
they were neither ejected from work and family roles nor separated
from their children, but able to enjoy some benefits from seniority in a
multigenerational kin group.

Another striking similarity concerns the timing of childbearing:
For the Gusii, as in nineteenth-century Essex County, a woman bears
children until menopause, rather than limiting childbearing to her
youth, as in the contemporary United States. This means that among
the Gusii, as in Essex, there are infants and small children in the
household to be taken care of for two or three fertile decades; the empty
nest does not come soon, and may never come if the parents die. Being
a parent of an infant or small child is not thought of as an exclusive role
of young adults, and full siblings can be as much as a generation apart
in age. These are characteristics of populations relatively high in both
mortality and fertility. From the viewpoint of the contemporary United
States, with its low mortality and fertility and with childbearing confined usually to women under 30, populations on the other side of the
demographic divide tend to look alike. And they are alike in the
lengthy restriction of women to the house by the demands of child care,
the prolonged maintenance of an age-differentiated household, and the
delegation of child-care tasks to older children. In short, in contrast
with the contemporary industrialized world, the concurrent integration
of parenthood with other activities must go on for a longer period and
cannot be seen as a temporary phase in the life of a married couple.

If demographic factors create similarities in the life course and
family cycle between the Gusii of East Africa and the Americans of
nineteenth-century Essex, economic and cultural factors create large
and instructive differences. The Gusii economy, though recently
monetarized and increasingly affected by urban employment, is still
basically undifferentiated in place, role, and organization. Families live
on their own land and grow their own food, as well as valuable cash
crops. The women, confined to the home by child care, are the primary
cultivators of the soil, although it is owned by their husbands and sons.
Their domestic roles as wives and mothers are not separated from their
economic roles in subsistence and market agriculture. When more
labor is needed to raise the crops, other members of the domestic production unit and their kinship networks are mobilized to do it, before

resorting to hired farm laborers. The economy of late nineteenth-century Essex County differentiated home from workplace, domestic from occupational roles, and bureaucratically organized production units from family-based consumption units. Married women generated income by taking in boarders at home, but in the urban centers they participated only sporadically in primary productive activity. From this viewpoint, they look much more like twentieth-century American housewives than like Gusii.

The cultural factors of patrilineality, patrilocality, and polygyny, as might be expected, only serve to widen the perceived gulf between the Gusii and historical Essex County. The localized patrilineal descent groups of the Gusii, their rigid rule that a woman moves at marriage to her husband's family and lineage, and the formation of polygynous domestic groups through a man's marriage to additional women, each with her own household, would seem to make further comparison with the West unnecessary if not untenable. Yet, I hope to show that application of the life-course perspective outlined in this volume renders the Gusii material comparable to that of the Western societies, illuminates both, and represents the advance over the family-cycle approach that Elder suggests.

There is a certain appropriateness, if an accidental one, about the choice of the Gusii as a preliminary non-Western case for illustrating life-course analysis. In 1949, Philip Mayer published a monograph entitled *The Lineage Principle in Gusii Society* that is an excellent example of the synchronic structural-functional approach of Radcliffe-Brown. In 1964, I published an article entitled "The Gusii Family" in a volume that was intended to illustrate the developmental cycle approach to domestic groups, as initiated by Fortes (1949) and Goody (1958), in its application to a series of African societies. Having returned to the Gusii in 1974–1976 after exposure to the concept of the life course as an analytic tool, I now use the same society to exemplify the virtues of yet another sociological approach. Future historians of the social sciences may want to examine the Gusii once again, as an illustration of how different the same society looks through various analytic lenses.

In proposing the life-course perspective for cross-cultural comparison, I follow Elder in referring to the life course as consisting of "pathways through the age-differentiated life span and subjective representations of it." These pathways embody both continuities and discontinuities for the individual, and their subjective representations can be collective or individual. The collective representation of the life course in cultural beliefs and values is a set of ideals that may not be realized but serve as standards against which individuals evaluate themselves. The individual's subjective representation of his life course includes his version of the collective standards and the conclusions he has drawn from retrospection and contemporaneous monitoring, concerning his place vis á vis those standards.

The concept I find of greatest utility in describing the life course is that of career, which Elder defines as a "patterned sequence of movements through social networks and settings." The subjective career as defined by Hughes (1971) is "the moving perspective in which the person sees his life as a whole and interprets the meaning of his various attributes, actions and the things which happen to him." I would emphasize again that the subjective career can be dealt with in both collective and individual representations and that individual representations of it are permeated with cultural meanings. Thus, the life course and its career pathways, as represented in collective and individual forms, comprise the basic conceptual framework for a cultural phenomenology of adulthood. In this enterprise the focus of interest is how people make sense of their lives with ideas drawn from their cultural environment, what kind of order they find there, and how they are affected by conclusions they draw from their culturally guided introspection.

For this conceptual framework to be used cross culturally, the following assumptions must be made:

1. All normal persons in all societies view themselves as continuous entities (physical, psychological, social) from their earliest memories to the present, despite physical growth, psychological development, social and residential mobility, changes of name, and ideological conversions.
2. All normal persons everywhere think about themselves in a chronological context and place themselves in relation to culturally derived standards.
3. At least two types of such standards are universal: cultural norms of age-specific performance (Neugarten and Hagestad, 1976) and long-range goals representing cumulative performance in a culturally defined career pathway.
4. The individual represents his continuities to himself in terms of the criteria and goals of his subjective careers and organizes his future behavior on the basis of these assessments. It is goals rather than roles that organize career activity, and an individual's movement into and out of certain roles may only be comprehensible in terms of career paths toward long-range goals.
5. The individual's self-evaluations in relation to age norms and

career goals play an important part in his sense of his own worth.

With these assumptions, we can take a preliminary look at the life course among the Gusii. Since the Gusii had no specialized occupational roles, we are forced to identify career paths without the familiar occupational career line that so dominates Western thinking on this subject. What meanings do people find in their lives when they have no occupational careers?

I found one clue to the answer at a Gusii funeral I attended in 1974, for a 68-year-old woman. Many hundreds of people attended, and, at the place where male mourners sat with her husband, I was handed a piece of paper on which were written the deceased's name, her dates of birth, marriage, and conversion to Christianity, and the numbers of her male and female children, grandchildren, and great-grandchildren, which were totaled at the bottom to yield the number of her descendants. This was her epitaph, the final public statement of her worth. In the past, her worth would have been represented by the number of people attending her funeral, for each descendant who marries increases the number of kin whose attendance is obligatory; but literacy has added the written, quantitative epitaph.

In my field research of the following two years I discovered how significant that epitaph was, in terms of both the public evaluation of someone whose life is over, and the self-evaluation of adults beginning many years before their deaths could realistically be anticipated. Gusii funerals, like those of other African peoples (Fortes, 1971) constitute definitive collective judgments concerning the meaning and value of the deceased's life. It is no exaggeration to say that Gusii people begin preparing for their own funerals as young adults. For example, a young man who becomes employed will soon invest his earnings in building a house for himself at his father's homestead, although he has no intention of leaving the city where he is employed and no early prospect of being able to take a wife. The most urgent reason for this is the prescriptive necessity of burial at home and the total disgrace of being buried without a house. The same sense of urgency surrounds the intentions of young men and women to marry and to have children until the wife reaches menopause. Any interruption in this sequence is treated as a disastrous, irreplaceable affliction requiring expensive remedies. Relaxation is only found among the old who have many descendants. One ailing man in his late sixties, a large landowner and polygamist whose land was now crowded with the houses of his quarrelling sons, grandsons, and their wives and children, expressed it well when he said that his main pleasure in life was counting the progeny residing on his land. He could be certain his funeral would be a good one.

Considerations of this kind led me to formulate career pathways for the Gusii that are recognizable to them but more explicit than they would ever make them. These formulations are based on evidence that there is a high degree of consensus concerning long-range goals, and that individuals pursue them with perseverance, urgency, personal sacrifice—all symptoms that their personal salience matches their cultural significance.

In my formulation, each Gusii man or woman pursues three related subjective careers: a reproductive career, an economic career, and a ritual career. Although there are some ritual specialists, everyone has a ritual career. The reproductive career seems to be the most significant for both sexes. Its goal is to become the ancestor of a maximally expanding geneaology. This means women have children as frequently between marriage and menopause as is consistent with child health, which the Gusii believe to be every 2 years. A man who fails to impregnate his wife that often will be publicly accused by her of neglect. The woman must have at least one son to take care of her in her old age and whose wives work with her; to have nothing but daughters (who move away at marriage) is second only to barrenness as a disaster. If her husband dies, it is her right as well as her obligation to have a leviratic husband to impregnate her regularly so she will continue to bear children "for the dead man." For men, the goal means not only maximizing his wife's offspring but taking additional wives as he can afford them and so appending their reproductive careers to his. If a man has been a monogamist, this becomes particularly significant when his wife reaches menopause, for he might look forward to a decade or more of continued procreation if he takes a younger second wife, and some men do at that time.

The reproductive career as I see it, however, is not limited to the individual's own procreation, but includes that of his or her offspring. Grandchildren are as fervently desired as one's own children and, not incidentally, play an essential role in the burial of grandparents.

The economic career is more differentiated by sex because men own land, while women do not, and men now participate in modern employment and business ownership while women do only to a marginal degree. The Gusii man's most cherished economic goal in the past was an ever expanding herd of cattle to be reared when young and to provide milk and meat when mature. Land was then abundant, and the raising of crops was considered essential but less important than animal husbandry. The ever-expanding herd is conceptually linked in

Gusii thought with human reproduction, but in the past it was eco-nomically linked as well. Bridewealth was paid in cattle; thus every daughter born represented potential cattle income. Each son, of course, represented a future demand for cattle, but the sons were permanent family members who served the father by tending his herds and pro-tecting them from raids. The expanding lineages of humans and cattle were intimately connected, and reproductive and economic goals were not entirely distinct. Furthermore, each additional wife of father or son brought in by bridewealth cattle was assigned new fields to cultivate and made possible cultivation of more available land, while also in-creasing the reproductive capacity of the family. Successful men had eight or more wives, large herds, and a private army of adult sons from their countless children, representing ideal outcomes of the desired cycle of ever-expanding exchange.

The man's actual role in pursuing these combined economic and reproductive goals was that of an investor and supervisor. If he had sons to do the herding and wives to do the cultivation, then his job was mainly supervisory; if he lacked the field hands, then he did their work himself until the domestic production unit had expanded. But the in-dependent mature man not living under the authority of his father always made all the investment decisions concerning the use of cattle for bridewealth (he negotiated with the bride's father) and the alloca-tion of fields among wives. The concept of an economically indepen-dent individual acting as supervisor and investor rather than worker has not died out among the Gusii; it is being applied in the modern sector. A man with some capital sets up a shop and then puts one wife in charge of it while another wife runs the family farm; if a surplus is produced, he starts another small business or buys some imported cat-tle for the farm. A man with some employment income invests in the education of his eldest sons, hoping they will be able to qualify for lucrative jobs and will in turn invest in the education of their younger siblings. The goal of a self-sustaining or self-generating family firm, with the patriarch as entrepreneur, has not disappeared, but has found new fields for application. The strategy followed in this economic career also remains the same; that is, exploiting the bonds of obedience that tie wife to husband, and sons to father, for economic gain. But patriarchs nowadays complain that cows are more dependable than humans: you rear them and they give you milk in return, but with your own children, you can never be sure.

In this description of the Gusii reproductive and economic careers, one aspect of change has already emerged: In the past the economic and reproductive careers were inseparable because their goals, though distinct, both required the birth of as many children of both sexes in the family as could be successfully reared to maturity. In the present economy, however, children are an economic liability because they are not needed on the small land holdings, they require school fees to become economically self-sufficient, and the bridewealth system is in disarray. We found otherwise intelligent Gusii parents in 1974–1976 pursuing what seemed blatantly contradictory goals in their economic and reproductive careers; they continued to pursue traditional reproductive goals although these have lost their economic rationale so completely that the benefits have all turned to costs, some of them quite severe. How can this behavior be understood?

Part of the answer lies in the subjective aspect of the life course I have not yet described, the ritual career. Its culmination is the posthumous evaluation of the funeral ritual, in which the reproductive success of self and offspring are given the highest marks. Its goals are the physical safety and sense of personal potency that can insure continuity from generation to generation. For the Gusii, as for many other African peoples, any instance of reproductive failure or incapacity, including threats to the survival or continued reproduction of children, is interpreted as a sign of an intent to destroy the entire domestic group. If the sign is ignored, everyone will die or be afflicted by sterility or psychosis. To diagnose the intent and discover a remedy, one consults a diviner or sorcerer, who attributes the affliction to a default in ancestor ritual or the malevolence of a witch and prescribes animal sacrifice or magical protection, respectively. If the remedy does not work, one goes to another practitioner, often while using Western medicine as well. Whether or not cure is effected, the afflicted couple eventually accepts an explanation of the event in terms of some evil or punitive intent, stemming in many cases from an ancient grievance that may give rise to future afflictions. Many adults regard themselves as being subject to a long-acting destructive intent that once caused an affliction but is temporarily in abeyance. They regard their ritual careers, that is, their long-range safety and potency and that of their children, as constantly jeopardized. Their need for reassurance about safety from supernatural harm is so great that they will not voluntarily give up what is to them the most convincing proof, successful child-bearing.

The ritual career is pursued because it offers psychic comfort in the face of danger. For those who experience extraordinary affliction, signaling greater danger, it offers an extraordinary remedy, to become a ritual practitioner with a special measure of power and protection. Those who had suffered chronic illness or a severe disability and were able to gain an apparent remission often took instruction in the particular form of healing that cured them and practiced it on others. We found an extraordinary number and variety of healers in the area, suggesting that as many as 10% of those over 40 years of age possessed some curative power that others knew of and might benefit from; virtually all of these healers began their ritual careers as afflicted persons (including mothers of diseased or disabled children) who had been cured. A parallel ritual career open to the afflicted is that of the witch, an unfortunate who gains invulnerability for herself or himself through killing and cannibalizing personal enemies and those more fortunate. Though it is difficult to ascertain, we became convinced that some persons pursued the goals of safety and potency through the adoption of this secret identity.

Another aspect of the ritual career that accounts for its persistence among contemporary Gusii is its economic relevance. Crop failures, business failures, the deaths of cattle, the loss of jobs, and other obstacles in the attainment of economic goals, are seen, like barrenness, disease, and disability, as signs of intentional activity endangering the family. Ritual practitioners are consulted and prescribe many of the same cures they use for bodily disorder. Thus, economic as well as reproductive failures can be remedied by ritual activity, and the ritual career can be seen as a compensatory or restorative line pursued when other pathways are blocked. What it seems to restore is the sense of personal potency that includes physical safety and a measure of confidence in the continuity of the family.

Gusiiland, like Essex County, Massachusetts in the nineteenth century, is under an onslaught of rapid social change. Young men have grown up under vastly different conditions than their fathers or even their older brothers, and their fathers had already grown up as the first generation under colonial rule. (The British conquered the Gusii in 1907.) The Gusii have in recent years been responsive to economic and educational opportunities, and their lives have been greatly changed by employment, migration, and schooling. Yet when one examines their subjective representations of the life course and the long-range goals of their adult careers, one is struck more by persistence than change. The explanation for this lies in the realm of their fundamental beliefs, what Brim (unpublished) has referred to as the "theory of self" derived from their cultural background and embedded in their individual personalities. Perhaps that is where inquiry into subjective aspects of the life course always leads; it represents an intriguing arena for future investigation.

References

Brim, O. G.
    Unpub-   "Notes on the theory of self." Unpublished manuscript, 1975.
    lished
Fortes, M.
    1949   "Time and social structure." Pp. 54–84 in E. Evans-Pritchard and F. Eggan (eds.), Social Structure: Studies Presented to A. R. Radcliffe-Brown. London: Oxford University Press.
    1971   "On the concept of the person among the Tallensi." Pp. 283–319 in La Notion de Personne en Afrique Noire. Paris: Colloques Internationaux du C.N.R.S.
Goody, J. (ed.)
    1958   The Developmental Cycle in Domestic Groups. Cambridge, England: Cambridge University Press.
Hughes, E. C.
    1971   "Cycles, turning points and careers." Pp. 124–131 in E. C. Hughes (ed.), The Sociological Eye. Chicago: Aldine.
LeVine, R. A.
    1964   "The Gusii family." Pp. 63–82 in P. Gulliver and R. Gray (eds.), The Family Estate in Africa. Boston: Boston University Press.
Mayer, Philip
    1949   The Lineage Principle in Gusii Society. London: Oxford University Press.
Neugarten, B. L., and G. O. Hagestad
    1976   "Age and the life course." Pp. 35–55 in R. Binstock and E. Shanas (eds.), Handbook of Aging and the Social Sciences. New York: Van Nostrand.

Index

STUDIES IN SOCIAL DISCONTINUITY

Under the Consulting Editorship of:

CHARLES TILLY
University of Michigan

EDWARD SHORTER
University of Toronto

Richard Maxwell Brown and Don E. Fehrenbacher (Eds.). Tradition, Conflict, and Modernization: Perspectives on the American Revolution

Juan G. Espinosa and Andrew S. Zimbalist. Economic Democracy: Workers' Participation in Chilean Industry 1970-1973

Arthur L. Stinchcombe. Theoretical Methods in Social History

Randolph Trumbach. The Rise of the Egalitarian Family: Aristocratic Kinship and Domestic Relations in Eighteenth-Century England

Tamara K. Hareven (Ed.). Transitions: The Family and the Life Course in Historical Perspective

In preparation

H. A. Gemery and J. S. Hogendorn (Eds.). The Uncommon Market: Essays in the Economic History of the Atlantic Slave Trade